D1593003

West African Travels and Adventures

WEST AFRICAN TRAVELS

AND ADVENTURES

Two Autobiographical Narratives
from Northern Nigeria

Translated and Annotated
by
Anthony Kirk-Greene and Paul Newman

New Haven and London,
Yale University Press, 1971

Copyright © 1971 by Yale University.
All rights reserved. This book may not be
reproduced, in whole or in part, in any form
(except by reviewers for the public press),
without written permission from the publishers.
Library of Congress catalog card number: 74–151578
International standard book number: 0–300–01426–0

Designed by John O. C. McCrillis
and set in Times Roman type.
Printed in the United States of America by
the Carl Purington Rollins Printing-Office of
the Yale University Press, New Haven, Connecticut.

Distributed in Great Britain, Europe, and Africa by
Yale University Press, Ltd., London; in Canada by
McGill-Queen's University Press, Montreal; in Mexico
by Centro Interamericano de Libros Académicos,
Mexico City; in Central and South America by Kaiman
& Polon, Inc., New York City; in Australasia by
Australia and New Zealand Book Co., Pty., Ltd.,
Artarmon, New South Wales; in India by UBS Publishers'
Distributors Pvt., Ltd., Delhi; in Japan by John
Weatherhill, Inc., Tokyo.

Contents

Illustrations

Maps

Acknowledgments

The original manuscript of *Maimaina's Story* (Part II of this volume) was published by the Gaskiya Corporation, Zaria, Nigeria, under the careful handling of Professor Neil Skinner and Alhaji Abdulmalik Mani. We would like to thank the Gaskiya Corporation both for giving us permission to do this English translation and for allowing us to reproduce the Hausa text. The excellent portrait of Maimaina included here has been reproduced with the kind permission of André Deutsch, Ltd.

In preparing this work, we have drawn heavily on the accumulated experience of our many years in Nigeria. We could not begin to mention individually all of the people who provided us with assistance and hospitality throughout those years. We would, however, like to express our appreciation to Mallam Muhammadu Dikko and Mallam Tata Askira, two of Maimaina's grandsons, for their valuable help (to K.-G.) in undertaking research in Bornu in 1957. For their careful work in typing the manuscript we wish to thank Mrs. Evelyn Jennings, Mrs. Evelyn Middleton, and Mrs. Helen Kyrcz, and for her help in preparing the maps, Mrs. Roxana Ma Newman. Finally we wish to thank Mrs. Barbara Folsom of Yale University Press for her encouragement and good humor in seeing the manuscript through the Press.

vi

Introduction

A review of the work of historians and social scientists in Africa during the postwar period reveals one major shortcoming in their coverage of the northern Nigerian scene. Although Hausaland has been the focal point for a number of scholarly studies which have, by their sustained quality, earned the Hausa people and their institutions a privileged position in the documentation of African cultures, the region has lagged behind in the realm of autobiography. For example, *Akiga's Story* (East 1939) and *Efik Traders of Old Calabar* (Forde 1956) have brought status to the history of the Tiv and Efik peoples respectively, and biographical interpreters such as Turnbull, Winter, and Fox, working elsewhere in Africa, have put "their" peoples on the map; but there has been only one narrative by a Hausa-speaker that has succeeded in securing a comparable position in the literature. This is Mary Smith's *Baba of Karo* (1954), a sensitive and insightful account of Hausa customs and social organization.

To some extent, however, this apparent shortcoming is a consequence of the dominant position of a few European and Asian languages in the world of books and scholarship. There do exist, in fact, two or three autobiographical accounts by Hausas and several biographies of eminent leaders; but apart from the political autobiography of the late

Sardauna of Sokoto, all of these have been written in the Hausa language. Hence neither of the better-known recent anthologies devoted to the examination of Africans' own personal observations as a new component in the interpretation of African history—Thomas Hodgkin's *Nigerian Perspectives* (1960) and Philip Curtin's *Africa Remembered* (1967)—includes excerpts from the two Hausa writers treated in this book. If the "fault" lies with the Hausa authors for preferring to work in the vernacular, the loss is undoubtedly that of English-speaking readers; and it is to help repair this loss by bringing instances of historical Hausa autobiography before a much larger public that we have translated the two manuscripts comprising this volume.

Dorugu's narrative (Part 1) is the story of a Hausa boy who accompanied the famous explorer Heinrich Barth on his travels across the Western Sudan between 1850 and 1855. This is an independent eyewitness account of places and events known for a hundred years only through Barth's scientific writings. Here for the first time we have glimpses —contemporary and non-European—of Barth the man, to supplement our derived assessments of Barth the scholar. And here we also find a rare description of Overweg, Barth's scientific companion, who seen through African eyes appears a much warmer character than Barth's slighting paragraphs suggest.

Maimaina's story (Part 2) is an account of the British occupation of northern Nigeria at the turn of the century told fifty years later by a Nigerian chief who participated in these events as a young man. The narrative offers not only a new viewpoint but also an extraordinary amount of detailed evidence—often complementary and very frequently corroboratory—which can serve to evaluate government and official reports of this traumatic and controversial period

in Nigerian history. In addition, Maimaina recreates a mood
of the period and thus is able to provide a sympathetic picture of what it must have been like to be a political agent of
the government in the pioneer days of Lugard's administration of northern Nigeria.

It should perhaps be emphasized that these manuscripts
were not selected primarily as examples of vernacular Hausa
literature. From a language point of view there are clearly
better texts to illustrate "better" Hausa stylistics. Dorugu's
Hausa narrative is too difficult to read: his dialect differs
considerably from the now-standard Kano dialect and the
orthography is old and out of date; while Maimaina's prose
is unavoidably turgid because of the wealth of factual ma-
terial packed into a short account. But for fresh perspectives
on the Nigeria of the times and for a new look both at the
people who traditionally lived there and the uninvited
strangers who came there—in short, for a much-needed
non-European contribution to the story of Hausaland—
these texts are unsurpassed.

When he returned from his travels in what is today northern Nigeria, Dr. Heinrich Barth was not alone. "I had in my
service," he recorded later, "two liberated slaves, Dýrregu,
a Haúsa boy, and Ábbega, a Marghí lad . . . the same young
lads whom on my return to Europe I brought to this country,
where they promised to lay in a store of knowledge, and who
on the whole have been extremely useful to me" (III: 22).
These two boys were probably the first northern Nigerians
ever to visit England and Germany. In any event, Dorugu,
to use the modern orthography, has shed considerably more
light on Barth and himself than Barth has done on any of
his informants; for while in England Dorugu narrated his
life story, which was taken down verbatim in Hausa.

Most of the information about Dorugu's early life is gathered from his autobiography. He was born about 1839 or 1840 in Damagaram, a traditional Hausa province now in the Niger Republic. Captured in a slave raid, as a young boy, he was carried off to Zinder and sold to a Kanuri merchant. His master took him southeast to Kukawa, the capital of Bornu, where he worked as a domestic servant for a time before being resold to an Arab in the city in order to settle one of his Kanuri master's debts. This transaction would have taken place some time in 1851, when Dorugu could not have been more than twelve years old or so.

At this time the famous travelers Heinrich Barth and Adolf Overweg were based in Kukawa. They had arrived in April and May of 1851, having survived the strenuous and hazardous trip across the desert that had claimed the life of their expedition leader, James Richardson.[1]

Dorugu's association with the explorers came about when he was hired out to Overweg as a camel boy on a journey to Kanem, the region north and east of Lake Chad. When later narrating his adventures, Dorugu provided a picture of his first impression of Overweg: "His face and hands were all white like paper, he had a red fez on his head, a long beard, and was wearing a white robe." On the return of the caravan to Kukawa, Dorugu reluctantly went back to his Arab owner, but Overweg was soon able to secure the boy's freedom for the sum of fifteen Maria Theresa dollars (about $25.00). Having been provided with a certificate of redemption written out by a *mallam,* Dorugu voluntarily entered Overweg's service as a houseboy.

1. On reaching the southern edge of the Sahara, Richardson, Barth, and Overweg split up and took different routes to Kukawa, their predetermined goal. For background information on the expedition, see Boahen (1964) and the introduction to Kirk-Greene (1962).

After Overweg's death from fever near Lake Chad in October 1852, Barth took over Dorugu and another freed slave of Overweg's called Abbega, who was some three or four years older. Together they accompanied Barth westward to Timbuktu and finally northward across the Sahara. Barth wrote, "Even during the whole of my journey to Timbuktu and back I conversed in this language [Hausa] exclusively . . . with the Hausa-boy Dúrregu or Dórugu, and even mostly with the Marghi-lad Abbega" (1862: xvii).

When Barth returned to Europe in 1855 he took the two youths with him. Dorugu was described by Barth's brother-in-law, in the most complimentary terms, as "a 14 year old Moslem Hausa with light-brown complexion, small and highly intelligent," while Abbega was simply described as "a coal-black muscular Marghi pagan, 18 years old but less gifted than the other" (Schubert 1897: 60). A portrait of the boys, drawn while they were visiting Barth's family in Germany, appears in Barth (1857–59, III: 22). A lesser-known photograph of the boys taken in an identical pose is reproduced in this volume.

Barth planned to educate the two boys in the Christian way of life, with the idea that they should return to northern Nigeria as lay missionaries to spread the gospel. But once the excitement and novelty of their European experience had worn off, the two youths felt homesick and began to pester Barth to arrange for their repatriation. We have a copy of the Foreign Secretary's instructions to the British Consul at Tripoli in February 1856, just six months after the party had reached Europe (Benton 1912: 253–54):

> Dr. Barth has applied to H.M. Govt. to assist him with the means of sending back to Africa two Blacks, named Abbega and Dyrgu, who had been bought out of slavery and made free in Central Africa by the late

Dr. Overweg, and after his death were taken by Dr. Barth into his service, as free men, and have accompanied him to England.

Dr. Barth's intention was to keep these Africans in England for about two years, and after they had learned English, and if possible some handicraft, and had become acquainted with European manners and customs, to send them back to Africa; but it seems that they have become home-sick and are desirous now to return to their native country.

In compliance with Dr. Barth's application the Board of Admiralty have been requested to provide these Africans with a passage to Malta and Tripoli, and I have to instruct you on their arrival at the latter place, and in order that their freedom may be sufficiently ensured on their return to their own country, to furnish them with an Arabic passport, such as liberated slaves generally receive in Tripoli, countersigned by the Kadhi; and to place them under the protection of some trustworthy man, going either to Kano or Kuka.

You will also furnish them with a camel.

You will draw upon me in the usual form for the expenses which you may incur in carrying out this instruction.

C. [Clarendon]

While the return travel arrangements were being made, the youths went to live and work temporarily with the Reverend J. F. Schön, a pioneer Hausa-language scholar who had taken part in the evangelical expedition up the Niger in 1841 (see Hair 1967). The secretary of the Church Missionary Society, Henry Venn, describes meeting the two youths to arrange for their move to Schön's home:

Went to see Dr. Barth, the African explorer. Had
some talk with his two African lads and arranged with
the Doctor to send them to Mr. Schön to be his interpreters for the Yoruba [sic!] language. They were both
of them evidently as home-sick as any Swiss, and to all
of my attempts to lure them to stay in England, their
answer was "Africa! Africa!" [diary entry of Feb. 2,
1856, taken from Hair 1967: 47n]

According to Barth's account, he was so preoccupied with
writing up his diaries for publication during that winter of
1855–56, that he had no time to devote to his study of
Hausa despite his love for and deep interest in a language
whose "easy character and rich development . . . caused it
soon to become a favourite with me." So he agreed to lend
Dorugu's services to Schön to help him with the Hausa
grammar and dictionary he was compiling. Barth was of
course aware of Schön's need for an informant since it had
been his own strong recommendation regarding the importance of the Hausa language and his praise for Schön's
earlier work that had led the committee of the Church Missionary Society to ask Schön to resume his linguistic work.

In February 1856, therefore, Dorugu was sent to Schön's
place in Chatham, Kent, to stay for a few weeks. At the
beginning of March, Barth sent a note to Schön asking that
Dorugu be sent back at once since a passage to Tripoli was
arranged for the fifth of that month. What happened next
is not entirely clear except that it plunged Barth and Schön
into an acrimonious personal dispute that was perpetuated
in their disagreement on matters of Hausa grammar. It seems
that when the time to leave drew near, Dorugu changed his
mind and informed Schön that if Abbega were also willing,
he would prefer to remain in England. Abbega agreed,

whereupon Schön broached the subject to Barth, who flatly refused.

Annoyed at the trouble the two boys had caused him in arranging their passage home, Barth would not countenance a change of plans. Apparently he was also embittered by a quarrel with the secretary of the influential British and Foreign Anti-Slavery Society, who had roundly accused him of importing two slaves into England (see Schubert 1897: 107). He insisted that they go to Southampton as planned and board the naval vessel *Hydaspes,* on which the British government had arranged their passage.

On the day of the sailing Schön followed the youths to Southampton, ostensibly "with no other intention than to see their wants supplied for the passage." When they saw Schön they reiterated their desire to remain in England and begged to be allowed to stay. Schön convinced the captain that this was indeed the boys' own free choice, whereupon the latter agreed to let them disembark to return with Schön to Kent.

Not unexpectedly, Barth interpreted Schön's actions as being far from straightforward and ethical, an accusation he leveled in public some six years later (1862: xvii):

> The two liberated slaves, with regard to whom I have said more in my *Travels,* would have rendered me great service in my linguistical studies even after my return to Europe, if other people had not crossed my intentions. For in the commencement I was not able to apply myself to this class of labours, as I was obliged, to work out my geographical material, and meanwhile the Rev. Schön and his friends preferred obtaining by artifice and violence, what they might have obtained much easier by fair means, and thus to take out of my hands those people, whom to my great inconvenience

and expense I had brought to Europe, that they might be useful on future expeditions.

Schön's reply to this charge and his own account of the episode, published in 1876, are worth quoting in full (1876: iv–vi):

> This charge, so seriously reflecting on my character, I most emphatically deny. It has been a source of pain to me to find myself compelled to defer my reply for several years, while even now I would prefer forgetting and forgiving a personal injury were it not a sacred duty to set myself right with the public . . . [otherwise] I may be regarded as pleading guilty to the charge. . . . The two young men alluded to had made up their minds, long before I saw or knew them, to remain no longer with Dr. Barth; an application for a passage in one of H.M. ships of war had already been made, when Dr. Barth told me of their being with him. He kindly allowed Dorugu to come with me until the vessel was ready, and to my surprise, he resided under my roof for several weeks. When the news arrived for his embarkation he burst out crying, said he would like to stop with me, and would rather be educated in England than return to Africa in a state of ignorance; and that if his companion Abega could stay with me too they would not then return to Africa. Abega agreeing to this proposal, I endeavoured to get Dr. Barth's consent, but failed. He declared, that "as they had given him so much trouble about a passage they should now return to Africa, and that he would not listen to my proposal." I then reminded him that there could be no *must* in the case, that they were not slaves in England and that they were at liberty, as much as he or myself, to choose

for themselves. Barth now spoke to them in Bornu [Kanuri], but what he said to them I could not then understand, and what was told me afterwards I will not repeat. Suffice it to say, he was in a rage and overawed the young men, who bade me good-bye saying they would rather return to Africa than be a cause of unpleasantness between Dr. Barth and me. The following morning [5 March 1856] they were sent to Southampton to embark. I followed them to Southampton with no other intention than to see their wants supplied for the passage, and to take leave of them. They both said, "had we known how to get to your house, we should have come to you instead of going on board; can we not go with you now." My reply was, "it is too late now." "Why cannot we leave the ship and go with you? go ask the Captain." I did so. All the Captain wished to know was, whether the request was made by their own free choice. He called for them, satisfied himself that such was the case, and then said they might return with me. No one could be more surprised than I at the turn affairs had taken. The lads ran to take the few rags provided for their comfort, and returned with me in great joy. Had I arrived a few hours later, the vessel would have left. At this time they were altogether out of Dr. Barth's hands, by his own choice, and he had no right to charge me and my friends with artifice and violence in taking them. They had done nothing but what they had a perfect right to do, as free men in free England.

After their abortive departure Dorugu and Abbega settled down in Schön's household, where they assisted him in his Hausa studies and began their own education.

I had made it my first business to teach them to read their own language by the use of a little Primer, published in 1848. But I must mention the assistance I have derived from Koelle's books in the Bornu language. As both of these lads spoke the Bornu language, they were able in a very short time to read the Bornu stories, fables, etc., etc. Nothing could be more suited to their taste, nor so likely to encourage them in their studies as the discovery of the practical use of mastering the formidable A B C, and to see that they could at once understand what they read. [Schön 1862: viii*n*]

For purposes of his own research Schön worked primarily with Dorugu who, unlike Abbega, spoke Hausa as a mother tongue.

I discovered very soon that Abbega spoke Hausa like a foreigner, being a Margi by birth; but being very communicative, I obtained many new words from him, besides collecting a small vocabulary and some stories in his own native tongue, the Margi. Dorugu is a real Hausa, speaks the language fluently and beautifully. Never was there an African coming to this country that was of greater use; full of information for his age, probably not more than 16 or 17 years old, energetic and lively in his habits, always ready to speak. He began relating stories to me, or rather dictating them, giving me a description of his own life and travels in Africa in his own language, very often dictating to me for hours together and even till late in the night; so that I had soon a Hausa literature of several hundred pages before me. [Schön 1862: viii]

Although Dorugu remained in England for another eight

years, all his work as a linguistic informant seems to have taken place during his first year with Schön. As well as can be ascertained, his autobiography and all the other stories that were eventually published in *Magána Hausa* were narrated in 1856, within a year of his arrival in England and before he had learned to speak English. Dorugu could thus not have been more than seventeen years old when he dictated his autobiography—very young, considering the sophistication of the narrative.

In May 1857 Dorugu and Abbega were baptized at the mission house at Chatham. Dorugu was given the Christian names James Henry, after Schön and Barth; Abbega was christened Frederick Fowell Buxton, after Schön and his godfather, Thomas Fowell Buxton, an ardent abolitionist known as "the friend of the African race."

Abbega left for Africa later that year but Dorugu stayed on in England. In 1862 Schön was able to write, "Dorugu is still with me, reading and studying, and by God's blessing, preparing himself for still greater usefulness" (1862: x). Finally, in 1864, Dorugu went back to his native country. Like Abbega before him he returned to Nigeria by ship rather than recrossing the desert. He met his old friend Abbega in Lokoja, worked with the missionaries there for a time, and then pushed on to Hausaland (Schön 1885: 265–69). Apart from Schubert's statement (1897) that he lived "an unsettled life in and around Kano," we have no further knowledge of Dorugu until the turn of the century, when we find him employed as a schoolmaster for the newly formed [1900] Northern Nigeria Regiment. We do know that by 1906 he was giving Hausa lessons to European civil and military officials in Zungeru, capital of the Northern Protectorate, and that during his last few years he was employed in the pilot government school at Kano for the sons of emirs and their titled courtiers. This school was the centerpiece of the experimental program of Western literacy devised for Northern Nigeria. There Dorugu worked with Hanns Vischer, the North's first education officer, who, because of his linguistic fluency, was known as *Dan Hausa* ("a Hausa son").

It is, indeed, through the Vischer connection that we have our only substantial description of Dorugu at the end of his life. Vischer's wife Isabelle had met Dorugu only once, but the strong impression that he made on her, plus his unique personal history, were sufficient to induce her to devote two lengthy diary entries to him. Since Isabelle Vischer's published diary is generally inaccessible, her rare and vivid description of Dorugu deserves quotation in full (Vischer 1917: 42–45, translation ours):

> *29 November 1912.* Old "Dorugu" died at Nassarawa [a quarter of Kano, outside the city walls] this morning. A highly original character thus disappears; nor was his passing a common-or-garden affair. It's fortunate that he died when he did, for a type of leprosy had just been discovered on his body which would have condemned him to isolation, and that would have upset the poor fellow terribly. Of a ripe old age, he passed away quietly. He is to be buried in the Christian cemetery, and since there is no pastor here my husband will have to read the burial service for him.
>
> Born in the Sudan,[2] Dorugu became a Christian but in his own fashion, rather wishy-washy, as so often is the case with half-Europeanised Africans. In 1851 he had been presented to Dr. Henry Barth by one of the

2. The term *Sudan* here refers broadly to the geographical region south of the Sahara and not to the present country of that name.

emirs as a gift.[3] He accompanied that famous explorer
in his journey to Timbuktu and right across the desert
as far as Europe, where he received first-class school-
ing. It was then that he adopted Christianity. He was
shown off in many places and was even presented to
Queen Victoria and the King of Prussia. During his
time in London he made himself useful in a number
of studies on Sudanese languages. After eight years of
exile, Dorugu returned to his own country with a group
of missionaries.

Afterwards, he accompanied various explorers, soldiers, traders and administrators, to whom his services
as interpreter were invaluable. Finally, he was taken on
[here] at [the] Nassarawa [School], where he drew a
small pension that lightened the burden of his old age.
During his far-flung travels he had met a lot of very
interesting people. Sometimes, but all too rarely, he
would talk of his memories.

I visited him once, and I shall never forget the impression that this strange apparition made on me. The
old man was sitting on his bed, a simple local couch
overlaid with rush mats and a few blankets. Half-
naked, his body was nothing more than a skeleton with
brown parchment stretched over it. His eyes were deep-
ly sunk into a horribly thin face, yet they showed a
gentle and intelligent expression. Pushed up onto his
forehead was a pair of spectacles. Ah! Dorugu's spectacles! Everyone has seen them, it seems, but nobody
remembers ever having noticed them on his nose! He
addressed me in English: his speech was formally careful and correct, without the trace of an accent. His

3. This is incorrect. As explained earlier, Barth took Dorugu
on as a servant after the death of his companion Overweg.

conversation, which was graceful and unlabored, contrasted singularly with the old man's fierce appearance. His wife, a devoted Hausa woman, stood by his bedside. She looked after him to the end, showing unlimited selflessness.

6 December 1912. I fear that during his lifetime Dorugu succumbed to the sin of avarice! People were surprised to find in his house a whole collection of objects gathered over the years: boxes full of biscuits, cocoa, jams, all unopened . . . and a dozen pair of spectacles! You could list the names of all the Europeans with whom he had lived from the initials that were on the clothes in his extensive wardrobe. They also discovered £250 sterling, in little rolls of gold and silver pieces, quite a fortune in the eyes of his compatriots.

Nobody was really sure what religion Dorugu's widow was. The Native Court would have to hand over to her the whole estate if she said that she was a Christian like her husband; otherwise she would only receive a small portion of it. The *alkali* therefore explained the matter to her. In the face of such strong temptation, would it not have been easy for the poor woman to have answered without too strict a regard for the truth so as to inherit all of Dorugu's wealth? She did not even hesitate. Not only did she declare that she was a Moslem, but she even distributed as alms the little that she did inherit. She will continue her humble existence in obscurity.

As we have seen, Abbega left England in 1857, a full seven years before his companion. After returning to southern Nigeria by sea, he made no serious attempt to reach his

native Margi country, which lay far to the northeast, hard
by the western slopes of the Mandara hills. Instead he attached himself to the Yoruba-Sierra Leonean missionary,
Samuel Crowther, in his evangelical advance up the Niger.
This was fully in accordance with Barth's and Schön's
wishes, as evidenced by Schön's proud testimony: "Abbega
has returned to Africa with the Gospels in his hand, has
given evidence of his zeal for the conversion of others, and
has hitherto maintained his Christian character" (1862: x).
Schön's praise notwithstanding, Abbega later reconverted
to Islam, finding Christianity "full of drawbacks." Abbega
served for a time as a native catechist at Rabba, then the
capital of Nupeland, after which he returned to Lokoja, the
mission center situated at the confluence of the Niger and
the Benue. There he became interpreter to the scholar-
consul Dr. William Balfour Baikie, the founder and driving
force behind the settlement.[4] At this time Abbega was con-
versant, we are assured, with five African languages as well
as with Arabic and English (Pedraza 1960: 61).

When Baikie left Lokoja in 1864, his successor, Lyon
McLeod, enlisted a select body of personal messengers in
lieu of an official company of consular guards denied him
by the Foreign Office in London. Among these was Abbega,
who used to accompany the consul on visits to Masaba at
Bida. In the 1880s we find records of Abbega's employ-
ment as personal courier to the agent-general of the Com-
pagnie Française de l'Afrique Equatoriale, who doubled as
French consul in the delta area. In his diary, this consul,
Commandant Mattei, provides an amusing comment on
Abbega's style as an interpreter: "In his capacity as an in-

4. Earlier, the calamitous 1841 Niger expedition had chosen
Lokoja as a site for a mission settlement, but it was subsequently
abandoned.

terpreter this good fellow imagines that it would be derogatory for him not to know the answer to every question put to him, and that he is therefore bound to produce some sort of reply to whatever is asked him about the manners and customs of the country."

Abbega seems to have been recognized as an unofficial go-between with the Etsu (emir) Nupe at Bida, with whom he conducted a number of diplomatic-commercial negotiations, including the agreement for the settlement of the Catholic Fathers of Lyons at Lokoja in December 1884.[5] It is not surprising, therefore, that agents of the Royal Niger Company entrusted with the firm's expansion on the Niger and lower Benue during the last fifteen years of the century should find the presence of this polyglot, literate, and versatile man a valued asset to their administration in Lokoja. In 1896 Abbega was appointed chief of Lokoja. He was deposed the following year, reinstated the next, and then deposed again finally in 1904 (Pedraza 1960: 98).

In 1873 Abbega's daughter Salamatu married a Hausa, Yerima Abdu, who was the grandson of Abdussalam, a scion of the royal family of Gwandu in Sokoto. A son was born to them in 1874, and named Muhammadu. On his father's death shortly afterward, his mother took Muhammadu back home to Lokoja, where he was brought up in the household of his grandfather Abbega. This was the boy whom northern Nigeria would come to know and remember as Maimaina, the "king-prince." This nickname, which was coined for him by the Kanuri, developed into something like a personal title when he retained it after his elevation to a chieftaincy in 1913. Because of his contact with Royal Niger Company personnel through his grandfather Abbega, Maimaina soon

5. Though developed and administered by Europeans, Lokoja was nominally under the jurisdiction of the Etsu Nupe.

learned to speak English. Literacy, he liked to tell us in his
old age, he acquired later from the talented Sierra Leonean
clerk attached to Biu Division in the early 1920s, J. Adol-
phus Palmer. Such was Maimaina's linguistic prowess that
among the Kanuri of Bornu he was also referred to as
Maina Turjiman, "the prince of interpreters," a profession
he had inherited from his grandfather.

In the text that follows, Maimaina has written about his
life between the ages of twenty and thirty, so we will sketch
his story only from 1913 onward. This was the year when
W. P. Hewby, the famous Resident of Bornu Province with
whom Maimaina had worked so closely as interpreter and
political agent, retired from Nigeria. About this time Maimaina asked to leave government service; as an acknowledg-
ment of his loyal service he was made Chief of the Margi[6]
District of Bornu Province. This district had just been transfered out of the former Maiduguri Division to a newly constituted "Pagan" Division with its headquarters at Biu. The
presence of the notoriously lawless Chibuk people in the
area made it a difficult district to control, and much credit
was due to Maimaina for his stabilizing leadership. A senior
administrator on tour of the area in 1916 recorded his impression of Maimaina—in a style characteristic of the period
—as "one of the most efficient natives I have ever had to do
business with."

In 1917, the administration decided that the Shehu of
Bornu had legitimate traditional claims on some of the more
important Margi villages in the district (including Mulgwai,
Maimaina's own family fief on his maternal grandmother's
side), and that therefore Maimaina's jurisdiction should be

6. Except in direct quotations we have adopted the modern
spelling *Margi* in place of the older *Marghi,* however the word was
spelled at the time under discussion.

confined to a complex of mostly Chibuk villages, which would remain in Biu Division. Maimaina refused to accept this demotion and resigned. Perhaps not unrelated to the resignation are references in the Biu Division files to Maimaina's alleged rudeness to the Shehu and to the disappearance of $1,500 from the Margi Native Treasury, to which Maimaina, as chief, held one of the keys. Retiring to Potiskum in Fika Emirate in 1918, he took up trading.

When the Bornu-Yola provincial boundary was adjusted in 1921 to allow for an extended Margi grouping, Maimaina was invited to become chief of the new Margi district. He selected a site for his new headquarters in the thick of the bush some thirty-five miles northeast of Garkida. When the village was completed—years later he used to recount how no fewer than twenty-four lions were killed while the area was being cleared—he called it Askira, a jubilatory name derived from the Arabic root *shukr* meaning "thankfulness."

Maimaina was installed as Sarkin Askira on February 2, 1922. There he was to remain for over forty years, as the first chief of Askira, a district later advanced to its present status as a Subordinate Native Authority within the Biu Native Authority Federation. Once the initial problems of pacification and administrative organization were settled, Askira District, with its small population, limited economic resources, and chronic lack of communications, took its place among the quiet, generally ignored outlying regions of northern Nigeria.

If the government forgot about Askira for forty years, happily the administration did think of Maimaina in the end. In 1956 one of us (Kirk-Greene) found an opportunity to spend the Christmas holiday weekend interviewing Maimaina. A tape of his reminiscences was made for the national archives in cooperation with the Nigerian Broadcasting Corporation, and Maimaina was encouraged to write down his memoirs. This he did with characteristic application, and it was, he used to say, a very proud day for him when in 1958 Gaskiya Corporation published the first volume of *Labarin Maimaina Na Jega, Sarkin Askira*.

More recognition was to come. Learning of this vernacular autobiography and of Maimaina's subsequent award of the Queen's Medal for Chiefs, General Sir Francis Festing, Chief of the British Imperial General Staff, sent to Maimaina a letter of congratulation for his "unparalleled record of service to the Government and the people of Askira." General Festing was the nephew of Major Festing, whose employ Maimaina had entered in 1895; and, by yet another happy historical coincidence, the Resident of Bornu Province who delivered the general's letter to Maimaina in 1960 was the nephew of a former Bornu Resident under whom Maimaina had worked in 1905–10, Major Augustus McClintock. Maimaina's reply to General Festing ran thus:

> Very many greetings and unbounded respect. I have received your letter and the photograph which accompanied it which were sent to me by the Resident, Mr. McClintock. I cannot tell you what pleasure it has given me to receive this and to have news of you. I was so excited that I was unable to sleep at all and spent the night thanking God that He had allowed me to live to hear news of a descendant of my first master, Major Arthur Festing, from whom I was separated nearly 59 years ago, and who I shall never forget however long I may live.
>
> I hope that one day I may be able to visit England and meet you face to face.
>
> May Allah grant you increasing happiness and well-being.

Maimaina's crowning achievement came in 1961 when he was appointed to the upper legislative chamber of the then Northern Region and became a member of the House of Chiefs. He died in 1964, shortly after his ninetieth birthday.

The Dorugu translation is based on the text in the 1885 edition of James F. Schön's *Magána Hausa*. The autobiography takes up about one third of that volume, the rest consisting of short narratives and folktales, of linguistic but not historical interest. Excerpts had appeared earlier in Schön's *Hausa Grammar* (1862) and his *Hausa Dictionary* (1876), but the full Hausa text was not published until 1885. The title page erroneously reads "To which is added A TRANSLATION IN ENGLISH"; in fact, the vernacular texts were published by themselves. An English translation of the entire volume did come out the following year, but despite its separate title page it was bound into one volume with the 1885 text and labeled (inaccurately) on the cover and spine *Magàna Hausa*. Schön looked on this as comprising

> a close translation of the Hausa text, published separately, but originally designed to be appended to it as sent, and published in one volume; chiefly with a view to supply students of the Hausa language with a connected literature in their own tongue: and at the same time, the acquisition of English being an object eagerly pursued by such students, to enable them to become familiar with it through the medium of their own language." [1886: v]

In 1906, C. H. Robinson, lecturer in Hausa at Cambridge University, issued a reedited version of Schön's entire text, but without the English translation. The editing consisted primarily in orthographic changes and would-be simplifications, such as the removal of diacritics and the elimination of capital letters, and in the use of double letters for geminate consonants that Schön had failed to hear and mark. (Robinson also used double letters in many places where Schön had been correct in not using them.) The major correction in the new edition was the addition of the feminine genitival linker *r* between nouns, absent in Schön's texts. We now know that Schön's error was phonological and not grammatical. Dorugu's dialect undoubtedly made use of grammatical linkers with feminine nouns but these would have been indicated by gemination rather than by an *r*—and Schön never distinguished double from single consonants. Thus, the title *Magána Hausa* should not be amended to *Magánar Hausa*[7] but rather to *Magánah Hausa*.

As regards English versions, the present volume is the first revised edition to appear since the original 1886 publication. The children's abridgments, issued in the Little Books for Africa series as *The Story of Dorugu* (1932a) and its companion volume *Hausa Tales Told by Dorugu and Others* (1932b), hardly deserve mentioning, as they consist of nothing more than disjointed fragments of Schön's translation lifted from the original and reset in larger type.

While by no means readily accessible, the Hausa text of Dorugu's autobiography has been studied through the years by a century of language scholars and its worth fully appreciated. Its understandably dated orthography does not make it easy reading for a non-native student of the language nor for a native Hausa speaker brought up on modern orthography, but it is still an important source of information about archaisms and dialect variants in the language. Sample pages from the original 1885 edition are reproduced in appendix A of this volume.

7. This is the way the title is cited, for instance, in the bibliography in Smith (1967).

By contrast, the richness of the autobiography as a socio-logical/historical document has gone almost entirely un-recognized. Interestingly, Schön, whose professed concern with the texts was primarily linguistic, sensed the significance and uniqueness of the content:

> As to their import when read in an English translation, it may be feared that some of them will appear trivial and hardly worth the trouble of translating; it is there-fore necessary to bear in mind that the *language* of the original is the main object of publication, and, of course, also to facilitate an acquisition of a knowledge of it. On the other hand, I can assure the reader that almost every story contributes something as regards *forms* or *words* peculiar to itself. At the same time, I cannot but think that many will find the book interest-ing and entertaining, sometimes even amusing. The Life and Travels of Dorugu supply many geographical hints, and will be read with interest. His observations on English cookery, dinner parties and customs, show a shrewd and observing mind. The narratives exhibit the native way of thinking and arguing, they lead us into the secrets of family and public life; we learn something of slavery, of the state, quarrels and disputes occasioned by the institution of polygamy, condemning the system in their popular songs and traditions; of their views of heaven and hell, sun, moon and stars; also the love of money, so characteristic of the Negro race; much of human cunning, and especially in wom-en. It is also interesting to know that what education there exists among the people is conveyed by narratives of this kind. [Schön 1885: vii–viii]

The Maimaina narrative is a direct translation of the au-tobiography published in Zaria, Nigeria, in 1958. It covers

the story of Maimaina's life up to about 1910 and was meant
to be a first part of his memoirs.[8] Up to the present time, the
remaining parts have not been published, although it seems
that Maimaina did complete at least part of them.[9] The
Hausa text was edited to conform to present-day standard
orthography by the North Regional Literature Agency
(NORLA) and therefore does not pose any unusual problems for students learning the language. It is reproduced in
toto as appendix B to this volume, by courtesy of the former
Gaskiya Corporation.

In cross-checking the two autobiographies presented here
with Barth's own account[10] and with established sources for
the early colonial period, we have been continually impressed by the remarkable accuracy of both Dorugu and
Maimaina with regard to dates, names, and details of events.
So much so, in fact, that we feel compelled to urge universities and research institutes, professional scholars, local
teachers, amateur historical research organizations, and in-
dividual historians to direct their energies to this valuable
and—literally—unique sector of oral history before it is too
late and those who can still give firsthand descriptions of

8. This fact is indicated both on the title page and on the last
page.
9. The present chief of Askira, Maimaina's grandson, reports
having seen additional manuscript, which he is now unable to
locate.
10. The citations from Barth's *Travels and Discoveries in Central
Africa,* which make such a fascinating control for parts of the
Dorugu narrative, are taken from the three-volume centenary edition published in 1965. The pagination of this edition is the same
as the standard American edition published by Harper and Brothers,
New York, in 1857–59, of which it is a photographic reprint. Unless
indicated otherwise, all Barth references will be to volume and page
of his *Travels.*

major historical personalities and events are no longer with us. Without in any way challenging the importance of historical research by means of archaeological and linguistic techniques, we believe that what is most urgently needed at this point is intensive work at the level of basic oral history. In the matter of priorities, sites that have lain undug for centuries will not suffer by waiting another year or two; Arabic manuscripts that have survived the past hundred years may likely survive the next few months; but men and women who have lived through the 1890s and experienced the traumatic events of the turn of the century are increasingly fewer in number. Unlike artifacts, these old people can leave behind no evidence of their rich and varied experiences unless individuals act quickly to record their memories and thus make a lasting contribution to the history of Nigeria and all of West Africa.

A.K.–G.
P.N.

Oxford University
Yale University
June 1970

"Frederick Buxton Abbega" and "James Henry Dorugu," Barth's servants.
Reproduced from G. von Schubert, *H. Barth: der Bahnbrecher der deutschen
Afrika forschung* (Berlin, 1897).

Abbega, chief of Lokoja, as an old man. Reproduced from Olive Macleod, *Chiefs and Cities of Central Africa* (Edinburgh and London: Blackwood, 1912).

Heinrich Barth. Reproduced by permission of the Royal Geographical Society, London.

Maimaina Jega, chief of Askira, at age eighty-eight. Reproduced, by permission, from D. J. M. Muffett, *Concerning Brave Captains: A History of Lord Lugard's Conquest of Hausaland* (London: André Deutsch, 1964).

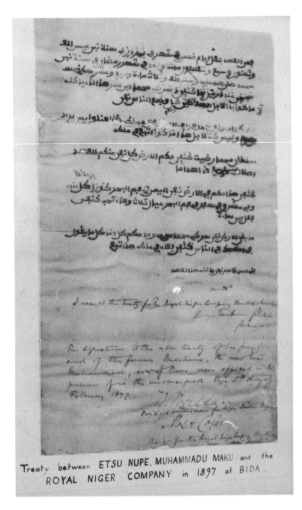

Treaty between Etsu Nupe, Muhammadu Maku, and the Royal Niger Company in 1897 at Bida. (Photograph by Anthony Kirk-Greene.)

PART I

The Life and Travels of Dorugu

TRANSLATED AND ANNOTATED

by Paul Newman

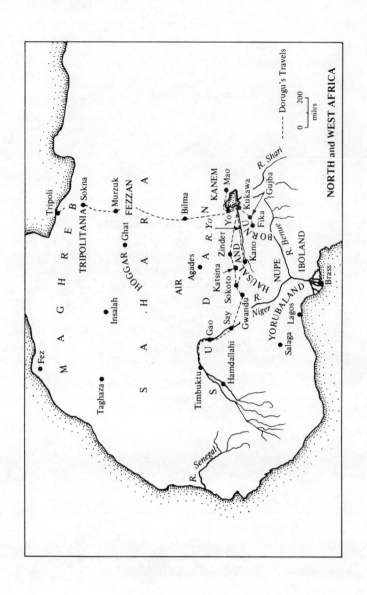

NORTH and WEST AFRICA

Dorugu's Travels ------

0   200
miles

MAGHREB

TRIPOLITANIA

Fez

Taghaza

Insalah

HOGGAR

Ghat

FEZZAN

Murzuk

Sokna

Tripoli

Bilma

S A H A R A

AIR

Agades

KANEM

R. Shari

Mao

Yo

Kukawa

R. Yo

Zinder

BORNU

Katsina

Kano

Fika

Gujba

R. Benue

Sokoto

HAUSALAND

Say

Gwandu

R. Niger

NUPE

IBOLAND

Gao

YORUBALAND

Brass

Hamdallahi

Salaga

Lagos

SUDAN

Timbuktu

R. Senegal

Chapter I

I was born in a village called Dambanas, about a day's journey from the city of Kanche.[1] My father, Kwage Adamu, and mother, whose name was Kande, lived together in Dambanas. I also had a younger brother named Hakurau and a younger sister named Taroko. The three of us were born in the same town. My father lived in that town for many years. He was a drummer, but he also had a small farm. We children were not able to do much work because we were not grown up.

When I saw that my father and mother were overburdened with farmwork, I said to my father, "I eat and drink but I'm not able to do anything. I wish you would give me a hoe so that I could help on the farm." He answered, "You're not old enough to work. Wait a few years, then I'll give you a hoe to use."

I started to cry because I wanted to work. So we went to town and he told a blacksmith to make me a hoe. When the blacksmith had finished making it and my father brought it to me, I was very happy.

The next day we arose early and went to the farm,[2] but my mother stayed at home preparing food. When she had finished, she brought it to the farm for us. Soon thereafter, they started eating their food, but I didn't want to stop and eat because I was enjoying farming.

My father took hold of me and said, "Eat your food; we've finished ours." Only then did I eat.

When we saw that there was very little corn in the farm that year, my father let it go and planted another one close to the house. We did get some corn from the one close to home, but not very much. In addition, we had a cotton farm which my father and I used to go to. My mother also used to go with us, but my sister was not well enough to go.

One evening when we were returning from the cotton farm, I spotted my brother from a distance—he had been left alone at home—along with another small child. My mother said to my father, "Look there at Hakurau and Taroko!" We were very much surprised. "How can she be well enough to come outside and play?"

But when we got home and entered the yard, I found that the other child was not my sister. I ran into the room calling her name, "Taroko! Taroko!" but she didn't answer. I was sure that she hadn't moved at all. The place where she was lying was filled with slime. Then I knew that she was dead and so I began to cry. When my father came in, he picked her up and looked at her until tears poured from his eyes. My mother was crying too, but my brother was too young to understand anything. My father asked him, "Did you give her *fura?*"[3] He answered, "Yes." "Did you give her water?" "Yes." After my father had questioned him like that, he didn't say anything. Finally he said, "Since she didn't die of starvation, it's all right."

My father called one of his friends and asked him to prepare a grave to bury her in. When the man had dug the grave, he put branches in it. They wrapped her in a cloth, then he picked her up and put her in the grave. He piled wood around the mouth of the grave and closed it up with wood. Then he poured on earth and closed it up completely.

The next day, my father asked my mother, "What sadaka[4] shall we do for her?" She answered, "We should buy some beans and make some *fura* so we'll have something to give away to important people." He said, "All right."

He went and bought beans and brought them to her. She made flour into *fura* and cooked the beans. Then we took them and carried them to the town square for important people. After they had finished eating the beans and the *fura,* some mallams[5] recited prayers. Then we went home and that was that.

Some time after the death of my sister, I heard news of war approaching our town.[6] We left in the night and fled a distance of two or three days' journey. But the rumor turned out to be untrue.

The next day people saw that their children were exhausted from traveling. As for me, I was also crying because I was tired. Whenever people heard an infant cry, they would say to its mother, "Give him a breast to suck so that he'll be quiet!" After we had been in the bush a while,[7] I think some people returned to town and discovered that no one had come to make war. They came back and told us, whereupon we returned to town.

It so happens that there was a thief who had stayed in town and had stolen a large number of things. He stayed there until we returned. When we came back, we found the town had been consumed by flames because the thief had set it on fire. Only my father's house and the house of an old woman had not been burned, although donkeys, goats, sheep, and chickens had gone into my father's room and were playing there. Close by there was a type of fig tree that we call *cediya* (it has large branches and bears a small fruit which very few people eat), whose branches had felt the fire and had dried up.

When I saw my dog, I chased it away. I didn't recognize it because it had grown. My father said, "Don't chase it away. Don't you remember that when we fled you left it at home?" I replied, "Yes, I remember," but added, "when we left it, it was little, but now it has grown up." He nodded yes.[8]

On returning we found that there had been no damage to the town except what had been caused by fire. When we resettled, the women looked all over for their pots, but they weren't able to find them until they finally discovered them at some man's place. Each woman then carried away her pot and went home with it. And that was my experience of war.

About a year later, we heard a rumor that another town was preparing to make war on our town. We fled to the bush again, but not very far from town, and there we slept. In the morning, we saw Fulanis on horseback some distance from our town. The way we were able to see them was by having a lookout climb a tree. One particularly careful person climbed to the top of a tree so that he could see everything. Whenever people came out of the town, he would warn us to get ready to fight them, with the result that our men did capture some people. While they set the town on fire, we watched everything they were doing. After destroying the town they went away. There was nothing left to see in the town except smoke.

The boy up above saw two men who had seen him in the tree running from the town toward us. He informed us immediately and my father and two other men intercepted them. When they met in the woods, they asked, "Are you one of us or not?" The two men answered, "Yes, we are one of you." They had come from our town, and since we knew them we were pleased to see them. We asked, "How did you know we were here?" They answered, "We saw one of you keeping watch in a tree." We asked them about news of the town. They told us that some people had been killed, some had been wounded, and some had been made slaves. We had seen some people carrying off booty from our town going toward their town (which was called Shagari). After they told us what had happened, we returned to our own town and remained there.

After this raid, we heard that the Shehu of Bornu, Shehu Umar,[9] was coming to make war on Kanche. He advanced without being seen until at midday he was seen in formation [with his men]. He came and made war on the chief of Kanche and totally defeated him. He set fire to the town, looted it, and then returned to his own town. We could hear the sound of their guns from Dambanas. In addition they raided another town called Tassawa.[10] The people of this town fought like fire and consequently were not conquered. Afterwards the Shehu went back to his town, but some of his men didn't go.

At that time, there was a famine. A man from another village, whose daughter my father had taken as a wife, came to my father and said, "I cannot allow my daughter to stay in your house, for she will die of starvation." He took hold of her and carried her away from my father's house, to a town called Bangasa. My younger brother and I wept because our mother had been taken away from our father.[11]

She was given to a certain man to be his wife, but because she didn't love him, she would run away to my father's house. Then he would come again and take her back to

Bangasa. But she refused to stay in that village. Whenever her husband went to the farm, expecting her to bring him food there, she would run away and come to our house, whereupon that man or her father would come and take her back again.

One day when her husband had gone to the farm, she stayed at home and prepared *fura* to take to him there. At the time, there were still some Kanuri around,[12] since not all who had made war on Kanche had gone away. When she was on her way, carrying the *fura* and her hoe, they ambushed her from behind some trees. They seized her and took her away. When my father heard the news he told us, "Your mother has been captured. There is nothing we can do but be patient and hope." Then he took my brother and gave him to a man from Tassawa to become like his own son. He said, "You needn't return my son to me until we meet again in the Afterlife." I cried because he had sent my brother there. I stayed quiet but I said to myself, "As soon as I grow up, I am not going to let my brother stay there."

I believe my brother was six or seven years old when he was given away. If I were to go there now, I would only be able to recognize him by his tribal marks, but he would not be able to recognize me (even by my tribal marks) unless I said something to him.

After a while, we heard that a chief named Tanimu was coming and that he would pass near our town.[13] When we heard this, people began to make preparations. When evening came, we heard them pass by. The men of the town set a crossbeam in place and brought support for the gate.[14] He [Tanimu] asked us to let him in so that he could get water to drink, but we refused. He became angry and went away. Some old men who were too tired to travel anymore remained behind. In the morning, we found them outside the town walls. Here is the song of one of them:

The night, the night, children of Kworgum,[15]
The night, the night,
If you do not know the night, hyenas will eat you.
There is no savior nearby,
Tanimu is a man of guns,[16]
The man of Yado is a bull.

Some time within that year, we heard that men of Bornu
had entered Kanche. I think that the chief of Kanche ceded
our town to them, but he warned them to be careful in trying to conquer us. Therefore, they were very clever. The
next day they entered the town one by one until our town
was full of them. My father told me to go hide, so I ran and
hid in the grass near the water and waited there. He came
to look for me in the grass and called me. I could hear him,
but I did not answer. Only when he called me a second time
did I answer. He reassured me, "Everything is all right now."
I answered, "If everything is all right, let's go home." We
went back and stayed there, but I was still very much upset.

I said to my father's wife, who was named Baka, "You
take your calabash and let me take my bow and my father's
straw hat and let's go to some other town." (This was my
father's wife but not my own mother.[17] My father told me
that he had married her when he was a young man and she
likewise was very young. I do not know what caused her to
leave his house, whether he sent her away or whether they
were separated by war. I think she must have been a slave,
because she could speak Kanuri.[18] Nevertheless, in the
house he treated her just like he treated my mother.) When
she heard what I had to say, she did not make fun of me.
(At the time, I think I was just eleven years old.) Rather, she
took her calabash and walked ahead while I followed her,
until we had even crossed a stream. My father was not at
home since he had gone with some men to listen for news.

When he came home and did not find us, he started running until he caught up with us and made us go back home. My heart was pounding furiously.

Some time later, he saw a man on horseback come and dismount at our house. He was a Hausa man. Afterward, another man came—a Kanuri man—who wanted corn for his horse, but we didn't have any. He spoke the language of Bornu [i.e. Kanuri] with my father's wife. Whenever he said something in Kanuri, I had to ask her what he had said to her. She told me that he wanted corn, and I told him that we didn't have any. He said that he was going to have some young men go into our house to take a look. When I heard this, I was frightened. A little while later, we heard that the chief was coming. In the evening about sunset, we heard that a man had come and was saying that all strangers should saddle up and mount their horses.

Then we heard the sound of the chief approaching with drums and horns.[19] At the moment the guns were fired, all the strangers started to capture their "hosts." My father had told me to go with him to a certain gate, but my head was all mixed up. I didn't know what to do, with the result that the Bornu man who had been in my father's house finally caught me. The Hausa man captured my father and someone else captured my father's wife, although who it was I don't know. All the children in town were crying. Mothers were separated from their children and husbands were separated from their wives.[20] And thus we were led away.

As we were leaving the town, he [my captor] dragged me through some thorns. Both he and I were in the briers. He took his horse by the hand and pulled me and the horse along until we came to a town. The briers had pricked my feet so that they were all bloody. He mounted his horse and then lifted me up and put me on the back. I really couldn't pay any attention to whether the thorns had pricked my feet or not since I was absorbed in worrying about what was going to happen to me. I saw a friend of mine riding on the back of his master's horse, and I called to him, "Do you see? We have become slaves." He replied, "There is nothing we can do except put our trust in God's works."

When we arrived at the war camp, we dismounted. As I was looking around, I saw my father's wife being led to the chief by a man with a knife in his hand. I felt my feet itching and then noticed that my feet were all bloody. They brought some nuts for us, but we didn't eat any. We weren't hungry because we were so unhappy. After they carried off everything from our town, they set it on fire. Chicken eggs were exploding like guns, as the fire reached everywhere. The fire continued burning in the town even into the next day.

They took us before their chief in order to show him the slaves that they had captured. When he had seen all of us they took us away. This was the beginning of slavery for me. If we had known they were going to capture us, we would have fought, but they outsmarted us. Our arrows are poisoned and the poison is very strong. If you were to lick it with your tongue it would kill you. So if we had fought them, many of them would have died, although they would have killed some of us too. But they didn't fight to take the town openly, but caught us secretly as one catches little chicks. I don't know whether even one of them died in our town or whether an arrow was shot.

When they left the hill on which they were encamped, they took along those of us they had caught, including me. I don't think that they had caught more than two or three hundred people (although they might have sent some away during the night). As we were going, we passed by another town close to ours. The people of that town were also captured and the town was set on fire. (I think there were about four hundred of them.) And so we proceeded together with them.

We arrived in a big town and spent the night there. The next morning they continued on with us to my grandmother's village, called Kunduwoshe. I saw my grandmother standing in her house. When she saw me, her whole body trembled. She asked me, "Where is Adamu?" I said, "I don't know." Then I simply said, "Good-bye." As I went on, I was crying. I saw a pair of twins lying on the road.[21] They were crying but they were too young to talk. And then we arrived in Zinder.

Chapter II

When we arrived in Zinder, we stayed there for many days, although some of the slaves were sent on to Bornu. I heard the news that the chief of Zinder had given my father his freedom and had said, "Go look for your son. When you find him, take him back to your town with you."[1]

My father took his drum[2] and went around drumming, because he knew that if I heard the sound of his drum I would come to him. From inside the house, I heard drumming that sounded like his, but I was not allowed to leave the house except when I went to get water for the horses. While I was in the house, other slaves belonging to my master went to fetch water and on the way met my father resting against a rock. He was waiting for me to come, but I had not gone to fetch water. He asked them, "Where is Dorugu?" They said, "He's in the house. We called him but he didn't hear us." They went on to get the water and then returned and informed me, "Dorugu, we just saw your father sitting there on the way to the water. He was waiting for you." I asked them, "Why didn't you call me?" They said, "We called you but you didn't hear us."[3]

I was given a new name. When they asked me my name I told them it was "Dorugu," nevertheless they called me by a Kanuri name, Barka Gana.[4] The compound in which I lived was divided into two parts. The quarters for the male slaves were on one side and those for the female slaves were on the other. There was no way to go from one to the other except by the one passageway in front of the master's doorway. I always used to go and chat with the women and we would laugh and play. No one else went except me, for I was very innocent. Every morning as I passed by, my master would call out to me, "Barka Gana, drummer!" I would laugh and continue on to the female slaves' quarters.

Our master had one slave, a concubine, who was the head of all the female slaves. Once when I went to them in the evening, my master's concubine was in her room. When she called me I thought she had something good to tell me. She climbed on her bed and said to me, "Barka Gana, get up on the bed."

I asked, "What am I supposed to do?"

"Come lie with me."

"I can't."

When she called me my body began to tremble. I was sitting close to the fire. The room was dark.

She called to me, "Come here!"

"I won't."

"Why not?"

"I don't know."

"Are you afraid?"

"Yes."

"What are you afraid of?"

"I don't want to sleep with you."

"I insist that you sleep with me."

I wanted to run away but she stopped me. I repeated, "I refuse!"

She said, "All right, but when you leave don't say anything to anyone. If I hear that you've told anyone, I'll beat you."

I said, "I understand. I won't tell anyone."

When I left, the female slaves were seated outside by the doorway. I think they knew what had delayed me like that. I sat with them a little while and we conversed in Hausa. When I saw her come out of her room, I got up and went away. Leaving, I ran into my master. He called me— "Barka Gana!" I greeted him and he gave me a kolanut.

I didn't visit these women after that, because of my master's concubine; but I have kept the secret until now. I think the woman behaved that way toward me on purpose because she thought I was accustomed to sleeping with female slaves in our town. Although she touched me, she didn't catch me. A day or two later, I heard I was to be sent to Bornu. I asked, "Am I being sent to Bornu?" They said yes. I replied, "That's good."[5]

They gave me a gourd to put water in, then they put me on a horse and went with me. They wanted to catch up with some men with cattle. When the horse ran, the water in the gourd made a sound, *blum-blum*.[6] They were laughing and talking to one another in Kanuri. I couldn't understand anything they were saying. It was just as if I were deaf. Finally we caught up with the men with the cattle, whereupon I was transfered to a bullock.[7] I immediately met a boy, or rather a young man, who spoke Hausa. On the whole, they treated me well all the way to Bornu.

I saw that Bornu was a large country. They stopped at a certain house, and there I saw Fara, my master's wife. The name of the city was Kukawa.[8] From Zinder to Kukawa is a distance of twenty days by foot and ten days by horse.[9] My master's wife had a four-year-old daughter and I think she and her mother both liked me. There was a large number of female slaves in that compound. Whenever the daughter of my master's wife had anything to eat, she would give me the leftovers. When she became ill with smallpox, it was I who stayed near her and brought things to her. In addition there was an old slave woman, in charge of the other slaves, who came and stayed with my master's daughter. The three of us stayed together until the daughter recovered.

One day as I was sitting in the room near the entrance to the compound, I began scratching in the sand, thinking that I might find a piece of kolanut, and I discovered a hole. I kept digging until I hit something hard underneath—a piece of a pot. I pulled it out and saw that I had accidentally found some cowries.[10] When I saw that there was a large number of cowries, I left them alone. I went and called the old woman and said, "Look at the cowries I found. But I don't know whose they are." I was speaking Hausa, but since she could not understand Hausa, I just said, "It was God who showed this to me."

She took all of the cowries—about a hundred, I think—and only gave me eight. Unquestionably the cowries belonged to someone else. She went and bought herself something with them. When people questioned this woman about the cowries, she said that I had taken them. I told them I had found the cowries, but that she had taken them away from me and had only given me eight. So they didn't say any more about it and let the matter drop.

Once I went to a compound where there was a woman

from my town. There was also a Hausa boy at her place.
Both of them knew Hausa, but since they had come to
Bornu they had almost forgotten how to speak it. I used to
go and see them. Once when I had gone, my mistress came
and saw me talking with her. She caught hold of me, took
off my robe, and tied me up with her cloth. I cried and
trembled with fear. She said to her son in Kanuri, "Kalur
kude shiga jer," which means "Bring chains and put him
in them." I could understand very little of Kanuri, but
that much I understood. Then her son went into the room
to look for the chains. When I heard him grab the chains, I
started to tremble. I carefully loosened the knot, and while
she was chatting in Kanuri I ran away.

I sped to my master's wife and threw myself at her feet.
She said to me, "Be still!" I was speaking in Hausa, so she
couldn't understand anything I was saying. She called a
slave who understood Hausa, whereupon I told her everything that had happened. Shortly thereafter, I saw that other
woman enter the house. She told my master's wife what she
had thought. A girl who understood [Kanuri and] Hausa
overheard them and related their conversation to me in
Hausa. She said, "That woman thought that, because you
were talking with a slave from your town, you were planning to run away with her." I think I didn't even reply. I
just went out and sat down, and then she finally left.

While I stayed in that household I didn't do anything,
even though there was work waiting for me, since they
wanted me to rest up from my journey from Zinder to
Kukawa. When I had rested, they took me to where my
master's slaves were house-building. They were building a
new compound there. I carried earth along with those who
were building the house. At certain times, we would go and
look after the horses, but in the evenings I would always

return to the house. Sometimes we would go into the city to get *tuwo* to eat.[11] In Kanuri, they call this kind of *tuwo* with sauce *bargashi*. When we had finished, we would go back to carrying earth.

After a while, I heard that my master was coming from Zinder with his slaves and concubines. All of us left the new compound and waited for him at the old house. In the evening, we heard them coming by the beating of the drums. That night we ate delicious *tuwo* with honey and butter. We welcomed them and then we returned to our new compound. The next morning, my master came to see how we were doing with this house. When he came and saw me, he said, "Barka Gana, how have you been?" I replied, "Very well, thank you." There were two or three rooms in that compound where he always used to go to rest.

I heard that I was to be given away because of a debt. I was told this by a boy who spoke Kanuri. I said all right. One day when an Arab came, the boy said to me, "Do you see that white man?[12] That's who you are going to be given to." I said to myself, "What can I do? I don't know what to do." The boy said to me, "When you see that white man coming, go into the bush and hide and don't come out until evening."

But I didn't pay close attention to what he was saying. Some time later, the man came when my master was also there. All of us slaves assembled and then they called me. The Arab examined my eyes, my tongue, my hands, and even my feet. When he had finished looking, they began to talk, although I didn't know what they were saying. The Arab mounted his horse. Then they said to me, "Go with him." "Why?" I asked. They said to me in Hausa, "Go and fetch some wood from his house." I told them, "You're lying. I know that you've sold me."

I went with the Arab—that is to say, my new master—all the way to his house in the city. He took me to his wife and she looked at me. He called one of his slaves who spoke Hausa and said to her, "Ask him where he comes from." I answered, "Hausaland."

She showed me where she and her husband lived and ate their meals, and I stayed there with them. She treated me as if I were her own son. In the mornings, I would go to the bush with two other slaves to find firewood and bring it home. Sometimes, we went to gather grass. Once the Arab asked me if I would take his horse to Kano to sell it. I refused, explaining, "I'm a slave myself. If I should go to sell a horse, won't they sell me instead of the horse?"

While I was in the Arab's household, a native man named Ibrahim came to his house. He asked my master if he would let me go on a trip to Kanem.[13] I think he agreed to let me go, although I could not understand what they were saying since I didn't speak any Kanuri or Arabic. My master and this man Ibrahim went ahead, and I followed them until we reached the house of a man called Tabib,[14] where Ibrahim lived. Ibrahim was this man's servant. When we entered the house I saw that supplies for traveling had been prepared. As we were sitting there, I saw a tall man come out. His face and hands were all white like paper. He had a red fez on his head, a long beard, and was wearing a white robe. He was looking me over. I was as afraid as if he were about to eat me. There was another man there named Yamadugana, which means "Little Mohammed," who spoke fluent Hausa. He asked me if I wanted to go with them to Kanem and lead my master's camel. Then he added that dates were found there in large quantities. They supposed that if they said that, I would be willing to lead my master's camel there in order to get dates to eat, but I wouldn't agree. They kept urging me, but I would hear nothing of it. My master and I returned to the house and slept.

In the morning, he gave me a *daura,* a slipover white shirt that we call *taguwa* in Hausa, and said, "Put it on." When I had put it on, we went to the house where we had been the previous day. They lined up the camels; then they gave me a rope to lead the camels out. We left town and went on until we were in the midst of the bush.[15]

Chapter III

Whenever my master went hunting, I saw him put the long metal rod in his gun, and watched him as he moved carefully. Once, when he saw a bird in the shrubs, he shot it and called to me, "Barka, Barka!" I ran and picked up the bird, but we couldn't find the gun rod. I took the bird to his servant, who cooked it and brought it back. I think he ate it with his friend Abdul Karim.[1] We spent that night in the bush because there was no town nearby.[2]

The next morning we got up and reached a town called Yo where we stayed for three or four days.[3] Yo is a town near the lake [Lake Chad], and so there were many very good fish to eat. They fished in groups. They would enter the water with two large gourd containers and a small stick. Whenever they caught a large fish, they would crack its head with the stick. We stayed in that town until we found some companions who were going to Kanem.[4] We crossed the river with them and eventually reached Kanem.

The people of Kanem came out to meet us, greeted us, and then returned to their houses. In the evening, the chief sent us some camel's milk, which we drank until we had had enough. We gave what was left over to the horses. They drank it and ate grass. We ate *tuwo* and dates and then went to sleep. In the morning we heard screams from a pit trap. The men mounted their horses and the herdsmen drove their camels home; however, when they didn't find anything, they came back and ignored the matter. We spent another day there, then we left and went to another place, where we stopped.[5]

The people of Kanem do not stay in one place.[6] Wherever they may be on Friday, the next day they will get up and go somewhere else, (in other words, they never stay anywhere longer than a week). They do not have farms; rather, they subsist on camel's milk. The chief had about twenty cows, and his horses were good and fast.

After we had settled there, I heard that our companions wanted to make war. They were going to raid some people a day's journey from Kanem, who were Tubu of sorts.[7] When they made their preparations, they carried nothing on their camels except empty sacks.[8] We also took two camels from our household. We loaded them with a tent and food and went along with the Kanem people. Night came while we were traveling. We stopped to sleep but didn't light fires lest they be seen in the night.[9] We got up in the middle of the night. I mounted a camel belonging to a Kanem man and galloped with another boy. Soon I tired of racing so I got down and went on foot with my master's camel. They stopped again, rested for a little while, then started again. The horsemen, however, went ahead to battle.[10] Some of them captured slaves, and others came away with cattle and goats. We went forward to meet them, whereupon they left the booty with us.

They rode ahead until they came to a large town.[11] When they saw how large the town was and the people coming out, they said to them, "We haven't come to make war on your town." The people withdrew to their town, but they were cleverer than we. When our men came back, they found that we had dismounted, so we spent the entire day there. Tabib and Abdul Karim drank coffee under the shade of an ox-hide, while we ate dates.

The men of the city hid their wives and children and cattle. They gathered all their belongings and carried them into a thicket of date palms. Only the men slept in town. But they didn't actually sleep, rather they lay in wait the entire night.[12] Our men rose very early in the morning before sunrise and saddled their horses. They loaded their guns, then headed toward the city. They fought, shots flying past, *kiu kiu,* until full daylight. The men of that town, the Tubu, repulsed them. When we saw them rushing toward us, we said, "Let's get up and make a run for it because our side is being overrun."[13]

I mounted a camel and Tabib gave me a small box to carry. As the camel ran, the box weighed me down until I fell off with it. I got up with the box and started to run on foot. We climbed a hill and there we stopped until they caught up with us. They passed the place where we had stopped to rest and where, consequently, goods had been left. They caught up with a man and tore open his chest with a spear, and they also killed another man there.[14]

After they pulled back, we returned to our campsite. They had taken all our things and had maliciously cut open the sacks filled with corn.[15] Since they took our tent along with the rest of our belongings, we had to spend the entire day in the sun.[16] When our chief came, he and his men galloped around our campsite three times, the chief followed by a man who was shouting and yelling. Only then did they enter and dismount. That is the war I saw in

Kanem. There was no other place to get corn except at the place where they had fought.

When we left Kanem, we followed our previous route, which led to Kukawa. We settled in our house which, however, was not near the Shehu's.[17] One night, my old master came to take me back to his house, but Tabib wouldn't let him. He said he wanted to take me back to my master's house himself. They were in the midst of making me a white cotton robe. He told Ibrahim to saddle his horse and that when it was saddled, he would mount by the door, which he did. Ibrahim went ahead of me, following Tabib on horseback, while I followed behind. When we all reached my master's house Ibrahim called my master, who came out and spoke with him in Arabic. I think Tabib gave him some money. Then I entered the house. When my master's wife saw me she was very pleased. Tabib and Ibrahim had returned to their house.

When my master sat down in his room, he called me and told me to give him my robe. I took it off and gave it to him, and I gave him my small knife as well. He took everything I had away from me and just gave me one small robe. I went and sat down, feeling very angry. I kept saying, "May God send me back to Tabib's household!" After I had stayed in his house for a little while, he sold me to another man, an Arab like himself, and so I fell into the hands of a new master. His name was Bohal, I think, and he lived in the Arab quarter. Every day, he would go out for a ride and I would follow him, so that when he dismounted I could hold the horse for him. I liked this new master of mine because he was good-natured. He liked many people in Kukawa and many people knew and liked him.

After some days had passed, I saw Ibrahim at my mas-

ter's house. He asked me if I would like to return to Tabib's
household. I said I would. He informed me, "Tabib likes
you enough to buy you."

I said, "I'd be very happy if he would buy me."

He asked my master if he would be willing to sell me, and
he said yes. He asked him how much money he wanted. I
think he agreed to sell me for fifteen silver dollars.[18] He
went and told Tabib and soon after he returned to us with
the money in a piece of cloth. He poured it on the ground
and they counted it and found it to be correct. Ibrahim called
me and we left. As we were going, we had a talk. He said
to me, "Now you are no longer a slave." But I didn't believe it until we reached Tabib's house.

He came out and I greeted him. He could speak a little bit
of Hausa. They called for a mallam named Madiarimami
and another mallam as well. They wrote out a certificate for
me; then someone said, "Give him his certificate." But
Madiarimami said, "If you give it to him he will lose it since
he is just a boy. It would be better if you gave it to Tabib
to hold for him until he grows up." So they gave it to him.
He said to me, "Now you are free, you are no longer a
slave." I thanked him. I was extremely happy that I had
been placed in his hands.

At night Tabib spread out a mat for me to sleep on in
his room. He, on the other hand, slept on a bed. In the
morning, I would go out and wash my face. He told his
servant to teach me how to make coffee, after which I used
to make the coffee and wash the things he drank it in. Sometimes when his horse was saddled, I would go with him to
the house of the vizier, Haj Bashir, the Shehu's top coun-
cilor.[19] When we left there, he would go to the house of
another friend of his named Alhaji, and then return home.
Whenever he stopped, I would take care of the horse until

he came out again, and so on until we finally returned home. Sometimes he and Abdul Karim went to the Shehu's palace. The Shehu used to give them horses and camels and food.

During the time I stayed with Tabib, he went out every morning and evening for a breath of air. He would take his gun and sling it around his neck, and we would go hunting. He had an excellent eye for hunting. Whenever he saw a bird or a gazelle he would kill it. I held his horse whenever he dismounted. When the sun began to set we would return home.

Once we went to a town near Lake Chad where he had a friend.[20] We went hunting there with his servant Ibrahim and his Kanembu friend. He shot a number of birds at the lake. We even found gunshot in a bird's heart. There were even hippopotamuses swimming in the lake. When we finished hunting we returned home. We left his friend in his own town and went back to Kukawa. The next morning, after a rain, we went back to Lake Chad. We met his friend there and then went on to the lake. We found that the fish had come out because there was so much water. Normally they hide in a place where there is only a little bit of water. We caught a great many and tied them on the back of the horse. Even the dog was catching fish.

Some of the fish we speared. Whenever Tabib's friend speared a fish he would say to him, "Nojirra nojinni?" and Tabib would answer, "Nojin," which means, "Do I know how to spear fish or don't I!" "Yes, you certainly do." As we were comnig out of the water, I saw a large fish. I went and caught it but it slipped from my grasp. Then Tabib's friend came and pierced it with his spear. We carried the fish and put them on the back of the horse; then we returned to Kukawa. The cook fried them and we ate until we were completely full. What was left we put away until the next day.

After we had been there some months, we loaded up one of our camels with goods and prepared to travel to Gujba.[21] Accompanying us were two of Tabib's servants, a servant of the Shehu, and a deaf slave whom the Shehu had sent to lead the way and take us to Gujba. We stayed in Gujba perhaps a month, then we left and went on to another town whose name I have forgotten.[22] There were many huge boulders in that town as well as many date palms.[23] We slept there. When we got up in the morning we went and climbed on a very high rock. When the people of the town saw us on the rock they sent someone to call and tell us to come down. When we climbed down and reentered the town, we discovered crowds of people talking heatedly and milling around because of us. They were angry because no one is allowed to climb up on that rock.[24] I think that these people were Mandara, although I couldn't understand their language.[25] We didn't stay there long because their chief was ill; nevertheless he sent us corn for our horse and *tuwo* for ourselves.[26]

As we were returning to Kukawa, one of our camels became ill, but we didn't know what kind of sickness it had. When we came to a small town we unloaded it, and it died there. When it was about to die, they cut its throat with a knife and killed it.[27] When they were carrying away the meat, there was a large amount of blood, so we figured out that it was an excess of blood that had killed it. Thus if we had bled it, it would not have died.[28] They carried the meat away and everyone took his share home. Tabib told the Shehu of Bornu's courtier to go and ask the chief of this town to let us have two pack oxen to carry our loads. The

Shehu's servant told the chief and the chief complied with the request. We thanked him and went on to Kukawa.

While we were in Kukawa, my master[29] called one of his servants to saddle his horse for him. When the horse had been saddled, he mounted it and Abbega,[30] one of his servants, carried his gun and they rode out. In the afternoon, before the sun went down, they arrived at a lake not very far from Kukawa. It was a campsite where merchants who came from Fezzan used to stop. They would rest there while some of their men went to look for housing. When they located houses, they would load up their camels and come into the city.[31] While there Tabib saw a white bird he wanted to shoot, so he took his gun from Abbega. He got up, followed it, and shot at it. He ran without catching it and his shoes got stuck in the mud. He didn't catch the bird, so he got out of the mud, but without his shoes. Abbega went to look for them and I think he found them and washed them. Then Tabib put them on again. I think this is what happened. I wasn't there with them but this is what Abbega told me when they came home.

That night, my master began to have chills.[32] A few days passed and his illness became more serious. He said that we ought to move to a Kanembu town near Lake Chad named Maduwari, where his friend lived. He supposed that if he went there he would feel better, then the next day he could go and bathe in the lake.[33] But that night he didn't sleep at all. In the morning, Abbega and I mourned for him. Someone was sent to Kukawa to inform Abdul Karim, but he did not tell him that Tabib was dead, only that he should come and see how he was.[34] On the way, Ibrahim and Abdul Karim passed some men coming from the town where we were. They asked them, "Is the stranger dead?" They answered, "Yes, he is dead."[35] Then Abdul Karim started galloping his horse and didn't stop until he reached us. When he got down from his horse, he went and shed tears over Tabib. After a while, he came to us and told Abbega and me not to cry: whatever Tabib had done for us he would do the same.[36] We replied that that was fine.

Abdul Karim asked Tabib's friend where he should be buried. He said, "Let's bury him under that tree." It was a big tree; I think it was an acacia. The ground around the acacia was very hard. They dug a grave there, about two feet deep, I think. His friend sent some boys and women to bring water in order to wash him. His friend was feeling great compassion. Not a single one of the people who were carrying the water felt like talking.[37] When they had brought the water, they lifted him up and washed him, then they wrapped him in a white cloth. Abdul Karim spread out a rug and put many other things in the grave before they placed him in it. They put in a big wooden bowl, then they laid branches neatly across the mouth of the grave, added leaves, and poured in earth. When he was buried, they cut trees and thorns and laid them over the grave.[38] When we finished, we left and got ready to return to Kukawa. One of his friends came and said to Abdul Karim, "Now that your friend is dead, don't snub us."[39] He smiled and answered, "I won't snub you."

Tabib had one servant who was in charge of all the servants. But he was a thief. As soon as our master died, he took our master's keys and went and stole money from among his things. Abdul Karim didn't know about it, but when he looked for the money, he couldn't find it. He called Ibrahim and said to him, "I think you took this money." Ibrahim insisted that he had not taken it. Abdul Karim said that if he did not return the money he was going to take him to the Shehu. I think this is what happened. He did

get some of the money back but not all of it. Abdul Karim
threw him out of his house because he was a thief. And so
we stayed with Abdul Karim and looked after him as we
had looked after Tabib.[40]

Chapter IV

We heard that Abdul Karim wanted to go to Timbuktu, a
town that I had never heard of before. The Shehu of Bornu
gave him provisions for the journey. He gave him some
camels and sent guides to lead them. Abdul Karim told me
that when we got to Hausaland, if I saw my father, he would
give me back to him. While we were making preparations for
our trip to Timbuktu, we lodged outside the town.[1] After
leaving Kukawa, it was twenty days before we arrived in
Zinder.[2] By horseback, the trip takes only fifteen days.[3]
When we arrived in Zinder, they provided us with a house.
Zinder itself is a small town set in a large area surrounded
by rocks.[4]

While we were in Zinder I saw some people from towns
near my grandmother's. On one occasion, I found a boy, a
friend of mine, and told him to go tell my grandmother that
I was in Zinder and that she should tell my father to come
and get me. However, I don't think he went, because if you
leave Zinder in the morning, you can be in my grandmother's
town by afternoon. When I failed to hear any news from
him, I met some Hausa men who said they would take me to
my father. I didn't agree to it because I was afraid that they
would sell me, since they were traders who had come to
Zinder to attend the market.

We stayed in Zinder about a month, I think, and then

we left there.⁵ We went and camped outside the town. There I saw the road leading to Kunduwoshe, my grandmother's town. I pointed it out to Abbega, "See that road? It leads to Kunduwoshe, the town where my grandmother lives." I added, "See that place way over there where there are a lot of trees?" He said yes. "That's where my grandmother lives. The town over there where you can see those big rocks is called Gawon da Rai, because of all the *gawo* trees⁶ found there." (The fruit of the *gawo* is red and when it is full-grown, it is quite long. People eat it, as do goats, donkeys, and sheep.)

When we left there, we proceeded along and camped on the road to Kanche. I asked some men there if they knew my father. They asked me, "What is his name?" I told them, "Kwage." They replied, "Are you the son of Kwage the drummer?" I said, "Yes." They said, "Your father passed by here yesterday on the way to Kanche." When I heard that, I felt very sad. But it was God who was leading me.⁷ We left that place in the morning and entered the forest. I don't think we stopped until that evening when we reached Katsina. We waited outside the town walls while a few men entered the city and informed the Emir that he had visitors outside the town.⁸ After telling him, they found housing for us. The Emir provided us with a house in which to lodge. It was a rectangular city-house made of dried mud.⁹

Katsina is a large city situated in the midst of trees. In parts of the city there are no people, because they have been dispersed by wars. In some places, there are even farms within the city. There are many tall silk-cotton trees there, the cotton being used to stuff war shirts and as tinder for starting fires.

One man in our household died, an Arab named Sharif, who had come with us from Bornu. We notified the Emir that a sharif in our household had died. He sent some of his slaves to dig a grave in our compound and they did so very nicely. They washed him, wrapped him in a new white cloth, and then laid him in the grave. After they had finished, they left us.[10]

A sharif is regarded as a man of God, for every black man says that if a sharif puts his hand in fire, it will not burn him. I saw two of them in Bornu. Abdul Karim sent me to take them something and they invited me to stay and drink coffee with them. I did stay and drink coffee, although there was no sugar in it. Perhaps they didn't have any more sugar. They were very kind people. When I was about to leave, they offered me a kolanut. I took it in my hand and left. I also heard the story of a sharif who found some boys who had caught a fish and had put it in the fire, whereupon he stuck in his hand and took the fish out. Whether this is the truth or a lie I do not know.

The market in Katsina is beautiful. Meat, cloth, cotton, thread, and many other things are sold there. When we left Katsina, a large number of people like an army went with us. They escorted us because the bush was dangerous due to the presence of highwaymen.[11] We started in the morning led by the people of Katsina, many on horseback and some on foot. When we came to a place where there was water, we stopped and loaded water on the backs of the camels. We went on and traveled the entire day until sunset. When night fell, we stopped for a short rest and ate our food with our hands; but we didn't unload the camels. Then we traveled the entire night.

I think that some of the camels died from hunger and exhaustion. When I became tired, Abdul Karim asked me, "Are you tired?" I replied, "Yes." He said, "Then climb up on a camel." So Abbega lifted me onto a camel. While I was resting there, I began to feel sleepy because I was tired. Some of the camels, moreover, refused to keep going because they were tired and thirsty. Then a horseman would have to get down from his horse and lead the camel. If a horse refused to go on, the rider would take the saddle off and throw it over himself, and then drive his horse forward. If a horse's strength gave out and he fell, you had to go on and leave it behind.

And so we traveled that way from morning until evening, when we finally reached a town. I can't remember the name of the town, but it was a large town full of people, and very pretty. We pitched our tents on the edge of town and stayed there about two days. People brought us a variety of things to buy: Bambarra groundnuts, corn, onions, peppers, rope, and many other things besides. They kept bringing them to us for us to buy. In every town we came to, they did the same. They brought many things in addition to those mentioned, such as grass for the horses, and stalks, leaves, and beans in the pod for the camels. But first we had to give them money or needles, although they didn't care too much for needles.[12]

When we left there, we entered another forest but it was not very threatening. We kept going until evening, when we arrived at a town where the Sultan of Sokoto was making preparations to go to war.[13] We pitched our tents in the same field where they had pitched theirs. The Sultan of Sokoto sent us four rams as meat and two leather bags of tax money.

While we were sleeping that night, some large hyenas came. An Arab saw them and shouted in Arabic, "Azurub, azurub!" which means, "Shoot, shoot!" Our young men jumped up quickly and fired their guns. They asked him, "What's the matter?" When he answered, "Hyenas," they burst out laughing. They had thought it was a thief. When I heard there were hyenas, I was frightened because we were sleeping outside the tent. I took a long cloth and rolled it up like a man's head, although it was bigger than my head. Then I put my head where my feet had been. A young man saw this and asked me in Kanuri, "Avi nanga ate dimin?" which means, "Why are you doing that?" I replied, "If a hyena comes, it will see the cloth and think it's my head. If it grabs it, I will get up and shout like that other man did." But no hyenas came, since they had eaten up all the bones the first time. It is only bones that attract them.

The next day, we were amazed to discover that the hyenas had not eaten the rams. However, that morning I heard that a man had rolled himself up in a mat because he was feeling cold. When the hyenas came, one grabbed hold of the mat and ran away to the bush with it, thinking it had caught a person. At that place if people didn't hide their children when evening came, a hyena might come in the night and run away with one into the bush and eat it. This was because the place was close to the bush and there were many hyenas there just like in Bornu. That is what hyenas do in Africa.

Once a hyena entered a town during the night. When it was about to leave, it got caught between the posts of the stockade around the town. A man ran and caught hold of its tail, so that it was unable to go forward or backward. Another man came and climbed on the fence with his sword drawn. Just as he was about to strike the hyena, it slipped out of the hands of the man inside the fence. When he was talking about it later he said, "If I had had a knife, I would have cut off its tail." But he had had a knife next to his thigh all the time. When he noticed this, he laughed and said, "The hyena must have been charmed."

The war camp was situated close to the village Whoever wanted to go to war got ready and came and joined them. Whenever people in Africa go to war, after they leave their town they do not go very far. When they tire, they stop, but only a short distance outside town, so that if they forget anything, they can go back and get it. For that reason, they never travel far the first day.[14] We stayed in that place about two or three days. When we started to travel, they told me to get an *agala* from some other boy in order to pull a camel that was walking too slowly. An *agala* is a rope tied to the lip of a camel under his two long protruding teeth. Sometimes people use horse halters on camels, but they are only used when riders are on their backs. While camels are walking, they continue to eat grass since their mouths are not tied up, so they move very slowly. As I was running, I came between some camels. One of them kicked me because it was startled, and I fell. I got up but couldn't walk because it had kicked me in the knee. An Arab came and grabbed my hand, saying, "Get up." When I stood up, he ran with me until my leg loosened up, then he let me go.

We arrived at a town where the Sultan of Sokoto used to come for a rest whenever he was tired of staying in the city.[15] We stayed there until the Sultan returned from the war. I think we were there about two months.[16] The town was pleasant to live in and was crowded with people. Many of the people spoke Fulani, but they knew Hausa even better than native Hausa people.

The Hausa of Sokoto: Whereas we say *wonan* ("this"), they say *wonga*.[17] Whereas we say *bial* ("five"), they said *biar*. I asked a boy there, "If you take twenty and add ten, what word do you use for the answer?" He said, *talatin* ("thirty"). He continued, "I thought you weren't a native Hausa since your speech is not like ours here in Sokoto."

I replied, "I know Hausa perfectly well because I am a native of Tuntume,[18] whereas you are a native of Sokoto." He said, "At first, I thought you were just learning Hausa." I said, "Just show me anything you want the name of and I'll tell you." He said, "You speak Hausa but I can't understand you." I replied, "You'll be able to understand me after a while." If we say *bashimi* ("bull"), they say *bazhini*.

Abbega knows Hausa, but since we didn't stay long in Hausaland whereas we spent a long time in Sokoto, he mixes things up when he speaks Hausa.[19] When we Tuntume people say *wonan mace* ("this woman"), they say *worga mace,* although they also say *wonan mace* and we likewise may say *worga,* if the words are squeezed together.

When we left there we went to Sokoto. The Sultan provided us with a fine house. I liked it very much, but I think Abdul Karim felt differently because their houses in London (England) are better and have better things in them than ours. But we think that they are the very best. Every day while we were in Sokoto, Abdul Karim would have his horse saddled and he and I would go outside the town and walk completely around it. It was large, but it was not crowded with people. These people keep cattle. The cattle in Africa are different from those of the English. Ours are tall and have humps and large horns. English cattle don't have humps or long horns—their backs are like those of the buffalo. Sokoto people also keep sheep. I will mention one difference between our sheep and those in England. Ours are tall, whereas those of the English are fat and have a lot of hair on their backs; moreover, their tails are short and their ears are short and stand up. The sheep in Sokoto have long large ears that droop down, and long tails. Their hair is short like the hair on our heads in Africa. In England sheep have white hair, not red like that of our sheep in Africa. We are not able to make cloth with the hair of our sheep; however, in Timbuktu they make cloth with the hair of their sheep since it is long like that of the sheep in England. The sheep of the Arabs also have long hair and large tails.

In Africa we have guinea fowls, which feed outside the town, as well as chickens. One guinea fowl lays fifty or a hundred eggs. Whenever she lays eggs, if there are two then you should take one and leave one. When she lays another one, you take away the one you left the previous day. And so you continue to collect eggs that way. If you don't do that, when she has laid about twenty eggs and sees them, she won't keep laying. I think one hen can hatch more than twenty-five chicks.

I don't think I have ever seen a woman in Africa eat a chicken egg or an egg of a guinea fowl or of an ostrich; but in England I saw women eating eggs all the time. One thing I don't like is to see someone eating a raw egg, for we like them hard as stones.[20] Similarly with the English way of cooking meat. As soon as it touches the fire, they say it is done and have it brought to the table; but we like it to stay until the fire has burned it. When we are in Africa, we do eat some raw meat, but don't make a complete meal of it. The part we eat raw is the stomach of a cow, sheep, or goat.

Chapter V

After leaving Sokoto, we went to a town called Gwandu[1] about four or five days away. The town, which is situated among rocks, is small but full of people. I think they were constantly in fear since they were close to the edge of the bush. They spoke Hausa as in Sokoto. I think we stayed there close to a month before we left.[2]

We went on to another town called Birnin Kaffi [i.e.

Birnin Kebbi]. One evening at sunset when we were there, we heard shouts from another village some distance from us. There was no question but that they were being raided, but I don't think one man went to help them, and so the raiders simply destroyed the village and left.

From there we went to another town that was on the other side of a large river.[3] They brought canoes and carried us across. Twenty people could fit in one of those boats.[4] These people spoke Fulani which, however, I couldn't understand.[5] From there we went on to yet another town, where we camped. The townspeople came to Abdul Karim and asked him to pray for rain. He replied, "Our prayers are different from yours. When you say a prayer you speak it out loud, but ours are done silently." I think that is what he said. Then he folded his hands while all of them, including their chief, stood around him. At the time, I was in the kitchen preparing coffee for him. When he finished praying they thanked him and went away. That night there was a heavy rain. The next morning they were astonished. How was a white man able to summon rain? They asked him again, "Do a prayer for us today." But he refused and said no. Nevertheless, they thanked him very much.[6]

When we left there we boarded a boat that was really like a house.[7] We were able to make a fire and cook our food right in the boat. At night, we would go ashore and sleep on the sand because we couldn't see to travel.[8] When the sun rose, we would board the boat again. The men whose boat it was were from Timbuktu. They spoke the language of Timbuktu [Songhay] as well as Fulani. They carried us all the way to a town a day's journey from Timbuktu.[9] People catch large quantities of fish there and they also kill manatees.[10] I ate some manatee meat, or at least some skin. It is oily and delicious, but if you eat too much it will make you ill.

This is how they propel their boats, whether large or small. If it is small and filled with a heavy load, then three men push it. Two men stand in the front of the boat and one stands in the back. They push it with long poles[11] since there are many hippopotamuses there. When we left the boat, we slept in the town near Timbuktu.

While we waited in Say,[12] our camels were brought to carry our supplies. We loaded them on the camels' backs and started out in the morning. Before sunset, we reached Timbuktu. We also had some donkeys that carried loads of rice Sid el Bakay had given us.[13] They found us an excellent house.[14] It had a solid door with a thing for knocking on the door like they have in England. It also had a lock on the inside like the doors in England. The house had eight large rooms with a courtyard in the center. Off the room in which Abdul Karim slept, there was another little storeroom to put things in. It was dark but there was an opening to let air in to prevent the items inside from rotting.

One day, Abdul Karim locked up the storeroom without remembering that he had left his keys inside. The day came when he wanted to open it and he couldn't find his keys. He asked his head servant, named Gatroni.[15] He replied, "I haven't seen them. Maybe they are inside." They tried to break down the door but it was too strong for them. When they succeeded in making a small opening, they asked me to climb in. I put in my head but it was a tight squeeze for my body. When I finally got in, I found the keys on top of a box. I stuck my hand out with the keys. One of them took them, opened the door, then I got out.

There was an upper room that could be reached by stairs, from which you could see all of Timbuktu. Another room was the kitchen, which led to the place where the horses were kept. Near there, was a room where we kept pigeons. Pigeons are kept in practically every house in Timbuktu.

There aren't many where pigeons are not kept. Their pigeons are delicious, and Abdul Karim liked to eat them every day.[16]

Timbuktu has a large population but the city isn't as large as some others are.[17] Their mosque is tall like those in England.[18] I only entered it once. It was very beautiful. We wanted to climb up to the top, but it was dark so we went back. At noon, a certain man climbs to the top to call people to prayer. In Hausa, we call him *alkali*,[19] the caller of prayers. When the people come for prayers, they assemble in one line and one man leads the prayers. First they wash their heads before going to pray. They lift up their arms and then drop them and stoop down. After they stand up straight, they bend down until their foreheads touch the ground. They do this five times before they are finished. While they are reciting "Allahu akbar,"[20] you hear their voices like thunder —and that is not a lie.

I think there are no pagans, Jews or Christians in Timbuktu, only Moslems. They tried to convince Abdul Karim to become a Moslem but he refused. The people who wanted to force him were not Timbuktu people, but rather Fulanis who lived there.[21] They didn't like to see anyone smoking tobacco. If they caught anyone smoking, they would take him to the Fulani judge, which is what they did to Abbega. Once when Abbega was smoking, two Fulani slaves saw him. One of them said to him, "Give me your pipe so I can take a look at it." Abbega gave it to him, thinking that he wanted to smoke. When he had looked at it, Abbega said, "Give it back to me." He said, "No, I won't." Abbega assumed that he was joking. But when he continued to refuse, they started to fight. They said that they should first go to the judge and then they would give him back his pipe. He said, "Let's go."

On the way they passed the Arab mosque, where a large number of Arabs were seated. Abbega said to them, "I am not going to go any farther than this." When the Arabs saw them dragging Abbega and Abbega struggling against them, they asked, "What's the matter?" The Fulani slaves said, "We caught him smoking tobacco. Our chief said that we should bring anyone who is caught smoking to him." The Arabs said, "That's the Christian's servant. He didn't know that you don't allow tobacco. Let him go and give him his pipe."

When Abbega returned to the house he told us about it. We laughed and said, "You narrowly escaped ending up in a Fulani prison." If Fulanis see an Asben[22] smoking, they won't bother him; if they see an Arab smoking, they won't bother him; but if they see a native of Timbuktu with a tobacco pipe, they will take him before a judge. If you want to smoke in Timbuktu, you had better smoke in your house before you go out.[23]

The salt of Timbuktu is excellent and tasty. If you pick up some salt and look at it, it is like glass. They do not dig the salt in Timbuktu itself but at a place far from there.[24] They bring it in the form of kantu's. (A kantu is a cone of salt about fifteen inches tall and twelve inches in breadth.)[25] They are as heavy as bags filled with earth.

How do they bring salt to Timbuktu? They load up camels there. The camels have nothing on their backs except salt, something to eat, and water in skin bags. The camels that I saw entering Timbuktu with salt on their backs numbered over forty. While men were unloading the salt they sang songs. They sell it in Timbuktu to traders who then go to other places to sell it.

The people of Gwanja bring large quantities of white kolanuts to Timbuktu. They are cheap in Timbuktu but they are expensive in Hausaland since we are not so close to Gwanja.[26]

The bread of Timbuktu is delicious. You eat it without anything else, or, if you want, you can dip it in meat broth. To bake the bread, they make something like a chicken coop of clay, then they prepare a fire under it and they place the bread above. And thus they bake it until it is done.

They have a type of long grass called *burgu*. Horses particularly like to eat it and (because it is sweet) people also chew it. The waters of Timbuktu are full of it. The people of Timbuktu make a beverage from it which is good to drink, or so I've heard. I never actually had any of the drink although I did chew the grass itself.[27]

I saw the Timbuktu market where they sell different kinds of meat, firewood, bread, and many other things as well.[28] There were also various slave markets. I went to see the slaves there—boys and men, women and their children— but not very many, as one sees in Bornu; there you will see hundreds in one place.[29]

When they build houses, they make clay into bricks, put them in the sun to dry, then take them to build the house. However, I never actually saw how they build one.

Sid el Bakay was a good man who was sensible in whatever he did. He didn't want to stay in Timbuktu. Perhaps this was because of the property he had with him, namely his camels, horses, and donkeys.[30] He had one wife and three male children that I know of. All three of them liked me and I liked them too. Speaking only of two of them, I think one was five years old and the other was three.[31] I think the oldest son was fourteen at the time. There were also two younger sisters, aged four. He had a tent he lived in outside Timbuktu with his family and his animals. These two sons of his were young. Sometimes they would refuse to eat their food if I didn't come. They liked me to lift them on my shoulders and give them a horseback ride.[32] They spoke Arabic and so I soon began to speak it with them. While we lived in the city, they used to bring us food. Sid el Bakay told us that whenever the corn for the horses was used up, we should tell him so he could give us some more. Whenever we went to his house outside the town, we would find them playing enjoyably. We even grew tired of eating, since whenever we went there, they would slaughter a ram or a cow for us.

While we lived there, there were bad feelings between Abdul Karim and the Fulani because he refused to become a Moslem. They threatened to kill him unless he gave them some goods. I don't think that Abdul Karim had much wealth with him. It was just that they saw his big boxes. He had two a foot long and a foot wide,[33] plus some little ones.

When we were living outside the town of Timbuktu, we heard the beating of *tambari* drums all day. That day, Timbuktu was filled with Fulani horsemen hostile to us. While we were there, I think a man came and told us that the Fulanis intended to carry off Abdul Karim's goods. About sunset, after we had eaten our evening meal, Sid el Bakay assembled about two to three hundred Asben people. Some were on horseback, each with a spear and a shield, and others were on foot with two spears and a shield. We were getting our guns ready. And that's the way we were when we started out. I was following on foot. Sid el Bakay had a gun with two barrels. Abdul Karim had a gun with two barrels and also a pistol with five barrels. He also had two on the back of the horse, hanging from the saddle, one on each side. His servants also had guns, while I had a spear. Earlier I had had a quiver with twenty arrows in it and a good bow, but Abbega, who was also carrying a spear, broke the bow. As

we were proceeding, we met a troop of Arabs with guns.[34]
They said to us, "Let's get to the city quickly."

As we approached Timbuktu, the sun had sunk but there
was light from the moon. We saw a group of Fulani singing
and drumming. We stopped. We were some distance from
them and they were some distance from us. While we were
there, Abbega went into Timbuktu with a gun hanging from
his shoulders. Some Fulani who saw him wanted to fight
him, but others prevented them. Abbega didn't have any
powder or gunshot, just the heavy piece of iron on his
shoulder. If they had attacked him, they would have torn
him to pieces like a hyena or a small goat. He came running to us and said, "Where's Abdul Karim?" I said, "He's
standing over there." When Abdul Karim saw him, he was
amused because he saw that Abbega was a man of courage.
I think he then gave him some gunshot and powder.[35]

While we were there, two Fulani men came and tried to
circle round our camp. Sid el Bakay saw them and inquired
whether they were Fulani. When they heard him say that,
they spurred their horses and galloped away to their own
camp. But some Asben men caught up with them. One of
them threw away his gun and the other fell from his horse.[36]
When he got up, he forgot about his gun. All he wanted was
to save his life. The Asben men picked up the guns and
brought them to Sid el Bakay, who held on to them.

When the Fulani saw that they were not going to achieve
a victory, they said they wanted their guns. Sid el Bakay
said, "I refuse to give them to you if you intend to fight us."
They said they were not going to fight us; everything was
going to be fine. But the Asben men wanted to fight, for
they were men of fire when it came to fighting. When they
clashed their shields, it sounded like the firing of guns.
Nevertheless, Sid el Bakay gave the Fulani their guns and
they returned to the city. When they approached our house

in Timbuktu, they fired their guns, sending gunshot into the house. One of the servants named Gatroni, whom Abdul Karim liked, was in the house and became extremely angry.[37] He loaded his gun and was about to fire it when another man, named Ali, tried to stop him; but he wouldn't listen to him. He insisted on firing his gun. He said to Ali, "The Fulani must think that we are cowards. If we don't stand up like men, they will have contempt for us."

That night, we returned to our house outside town. I was so tired from running around that I began to cry, so they lifted me up on the back of a horse. And that was the end of our fight in Timbuktu.[38]

Chapter VI

We stayed in Timbuktu about eight months; then we began to prepare our goods for departure.[1] Abdul Karim loaded up all of his belongings in four large boxes and some sacks. We left Timbuktu safely, for which we thanked God. We arrived at the tent in the field where Sid el Bakay lived with his family. There we spent the night and loaded up our camels the next morning. We had a large number of people along with us, including Sid el Bakay, who escorted us for ten days.

During the entire period, we traveled among Asbens. Wherever we stopped for the night, they would kill a cow for us and we would eat meat until we couldn't take any more. Many people went to see Sid el Bakay to have him put his hands on their heads and bless them. Some, moreover, filled their hands with earth and he placed his hands on the earth and said a prayer for them.

Some Asben women are thin and some are quite fat,

while others are so fat they can hardly move.[2] I saw a great
many Asben women, so let me tell you how fat they are. One
woman I saw had an arm bigger than my thigh. I wouldn't
have wanted to be slapped by her, because if she slapped
you, you would stay wherever you fell, and not think about
getting up again. Her body was as big as a man and a boy
put together, and her thighs were as big as my whole body.
I saw another girl about ten years old who was almost as fat
as my mother. Whenever an Asben woman wants to mount
a donkey, someone must bring a wooden mortar for her to
step on in order to get on the donkey's back. Although their
donkeys are strong, Asben women nevertheless travel with
two, so that when one of them becomes tired they can ride
on the other. Then while the second one is getting tired, the
first one is resting up. I saw all of this with my own eyes.

If you travel among the Asbens of Timbuktu you will
find these women are like hippopotamuses. They are not
beautiful at all. Hausa women are much more beautiful—
and it is not just because they are my own people that I say
this.[3] These Asben women, who are so fat, eat lots of meat
and drink lots of milk. Milk there is as plentiful as water.
From the time they are very small, their mothers force them
to eat. Asben men, on the other hand, are fine people when
you get to know them (unlike the Fulani), except that if you
meet them in the desert they are something to be feared.

When we came to another place, we camped on the banks
of a river where there were many hippopotamuses. Our
horses did not like to see them, nor did they like to see the
horses. They put their heads in the water so that their whole
bodies were then under water. When they made noises they
frightened the horses. When the horses heard these cries
they ran off into the bush, some of them even snapping their
ropes. I saw three hippopotamuses fighting in the water and

saw six or seven raise up their heads. Abdul Karim took
out his gun and shot at them, three times I think. One shot
went across the river and fell under a tent where some men
were sitting. When they saw the dust rise, they picked up
the bullet. No one was hurt. Then they brought the bullet
to Abdul Karim. I don't think they said anything; they just
showed the bullet to him.

After leaving that place, we came to a very fine old city,[4]
where they had many fish. After leaving there we proceeded
to the end of Asben territory, at which point Sid el Bakay
left us and returned to Timbuktu. While he was with us we
saw him regularly as we had in Timbuktu, so we were sad
to part from him. He was kind to every one of us. This man
acted according to the word of Jesus:[5] "He who shall give
a cup of cold water to one of my disciples in my name shall
not lose his reward."[6] Before he left he assigned two of his
workers to go ahead with us.

After that, we came to another place by the water's edge
and camped there. That night, we heard something coming
toward us in the water like the sound of a canoe. I said to a
woman, "There's a canoe." But she said, "No, it's too noisy
for a canoe." After a short while, we saw that it was a hippopotamus. It had come out of the water in order to feed. As
the hippopotamus left the river we followed it. The young
men loaded their guns and I took a short stick with me. Two
went around in front of it and six of us stayed by the river.
One of those two shot it. It fell, but then it got up again and
started running toward us. The moon was clear and bright
above our heads. When we saw it coming, we began to pull
back. When it came closer, they shot at it with their guns. It
wanted to stop and fight. I threw my stick at it and ran away
without stopping. It reentered the river and we returned to
our tents.[7] We left that place while it was still dark and

reached the town of Say where we had boarded the boat before.

I heard that there was a man there who wanted to kill Abdul Karim. A young man who spoke the Europeans' language told me. There aren't many people who speak the language of the Europeans, and there was only one in Timbuktu. He was a mallam, but he was a good-for-nothing scoundrel. He said that formerly, when he was young and went to the European regions, he was able to speak their language but now he had forgotten it all. He was a handsome man but one of bad character.

On leaving Say, we crossed the river and proceeded to another town a short distance away from where we had spent the night. On leaving there, we traveled many days before reaching Gwandu. The people who knew us were happy to see us, and we were pleased to be there, for we had arrived at the border of Hausa country. I think we stayed there four days. The house they provided us with was not the same one we had stayed in on our way to Timbuktu,[8] but it was comfortable and had an inner courtyard.

Baobab trees were very common there. The trunk of one baobab is like thirty men. Baobabs are large but they are not as tall as silk-cotton trees. We make sauce from the baobab leaves, both fresh and dried. The fruit is very large. If you pick one up and put it between your two hands, they will not touch. The length of one is about like a man's upper arm, although some are even longer. If you pick up one of the fruit and the prickles on the back touch you, you will keep scratching yourself until you are worn out, but it does not do anything serious to you. If you break one open, you will find the inside to be very white, like milk. There are seeds inside that you can eat. They are usually sour, although some are not too sour.

We have something else that is called *dankali* ("sweet potato"). Its body is red, it is as long as from the wrist to the end of the middle finger, and it is as wide as three or four fingers. It is sweet, and when you cook it, it is soft and tender. I like it very much. I don't know whether Abdul Karim ever tasted it or not.

We left there and proceeded to another town where we stopped. Many people came to visit the market in that town. There were numbers of silken cords and white robes, cattle, milk and butter, and large amounts of firewood. It was a small market with large trees, but it was crowded with people. I can't remember all the towns we passed through between the time we left that town until we finally reached Sokoto.

When we arrived in Sokoto again, we didn't stay in the same house we had stayed in before. I noticed that the place had changed because of the fact that the rainy season had come.[9] Both corn and grass had grown up. I couldn't recognize the place where we had stayed the first time. On leaving Sokoto, we descended to the bottom of a hill. When we got to the bottom, we were prevented from going on by a swiftly moving stream.[10] Before, when we had crossed there, it was the hot season but now it was the rainy season. We unloaded the camels, put the goods in canoes, and got in ourselves; and so we managed to get by. That place was very rough for the camels. If a camel stepped in the mud, it would sink all the way in. Then if it became angry and lifted out a leg to shake it, it would fall down with its load. While we were there, it constantly rained on us. But we didn't mind since we were used to it, like a fish in water.

We left that place and then traveled through fields of corn and rice until we arrived in Wurno and stopped at our former house.[11] The people there greeted us warmly. I pre-

ferred living in Wurno to living in Sokoto. One valley there
was filled with cotton plants. Close to Wurno is a stream
where the men catch fish and the women fetch water. They
bring water from the river to their houses in large pots that
they carry on their heads. While we were there I heard it
said: "No one may go to the banks of the river tomorrow
morning until the time to water the horses, because water
spirits are passing by."[12] And that is the way it was. No one
went until midmorning when it was time to water the horses.
I asked them, "Why aren't people allowed to go?" They said,
"If you see the water spirits you will die." They added,
"They are short and they have long hair."

While we were in Wurno, some people took a message to
Aliyu, the Sultan of Sokoto, saying that there were some
traders camped near Gawasu. Sultan Aliyu sent some of his
soldiers with their commander and said, "If they have come
in peace, do not disturb them; but if they are warlike people,
carry off all their goods." They left at night by the light of
the moon. When they reached the traders—I do not know
whether they questioned them or not—they looted all their
goods and carried them to Wurno. In the morning, they
learned that they were peaceful men, traders on their way
to Kano. Sultan Aliyu told his men that anyone who had
taken any of their goods must give them back. So they
brought back all of their goods, after which they left
Wurno.[13]

When we left Wurno, we crossed the stream and went to
Gandi, where fish were plentiful. There we replenished our
provisions for the journey. After Gandi we entered the
forest, accompanied by a large number of people.[14] We
arrived in Kano fourteen days later.[15]

Chapter VII

Kano is a city of children; but some people say "Kano is a city of young ladies" because their girls are beautiful. This was my first trip to Kano.

Every morning in Kano, Abdul Karim and I would go out by one gate, circle around, and reenter the city by some other gate. Outside of Kano there are many farms. They also have woods and in some places many streams. I believe that Kano has fourteen gates to the town. The buildings in the city are tall and built of clay.

They have Egyptian pawpaws there. An Egyptian pawpaw tree is tall, but not too tall. The fruit is about as large as a man's head. When it is ripe, it is not red and it is not green, but it is like a certain kind of pumpkin. When you break it open, it is sweet and soft, and its skin is not thick. There is also another kind of pawpaw that we do not call "Egyptian pawpaw" but just plain "pawpaw." The trees are about as tall as a man, although some may be taller. They grow wild in the bush and don't belong to anyone. The leaves are no larger than a man's hand. When the fruits are small they are green, and when they ripen they become red, although some remain green. If you go to pick the fruit you must be careful of snakes, because snakes like to eat it, as do birds. The fruit is about the size of a ball of mud and it has black seeds inside. We also have another kind of tree, called lime,[1] which is quite sour. Every Hausa man likes to carry limes in his pocket and to suck them. Some are as big as wild pawpaws, but some are quite small.

Within the city of Kano is a hill called Dada.[2] Before you see the city, you can see the top of it. If you sit near it with a white robe on, the color of the robe will change as if you had chewed kola and had spit on it. I heard from some Kano people that one man, an Englishman, had come and told the Emir that he could extract gold from that rock, but if he did so there would be a famine in the town.[3] The Emir said, "If it will result in a famine in the town, then don't touch the rock. Just leave it as it is." Whether the story is true or not, I cannot say. That is what I heard and that is all I know about it.

In the Bala district there are no houses, only open spaces where grass has sprung up in the town. Camels, cattle, and donkeys graze there, and slaves cut the grass to take home. There is a lot of water there where people catch mudfish. When you catch a mudfish, you cut off its head and clean out the insides. You put a sharp stick through it and set it up close to the fire. When the fire has browned it you turn it around. You pour salt, pepper, and/or bran sauce all over it. While you are chatting with your friend, it continues to roast. When it is cooked, you put it away until the next morning. When you get up in the morning, you tear off the tail since that's the tastiest part. All of the fish is delicious, although the tail is the best. There are no bones in its body except the one that runs down its back, and, if I am not lying, its teeth are like those of a man. Once, one of them caught hold of my finger and nearly broke off my fingernail. It doesn't have legs like a crocodile or a fish, but only some things like reeds in its body. It has two of them near its ears. When the dry season comes, it crawls in the mud and lies down in a place that will not dry up. It coils up its body like a snake. It has nothing to eat except its own tail and mud, and that is what it eats throughout the dry season until the rainy season begins.[4] When the rainy season starts, it comes out of its hole and catches small fish to eat, and that is how it feeds itself. Some of them are as fat as a stout man, if not fatter, and are nearly a foot in length. When they are in water, we kill them with spears and when in mud, we dig them with hoes. At the place where a mudfish is, it is possible to hear a slight noise, but there aren't many people who can because the ground they lie in is always shifting.

The Kano market is very large.[5] It has leather pouches, Kano shoes, antimony bottles,[6] antimony, peppers, salt, meat, wood, robes, cloth, mirrors, silk thread, swords, candies, cattle, camels, fruit, cakes, corn, needle cases, and needles themselves, waistcloths for girls,[7] ornamental stones, and sugar cane. The market is filled with blind people and seeing people all mixed together.[8] There is a large marsh in the middle of the town close to the market.[9] Sometimes it fills up like it is going to flood the town; then they pile up earth on the edge of the water so that it doesn't flow into the market.[10] It is said that all of this water is covered with an iron lid, and that if this were not done, the town would be destroyed, or so I heard. I noticed, moreover, that the surface of the water was covered with water-lettuce.

When you go to the dye-pits of Kano, you find many people.[11] Some are dying silk and some, thread. Some are dying robes and some are sewing. Some are beating strips of cloth while they sing. That is where leather-work and garment-making go on, and there are beautiful things to see there.

Here is how they dye robes. They dig a hole five or six feet deep, sometimes even more. They line the inside with mud. When it dries, they pick indigo and, after putting water into the pit, they add the indigo until it is half full. They take four long sticks and begin to beat the indigo until it becomes blue coloring. They then cover it and let it sit for four or five days before they open it. They wash a white cloth and when all the dirt is out they put it in the dye-pit. Men who dye cloth have hands as black as ink. When a dye-pit begins to get old, it doesn't have a pleasant odor. And that is the way we dye our clothes.

The place where indigo grows is good land. It grows in the bush, close to the edge of water. Its leaves are small and when full grown are red and have sharp edges. My home area is filled with indigo, as well as cotton, peppers, and to-bacco.

There are many different kinds of people in Kano: Arabs, Asbens, Kanuri, Nupe, Fulani, Yoruba, Wadais, Adama-was, and slaves speaking many different languages.[12]

When you enter Kano, you should be careful of your small belongings, because a dish of ours was stolen while we were there. Someone just put it under his big robe and walked away with it.

The calabashes they have there are the things we drink water out of. The gourd seeds are sown, then when they grow and become ripe they are picked. Some are made into bottles for carrying water and others are made into cala-bashes. You prepare the inside by cleaning everything out, after which you carve the inside nicely. Then you hang it up in your room, if you are a young man, that is.[13] There are other kinds of gourds that grow inside a compound. Before they get hard, you can cook them and eat them. After they get hard, you can make ladles from them or small bottles that you can fill with *fura* or water and take with you when you go to the farm.

They also make leather in Kano, and I will describe to you how they do it. You take an iron pot and fill it with water, then you pour in ashes of reeds or wood and mix them all up. Then you take a skin with the hair still on it and put it in the pot with the ashes. After you have left it a day

or two, you take it out. When you take it out, you test it to
see if the hair rubs off—that is to say, when you scrape it
whether it separates from the skin. Then you lift it up and
spread it on a tanning block, which is called *majemi* in
Hausa, and go split a small stick which is called *dan majemi*.[14] When you have spread the skin on the *majemi* you
kneel down on it, then you take up the *dan majemi,* grasp-
ing it in both hands, and begin to scrape.

After you have finished scraping off the hair, you go and
wash the skin. You pound *bagaruwa*[15] (a certain tree that
has pods) and pour it into an iron pot and close it up and
leave it. After a day you come and look at it. If you find
that the skin has changed and has become stiff, you don't
allow it to soak in the tanning fluid any longer, but take it
out to air. When it has dried in the air, you pour oil on it
and rub it until it is soft. If you hear it making sounds, you
know that you have tanned it long enough. When you rub
it, you take care to see that every part of it is soft and
properly oiled. Then you make a leather bag[16] out of it or,
if you don't want to do that, you can make a loincloth, or
you can put it away in your house.[17] When a skin has been
tanned, we no longer call it *fata,* but *kirigi*.[18]

Chapter VIII

After leaving Kano, we traveled a month, or perhaps more,
before we reached Kukawa.[1] When the people there saw
us, they were pleased, and said to us, "We heard that you
had been killed in Timbuktu." We replied, "We didn't die
but we did have a lot of trouble in Timbuktu."[2]

The city of Kukawa is well populated although it is not

as large as Kano. Outside the town walls all you see are
human bones, the skulls of people and horses, and donkey
bones filling up the place. The city of Kukawa—and I am
telling you the truth—is a slave city.[3] Once, when the
mallams of Bornu saw that they were not getting any rain,
they told the Shehu, "If people collect all of these bones and
bury them, we will get rain." That is what they did and that
year they had plenty of rain.

There are three markets in Kukawa. One is right in the
middle of town and the other two are outside. One is larger
than the other and they call it *kasugu kura,* which means
"big market." The one in the town they call *duria* or "little
market." The other one, which is located between *garugidda*
and *garufute* and is between them in size, is also called
duria.[4] The things in their markets are no different from
those in Kano, except that they also sell large fish and natron.

There is one thing the women of Bornu do that I know
about. Whenever they have finished carrying water, they
take tobacco blossoms and kolanuts and sit in the cool shade
and dab at their teeth with the blossoms. First they become
red and then turn almost black; however, when they rub
two upper teeth, they are as white as milk. Hausa women
also do this but not as much as the Bornu women.[5]

When I was talking about things in Timbuktu, I forgot to
describe their women. Some of their women fill the fingers
of their hands with rings, except for one or two fingers.
Some of these rings are brass, and some are white, and some
look like they are gold.[6] The women of Bornu have different
things on their hands, but they are also beautiful. Some of
them are made of clay, some of hippopotamus hide, and
some—which they wear on their fingers—are made of elephant tusk. As for the Hausa women, they like to put antimony in their eyes to make them blue.

Chapter IX

When we left Bornu, many people were sorry to see us go.[1]
After leaving Kukawa we came up to Yo, I think about six
days from Bornu [i.e. Kukawa]. It is a small town, but when
you get there you have to take in provisions because when
you leave it, you won't see another town its size for a
month.[2] There is a stream near it that dries up during the
hot season when there is no rain. In Kanuri that time of
year is called *dunyabe*. I think we took the following with
us: dried meat, dates, rice, flour, corn, water-skins filled with
water, and many other things besides these. There was a
Tubu man with us who had close to twenty slaves. We wan-
dered around with him everywhere.[3]

We stopped wherever we could find a well with good
drinking water. Sometimes we would find that a bird had
died and rotted in the water, but we would be forced to
drink it anyway because we couldn't find any better. We
would start in the morning before the sun had come up and
travel until sunset. Sometimes we would sleep—or shall we
say drowse—while we were traveling, but not many people
on camels did so, nor I myself who was traveling on foot.
We never liked to stop at a place without a well. There was a
guide with us who knew the area. We entered a desert where
there was nothing but sand with a little grass on it. There was
even a village there, although a small one. Those people
don't eat anything except the meat of a deer (called *ar* in
Arabic).[4] This wild animal is large and fat and has long
horns. You can see a hundred of them traveling at one time.
When we left that hamlet, we began to enter the desert. The
wind was blowing sand, which gets in your eyes. We had
something that we call *rawani,* which is a scarf we wrap

around our heads and over our mouths so we don't feel thirsty. We also wore a girdle around our waists so we would not want to eat. The desert is the end of the road for the glutton if he cannot control his gluttony.

When we came to one place, sand had covered the well, so we had to dig another one before we could get water. At another place, the camels weren't able to go on because sand had become like a mountain in front of them.[5] I heard some people say, "Clear the sand away and make a path for the camels." But we didn't do that because we knew it would be too much trouble. We pulled our camels along the bottom of a slope and then we climbed up the sand dunes little by little until we reached the top. In that desert you couldn't even get enough grass to pick your teeth with. Wherever you looked, there was nothing to see except sand-hills, and the heads of people, horses, and camels all mixed up. Everything was killed by thirst and hunger. Whenever we came to a place where there was some grass, we cut it and tied it on the backs of the camels to last us until we reached the next place. You could see the peaks of some mountains a distance of five traveling days away. They were higher than those around Timbuktu. When it rained on those around Timbuktu, you could see clouds rising after the rains had stopped.

While we were traveling, we came to a certain town. We showed our pleasure at arriving by firing our guns. There was much salt in that town since they mine it there.[6] The people of the town are Tubu, and that is where we parted from our Tubu friend, who went to his village with his slaves. Dates were plentiful there but they weren't ripe. We took them with us anyway.

We entered another desert and I think we were without a guide. The desert was hilly but there wasn't too much sand. Abdul Karim's servant was the only one who knew the place.[7] Finally we arrived in Gatron, a not very large town. The people there were date-eaters, and I even think they didn't have any farms except date farms.[8] From there we entered another desert, this one very sandy, and then we came to a town near Murzuk, where we were met by the consul.[9] I saw him embrace Abdul Karim. However, when I saw him I didn't know that he was an Englishman because he was dressed like an Arab and had an Arab-type gun. We left there and went on to another town where we spent the night. That evening, Abdul Karim gave each of us a dollar. That was the first time silver had entered my hands. In the morning, we left there and proceeded to another town where we slept. During the evening it rained. After leaving that town we entered Murzuk and found a place to stay in the consul's house.

There was a large clock in the consul's house. Once when I was sitting in the house, I heard a crying sound. I took a look but I didn't see anything. I asked the consul, "What made that sound?" He said, "Come here." When I went, he touched a small thing and it began to sound. I said, "That's amazing!" I think he was an Englishman, although he could speak Kanuri.

There were some Arabs there who knew Hausa, but not many, and also there were some Hausa slaves. They had soldiers there, all Arabs.[10] They wore white trousers that were like sacks, and their jackets were red. They had guns, but I didn't see any cannons except the one I saw in Kukawa. Outside the town there were date palms everywhere. I won't say that the town is large, but it is good-sized. I don't think we stayed in Murzuk more than a month before we left.[11] The consul accompanied us and spent the night in the same place with us. We proceeded to another place, where he left us and from which we continued with some other people until we reached Sokna.[12]

Sokna is a small town but there are many Arabs there. We didn't lodge within the town but rather in a house outside it. The camels and donkeys were suffering. They had beanstalks, but there was no water except from the well, and the sun was very hot.[13] When the Arabs dig their wells, they must dig for twenty or thirty fathoms before they reach water. They sew large well-buckets the size of two goatskins. When they put a bucket in the well, they tie the rope to a camel and dig a trench. Sometimes they use donkeys instead of camels. There are dates and berries and pumpkins in Sokna. When we left there, three or four men accompanied us whose camels Abdul Karim had hired to take us to the town we were going to.[14] On reaching there, he would pay them and they would return. One of them was a boy who was an expert at shooting a gun. Every day he shot one or two antelope. There were many ostriches in the bush there but he didn't kill any because they were smarter than he and had long necks.

When they had led us to the town where they were going to turn back, they stole my cloth. From that day on, I knew that Arabs are thieves. If you are traveling and are an anxious person, you can't allow yourself to sleep. You must sleep when the sun is up and keep watch on your belongings at night. If you don't do that they'll cut your throat like they do a chicken's. They are deceitful people. If you give them something, they won't be satisfied unless they get more. Also, they are miserly. If they have something themselves, they stay some distance from you. They like to shoot guns in the air like children and they like to play on horses. We came to a town in a valley, the name of which I have forgotten, and when we left there, they stole our cups. After leaving that place, I don't know the names of any of the places we passed until we arrived in Tripoli.

Chapter X

When we reached Tripoli, I saw a market outside the city and many soldiers,[1] everything being near the sea. When I saw the sea, my heart beat with excitement because I had never seen a body of water as large as that. When the sun rises, you would think that it is coming right out of the sea. When we entered Tripoli we went to the house of another consul.[2]

Outside Tripoli, there is a small town of slaves who have been set free but who are unable to return to their own countries.[3] The market in Tripoli tops all of those I have seen in all the places where my feet have carried me. Some black people asked me, "Are you going to travel on the sea?" I said yes. They continued, "You won't see another town again." I said, "I'm not afraid of that."

Abdul Karim bought new clothes for Abbega and me, suits of red wool. They were short and tailored rather than full, and from the neck downward they had buttons of white metal that looked like gold but weren't. Around the neck near the buttons were stripes of gold thread, and similarly on the sleeves, which did not have many buttons, just four on the shoulders, two on each side. The woolen trousers were soft and blue and very beautiful. They were big enough to put ten children in, and I am not lying. Finally there was a cap of red wool with a blue silk tassel on top.[4] Abbega and I were very pleased to have received these things.

The Hausa people there would like to return home but

they don't have enough money to get back to their country.
When some of the slaves get money, they hide it away; then
when they see that they can buy themselves from their own-
ers, they go to them and do so.

I don't know how large Tripoli is, but it is full of houses
which, on account of their height, are unlike any I have seen
built in Africa. There was a mosque near to us. Abbega and
I and an Arab boy went into it. It was beautiful inside. There
were lamps hanging, which I think they fill with oil. I saw
an old man there praying. He put his head on the ground
and raised it just the way that I used to do.[5] Everything I
saw was different from the things in our country, so I could
not help but be amazed. We spent four or five days in
Tripoli, then we boarded a small boat from which we em-
barked on a large one that we call a "smoke boat."

Getting on board I saw a large cannon. When we went
below, I saw rooms with places to sleep. I said, "This is
just like a town." We went up and walked around the deck.
In a little while, it began to make a noise like it was going to
swallow us up. The entire boat was shaking. We said, "We
have entered a new world." When the boat began to move, I
was confused. What was pushing it? The water had all
become white. After a while Abbega said to me, "Dorugu,
come here." When I went, I saw a large iron thing beating
up and down. I asked, "What kind of boat is this?" There
were two slave boys who spoke Hausa. I asked if they were
free. They replied in Hausa, "Oh, no." They said that they
were traveling to Istanbul. I was happy to meet people who
spoke Hausa, but I felt sorry because they were slaves. One
of them said to Abbega, "This is the boatwork of Moslems."[6] I said, "Perhaps they do the same in the Christian
countries." He said, "They're learning. Who can take such

large pieces of iron and join them together?" I didn't answer him.

After a while, my stomach reacted against the odor of the water and I began to vomit.[7] I tried eating some dried bread, but it didn't do me any good and my head kept spinning round. I went below to Abdul Karim and said to him, "Could you give me something to eat? My head is spinning round, I feel nauseous, and my mouth is bitter." He answered, "Oh, oh! Lie down here." When I lay down I began to feel better.

We slept that night on the boat. When the sun began to rise it looked to me like it was rising out of the sea. Toward evening we arrived at Malta, where we lodged in a large house. When Abbega and I saw the houses in Malta, we were astonished because they build their houses so beautifully. Their streets are swept and the market we saw—we did not want to look at it anymore; it was impossible to make up our minds because we wanted too many things. I won't be able to tell you the names of the things in their market because all the things were new to me.

When it was time to eat they called us. We killed the chickens in the way that is customary among Moslems. We took a knife and cut off the chicken's neck and threw it away. It kicked until the life went out of it. After they pulled off the feathers, they cooked it and brought it just for the two of us, Abbega and me. We sat down and were pleased that we were eating according to Islamic custom. If they had brought us any other kind of meat we wouldn't have eaten it because it would be *haram* rather than *halal*.[8]

Abdul Karim told us not to leave our shirts out like we did among the Arabs, but to tuck them into our trousers. Once when I went into his room, part of my shirt was hang-

ing out behind me, although I thought that I had tucked it all
in. When Abdul Karim saw it, he tugged at it and the rest
began to come out. He said, "Is this how you dress yourself?" I answered, "I didn't know that I had left part of the
shirt hanging out."

He took us to the house of the governor of the town. It
was a fine house with large rooms without even the least
amount of sand, unlike our houses, which are in a dusty
place. I saw a woman passing by. She had a full dress but
her body was small. If you put your two hands around her
waist, they would touch. Her hair was braided and hung
down her back, and her face was white as chalk.[9] I can't
remember now what she was wearing. When we went out for
a breath of fresh air, we saw a cannon and cannonballs.
We commented, "This town is strong." Then we returned
home.

Chapter XI

We stayed in Malta five days, or perhaps not exactly that.
We boarded another steamboat, which was full of people,
although not soldiers I think. When we left Malta, I began
to feel nauseous again. I asked Abdul Karim to see if he
could find a lemon for me. He said, "This is a boat. Where
can we get any lemons?" He went and asked a crewman
and he gave him a lemon which he brought to me. I divided it and gave half to Abbega because he wasn't feeling
well either.

After three days, we came to another town whose name
I didn't catch at all, since it was as if I were deaf to those
people.[1] We saw a large number of horses. One man was

leading two horses and riding on the back of another one. We lodged in a fine house, although I can't describe its appearance. I think it was an inn. At that place, a woman gave me money because she was pleased to see a black person in her house.[2]

When it was time to eat, they would ring a bell. When we went for a meal, we didn't know how to hold the knife and fork. (A fork is a metal thing like a spoon, but it is split like three fingers of a person, though with one handle.) We had trouble cutting up our meat to eat when we weren't able to mash it with the back of the fork.

When it grew dark, we took our belongings and went to a place where there were a lot of lamps. We saw people entering small rooms. We saw Abdul Karim rushing from one place to the next, sticking in his head. Finally, we also entered a room that was crowded with people. After a while, we felt some motion under us, and so we began to travel in the night until the sun began to appear. Abbega said to me, "What is pulling us?" I answered him, "The horses that we saw are pulling us." Abbega said, "If they're the same horses tomorrow morning, we're going to find some of them dead."

During the night, they stopped at a few places. I was feeling very thirsty. I heard a sound like white ants in an anthill[3] and I thought it was water I could drink; but when I went out I didn't see any. I was afraid to go far away because I might get lost, so I returned to Abbega. He said to me, "Go farther on. Are you afraid that you're going to get lost?" I said, "No, I'm not going to go any farther than this." And so we left that town.

In the morning, I stuck my head out to see what was pulling us. I saw a long piece of iron going forward and backward. I called out, "Abbega, come take a look!" When he put his head outside, he said, "I told you that we weren't

being pulled by horses." We never seemed to tire of riding
with our heads outside. When we entered some rooms,
which we called "dark rooms" [tunnels], I said, "The people
in this country are clever. Look how they dig under the
earth like squirrels!" When we stopped again at another
place, he asked, "Why do we stop so often?" I said, "Perhaps
they want our bags to catch up with us." In saying this, I
was thinking that our bags were coming in horse wagons,
because they didn't allow us to carry our bags right with us.
But they were following right behind us like the tail of a dog.

We got out at one place to walk around and we went into
town, where we had something to eat. I can say that Europeans are kind, because wherever we went they quickly
prepared food for us. When we left there, we asked Abdul
Karim the name of the thing that was pulling us. He said,
"Victoria's horse." I said, "Very well." As we were traveling,
we passed many towns whose names I don't know, nor can
I remember what they were like. If Abbega were here, he
could help me.[4] At night, I didn't know what town we
entered, although we stayed in a well-built house. In the
morning, I don't know who it was who told me the name of
the town—perhaps it was Abdul Karim himself, I don't
remember—but the name of the town was London.

Chapter XII

The house we stayed in was an inn, since travelers to different places stop in houses like it. We do not have any houses
like these and this is the reason: our travelers stop outside a
town. If they want to lodge in a good house they come and
look for one, and then when they have found it, they go

there with all their baggage. But in London you don't wait for anything; you just go and throw yourself into one of these rooms. They have plenty of servants and they have bells hanging up all around. If you want to call a servant, you ring one of these bells and very soon you will see a young man come up and ask you what you want. And another thing, when it is time to eat, they beat a large gong and everyone who hears it comes to the meal.

An English dinner is pleasant. Perk up your ears and hear about the pleasantness of an English dinner. They have a large table, five feet long, four feet wide, and three feet high. The first thing they do is to set the table just right. They spread a white linen cloth on it and put knives, forks, spoons, and napkins close together all around the table. They have chairs at every place where they put the knives.

A man sits at the end of the table and a woman sits at the head. The wife is seated first. Then the master of the house, on sitting down, says to the boys and girls, "Be seated." He has a large platter in front of him, if it is meat; but if it is something soft, it is placed in front of his wife. Men in London don't like to see their wives hurt in any way. If one of their women hits her hand on the table, her husband will say, "Oh, my dear, what is the matter?" When you see them doing this you can't keep from laughing, but if you laugh they say, "How rude you are!"[1]

Up to now, I've still not forgotten how they eat their food. They use dishes, some of which are silver, and some little things, gold. Their plates are more beautiful than ours. (I will tell you about it when the time comes.) When they start to eat, you don't know when there will be an end to it. They slice meat for you and have a servant bring you a plate of it. He also brings you potatoes, but they're not as tasty as ours. Then they bring you gravy, which is better than ours. In addition, they bring bread, rice, and many other things besides, but I cannot tell you the names of all of them because they have more types of food than we do. I think they eat every kind of leafy vegetable.

They take away this meat and bring something else that is white as can be, and since it is soft, they put it down on the table in front of the wife. Even if you don't know what it is, you will eat it because it looks nice and clean. They have something else called "pie" which I think is made entirely of sugar. I like it very much. When you have finished eating these, they take them away. Then knives are brought for every one of you and they bring cheese and bread. The head of the house cuts some, then a servant takes it from him and carries it around to all the people. When you have finished that, they take it away. Then they bring small bowls of glass, which, however, you cannot see your face in.[2] They set them on plates and put them in front of you. They bring nuts and wine of different kinds, and something similar to limes and some dried grapes. When you have finished eating, you dip your hands and wash them and dry them on a white napkin. When you see them eat all this food, you don't know where they are putting it, so you imagine that what they are eating is actually being taken away from them. The young ladies only eat small amounts of this food. I suppose that is why their waists are so thin.

After eating, the women leave the dining room and go to the living room. That is the largest room in the whole house. When they leave, the men drink up the rest of the wine, stroke their moustaches or beards, and converse casually with one another. When they finish, they join the ladies, who are playing an instrument called "piano." It sounds something like a *sarewa*[3] but even better. They have a book they put in front of them, and they sing while they play. If you want to ask them anything you must say, "If you please," because if you don't, they will say, "Rude young man."[4] But when you understand the type of playing they do, you enjoy it. Some of the men dance with the ladies and drink more wine. Also, some read newspapers. They read about news from every country, and they will show you printed pictures of people. When the time comes to leave, you go home.

Now I have told you many stories. Do you like them, you lover of the Hausa language? Have you discovered any new words? If you find a new word, you jump for joy. As far as I'm concerned, if I got gold I would jump for joy because gold has value, but what value have words? I am tired of talking; I am going to sleep. Isn't your hand tired from writing yet? I am going to sleep. If I talked the whole night, you would keep on writing throughout the night. Sleep well, you lover of the Hausa language. Tomorrow morning, if I get a lot of money, I will tell you many stories. Sleep well. I cannot add another word now.[5]

An African meal is a pleasant thing. When your wife makes *tuwo* and *miya*,[6] she makes them in separate pots. She makes the *miya* from baobab leaves and adds salt and pepper. When she makes that *miya,* if an Englishman were to taste it his mouth would burn up because of the pepper. She puts the *tuwo* in a dish and arranges the *miya* all around it. She carries the dish and brings it to her husband. She kneels and puts it down for him. If her husband has any friends with him, they eat together. His wife stays in the cooking room and eats with her children. Men in Africa do not like to eat with their wives. I don't know the reason why, so if you want to know, you must go and ask them.

After the men have eaten, a child takes away the dishes and carries them to his mother, who says, "Thank you, my child." Then she takes water to her husband. We eat with our hands. Children get burnt because the *tuwo* is hot, but men are used to the heat—or maybe it is because men's hands are tough from work like the skin of an elephant. When we work, our women also go to the farm to help their husbands. When we eat, we don't sit on chairs (because we don't have any), rather we sit on the ground, where some people spread mats or skins to sit on. We eat our meal in the evening at sunset. After eating, we go to sleep. In the morning the leftover food is mixed up in one pot and cooked, and when it is cooked it is taken out. It is more delicious than any kind of food in England. They think that since we sleep on the ground we don't appreciate good things.[7] After eating this meal, we don't have anything for the rest of the day except *fura*.[8] Then in the evening we have a meal. Children who do not like *fura* go into the bush and eat fruit in the cool shade of a tree. Toward evening, they bring home wood to cook the food.

While living in that house, I received a small flower on a box. I pulled it but it would not come off. I said to Abbega, "Look at this flower; it won't come off." He said, "Bring it to me so I can tear it off." I gave it to him and he pulled at it. When he found that it wouldn't come off, he bit it. He discovered that it was cloth that had been sewn on.

The maidservants in the house gave us something with bristles to clean our teeth. When we ate with them in the kitchen, if we wanted something they would say, "Say 'if you please.' "[9] Since we didn't know English, we would just stare at them and they would stare back at us. They used to ask, "What happened to your hair?" We explained, "We had our heads shaved in Tripoli."[10]

Chapter XIII

We left London and went to Hamburg, a city in Germany where Abdul Karim's father lived.[1] When we arrived at the gate of his father's house, he opened the door of the carriage and ran into the house. You could hear a lot of noise in the house. When Abbega and I went into the house, they took us upstairs. We put away our luggage, rolled up our dirty clothes, put on some clean ones, and came back downstairs. They brought us coffee and black bread and butter. I didn't enjoy eating that bread because it was dry and tough. I met Abdul Karim's mother, father, and grandmother. That day many people visited there and drank tea. We were outside in the hallway eating and drinking, so I don't know what they did inside.

When they finished, Abdul Karim called me to sing something for them. I sang one of Dan Karama's songs called "Is Dan Dauda at Home or Isn't He?":

> When he had a question,
> He gave a little call for the Prince.
> The Prince felt no fear.
> Enter without mercy,
> The battle is tomorrow.
> Song and drums of the night before dawn,
> Kande wails her cry.
> A crocodile skin,
> Death to your sacrificial ram.

When I finished they clapped their hands. I didn't understand why they did that until Abdul Karim explained that it was a sign of appreciation. While I was singing, he was in his room alone. On returning, he said, "That's enough." So

I left. In the morning, he called in a shoemaker to make shoes for Abbega and me, and a tailor to make short gowns for us. They were heavy so as to be adequate for us in Germany, for it is very cold there. If you cut your finger— and I'm not lying to you—not a drop of blood comes out.

One day, a man came and Abdul Karim told us to put on our white robes. We did so and went to his room. Abbega sat on a chair while I stood next to him with one hand close to my pocket.[2] I saw that the man had a pen, and when he looked at us he would lower his head toward the white paper he had in front of him. When he finished we went away. I didn't know what he was doing but Abbega thought he was making a portrait of us.

Abdul Karim's father took us to a church, but men were working there. There were many chairs inside all set up in rows. We left that church and went to another place near the water where we passed some fine houses and shops. We entered a certain house which was full of people. I think all of them were smoking tobacco and they had small pieces of paper in their hands. We were up above, but when they saw us they all lifted up their heads. All of them had white faces but I don't know why they were all wearing black caps. Then we returned home.

Some days many people milled around us, in fact they frequently did this. Once I snatched a stick from a boy and hit at them with it; then they all ran away. Abbega came and grabbed the stick from me and gave it back to the boy. On another occasion when we were going to Abdul Karim's brother's farm, adults and children crowded around the door like a swarm of bees until we got in the carriage, rode away, and left them behind.

When Abdul Karim saw a house that had been built for the common man, he said to us, "That gift for the common man is much better than the one the Sultan of Sokoto gave me." This is because the Sultan of Sokoto had only given him a small horse.[3] The house looked good from the outside but I didn't go inside it. When we arrived at the house, some of his friends gave us silver money. We left his father's house and went to his brother's farm in a carriage. His brother is married but doesn't have any children. On his farm he has dogs, cattle, and horses. When his servants were churning cream we helped them. As we were leaving, Abdul Karim gave me one of his brother's coats. It was heavy as armor, but even though I'm not too strong I took it with me.

After leaving his house we arrived in Gotha where we stopped at an inn. In the morning we went to the kitchen and spent the whole day there. We went out for a walk with a servant so he could show us new places, and we came to a place where there was water rising in the air. I just stood and looked at it. We went on and came to a large road, close to which there was a church.

Abdul Karim has a friend named Petermann,[4] who took us to the house of a woman named Dorothea Baker. We found children playing there and we too played with them. She gave me a book entitled *Naturgeschichte,* which contained pictures of monkeys, hedgehogs small and large—if you come close to one it turns its head in, then you can't pick it up quickly because it has bristles like a porcupine— bats, hyenas, lions, mice, monitor lizards, elephants, wild boars, male and female hippopotamuses, camels, giraffes, owls, ostriches, storks, tortoises, chameleons, crocodiles, snakes, scorpions, and crickets, date trees (anyone who travels in Arab countries gets tired of eating dates), cotton plants, tobacco plants, and many more kinds of things which I don't know the names of. We thanked her and went home.

I don't think that I know any other man like Petermann.

He is truly a good man. Sometimes he tried to speak Hausa
with us but he couldn't do it.[5] He gave me a book of the
world and wrote in Hausa, "Friend Petermann to his friend
Dorugu." I don't know what is in the book because I can't
read or write[6] but I took it to have something to remember
him by.

When we left Gotha, we went to Berlin where we stayed
in a large inn. There Abdul Karim took Abbega somewhere
with him. I didn't go but Abbega told me about the things
he saw. He said they went to the house of a great man who
wore a coat covered with gold and a sword down to the
ground.[7] Abdul Karim greeted him and gave him a beautiful
Kano pouch. When the women came, the young men would
take their shawls from their shoulders.

In Berlin I saw soldiers every day. The buildings there are
beautiful, tall, and strong. When they want to call a carriage-
man they blow a little thing like a whistle. Whenever a
coachman hears it he looks around. The man who blew the
whistle raises his hand, and when the coachman sees him he
goes to him.

In Germany I saw the father of Tabib, my former master
who had set me free. He was old but still strong, and his
height was like that of a well-grown man. He was not too
fat. His hair was white, or perhaps gray, and he wore a
black hat. His face was drawn. Abdul Karim said, "That
is the man whose son gave you your freedom."

While we were traveling in Germany we asked Abdul
Karim, "What is that white thing?" He said, "Sugar." When
we arrived at the inn, Abbega said, "If that's sugar, I am
going to fill up one of their ships with it and take it to our
country." When we had settled in the inn, I saw that white
thing on the roof, so I went and tasted it. He asked, "Is it
sweet?" I said, "Come here and eat some." When he tasted

it, he said, "It's nothing but water." I laughed and said, "Abdul Karim fooled us."

We met a young man there who spoke Arabic to us, and we answered him. The first thing he said was "A sallama alaikum" and we answered him, "Malaikum masallam," which is the normal Arab greeting. He invited us to his room and we sat with him. He was smoking tobacco and said to Abbega, "Take one." The kind of tobacco they smoked was rolled like a finger. Abbega loved tobacco. Whenever he got any, he smoked it just like he ate food. I have never seen a country where people like to smoke as much as they do in Germany. You can even meet a young boy about twelve years old with a tobacco pipe stuck in his mouth. They gave me tobacco but I wouldn't smoke it. I would take it and give it to Abbega.

At one place where we had gone in a railroad carriage I said to Abbega, "Come look at the road." When he came, he didn't think that there was any glass in the window, so as he started to stick his head out he shattered the glass and the whole think broke. I began to laugh. He reproached me in Kanuri, "Aviro kasutu dimin?" which means, "Why are you laughing?" I said, "Because the glass broke." A man came up to us with a fur coat and a fur cap. If you looked at the cap it appeared to have ears. He laughed. Abbega said, "That laugh sounds bad." Abdul Karim gave him some money on account of the glass. When Abbega broke it, he jumped back and stood still. He opened his mouth and eyes wide and said, "Oh, I didn't know there was glass there." When the glass fell to the ground, it sounded, *kilin, kilin,* like when you tap a dish. Whenever we went in a railway carriage after that, Abdul Karim would say, "Be careful of the glass."

I forgot to mention that Abdul Karim's father took us

to a place in Hamburg with many seats and lamps and with people sitting around on all sides. The first thing they did was to bring out a horse. A man was in the center of the ring with a whip in his hand. When he cracked the whip the horse would run. It ran around the ring five times, then they put it back. When they rang a bell, another horse came out with a saddle on its back. A girl came and they put her on it. I said to Abbega, "That's not a real person." Abbega said, "Yes, she's real." I said, "Look at her and see for yourself. Her legs are no bigger than three fingers." She dismounted, then she and the horse went out.

After that, a monkey came out riding on the back of a dog. He had a sword hanging down like a soldier and wore a tall cap which hung down in the front and the back. He galloped round the ring with his sword drawn. A man was chasing the dog. This man loaded a little gun and handed it to the monkey. I said, "Today, we are seeing something marvelous!" The monkey stood over there and the man stood facing it. He was a man who makes people laugh. He said something in German, whereupon the monkey put the gun to his shoulder and fired it. The man fell down and all the people laughed. To the accompaniment of music above, the monkey and his horse (the dog) left the ring. An elephant came out and they made it lie down like a camel. A man mounted it, then it walked around the ring and lifted him down. They brought something to it in a cup. It took the thing and swallowed it. When it took the cup, I thought it was going to swallow it too, but it gave it back to the man. There were some bells near it. Whenever it ate up something, it rang the bells for them to bring it more. We didn't see the end, for we left. That night, we enjoyed ourselves because we saw wonderful things that we had never seen before.

When we left Germany we boarded a boat and then a train. We arrived in London and lived there. I shall tell you about London by and by. I have told you many things. What are you going to give me now? Ah, you have given me many things, for which I thank you. Till another time. This ends the life and travels of Dorugu.

NOTES TO DORUGU'S NARRATIVE

CHAPTER I

1 Dorugu was born ca. 1839–40. Kanche is located about forty miles southwest of Zinder, the capital of the state of Damagaram in what is now the Niger Republic. Dambanas, which I have been unable to identify, must have been south of Kanche in or quite close to the traditional Hausa state of Daura, since Dorugu was on occasion referred to as Dan Daura, "a son of Daura" (Schön 1885: 265).

2 The normal settlement pattern in northern Nigeria is for people to live in compact villages and to work the surrounding lands within moderate walking distance of the village. In its Nigerian usage the term *farm* is limited to clearly specified plots of land actively under cultivation, and does not apply to people's homes or to farm-related structures such as granaries and animal pens.

3 Balls of cooked flour, usually eaten in sour milk.

4 Alms or charity given as a religious act.

5 Strictly speaking, a *mallam* is a religious teacher, although as a term of address among the Hausa it is more generally used for any educated, respected man.

6 In the mid-nineteenth century, Damagaram—which like the neighboring states of Daura and Maradi was caught between the empires of Sokoto and Bornu—was in a constant state of turmoil, being continually subjected to armed attacks and slave raids. For a good account of political events in the area at the time, see Smith (1967).

7 The term *bush* refers to any large uninhabited area of

brush-covered or forested land. The term is standardly used
in West Africa in opposition to *village* or *town*.

8   It is hard to believe that the dog could have grown so much
in a few days that Dorugu could fail to recognize it. Since
Moslems are normally very contemptuous of dogs, Dorugu's anecdote may be indicative of the lack of Islamic
impact on traditional rural Hausa areas at the time (Greenberg 1946, Smith 1967).

9   The term *shehu* (a Kanuri variant of *sheikh)* has been the
standard designation for emirs of Bornu since the dynasty
that still reigns was founded at the beginning of the nineteenth century by the famed Mohammed El Amin El
Kanemi. Umar, the second Shehu of Bornu (1835–80),
was the eldest son of El Kanemi. During most of Umar's
reign Bornu exercised some degree of suzerainty over
Damagaram.

10 Tassawa was a large town with an estimated population of
fifteen thousand in 1850. The chief of Tassawa was a semi-
independent vassal of the chief of the Hausa state of
Maradi. It is still a major market in the area.

11 Dorugu relates the episode as if the man from the other
village were a complete stranger, but presumably he was
Dorugu's grandfather.

12 The major people of Bornu. Today they number nearly two
million.

13 "The rise of Damagaram dates from the accession of the
Emir Tanimu in 1841. Although deposed two years later,
he recovered his throne in 1851 and then ruled the country
until his death in 1884" (Johnston 1967: 197).

14 Even a small town like Dambanas would have been walled
in those days.

15 Kworgum was located about fifteen miles southwest of
Kanche. It was tributary both to Zinder and to Maradi,
although it was actually ruled by the Emir of Maradi
through a slave.

16 "[Tanimu] grasped the importance of fire-arms much

earlier than any other Chief in the central Sudan and by building up an armoury of 6,000 rifles or muskets and 40 cannon he created a force that came to be feared even by his more powerful neighbours" (Johnston 1967: 197).

17 The Hausa practice polygamy; a maximum of four wives is permitted.

18 Dorugu probably means that his father's wife had at one time been a slave in Bornu where she would have learned Kanuri (as Dorugu himself later did).

19 Dorugu mentions the following instruments by name: *kotso*—a small, single-membrane drum played with the fingers; *kalangu*—an hourglass-shaped, double-membrane tone drum; *ganga*—a large barrel-shaped drum; *algaita*—a double-reed woodwind instrument; *kuge*—a V-shaped metal instrument used like a gong.

20 Dorugu was made painfully aware of this common and tragic aspect of slavery, the breaking up of family units.

21 The Hausa, unlike many tribes in southern Nigeria, consider twins to be good luck. Special pairs of names, such as Hassan and Husseini, are used for twins.

CHAPTER II

1 Dorugu offers no explanation of why his father was set free. Perhaps his father, being a drummer, was already known to the chief and was thus released in recognition of some previous service. In general, the system of slavery in Hausaland and Bornu was more humane than its harsh North African and American counterparts.

2 Specifically, *dundufa* (or *tudara*), a long narrow drum.

3 There is something peculiar about the matter-of-fact way in which Dorugu relates how he barely escaped making connections with his father. Dorugu describes a similar case of just missing his father in Chapter IV. In neither incident does he describe any serious concerted effort by him or his father to get back together.

4 The Kanuri name literally means "Little Blessing." "Do-

rugu" is not a common Hausa name. It was perhaps given to Dorugu as a nickname equivalent to the English "Shorty." Bargery (1934) lists a word *durgu* with the meaning "a short-legged person or thing."

5 Schön, being a missionary, omitted the seduction scene in his translation as being unfit for publication. He explained why he did not censor the original Hausa: "We might have passed it over altogether, but as the event had consequences affecting the whole life of Dorugu, we thought it right to mention it. It was owing to the influence of this concubine that Dorugu was sent to Bornu; and after the arrival of the same woman in Bornu, was sold again into other hands, and thus at last got into the hands of the German traveller, the late Dr. H. Barth, who brought him to Europe" (Schön 1886: 16).

6 Sound symbolic words are not coined on the spur of the moment in the course of speech. Rather they exist in the lexicon of a language (perhaps as a distinctive subset of the total lexicon) and persist over time. Cf. Dorugu's *blum-blum*, with Abraham's entry *"bùlum-bùlum:* the sound heard when stirring indigo" (1962: 118).

7 The use of oxen to carry loads and people is a distinctive characteristic of the peoples of Bornu, particularly the Kanuri and the Shuwa, and is not often found elsewhere in Nigeria.

8 Founded in 1814 by El Kanemi, Kukawa remained the capital of Bornu for the next hundred years. Some thirty years before Barth made Kukawa home base for his African travels, it had been visited by a British expedition (Denham et al. 1828). For an account of the various capitals of Bornu see Kirk-Greene (1958a).

9 Approximately three hundred miles.

10 Although cowries had long constituted the common currency in Kano, it was not until after 1848 or so that they became important as currency in Bornu. In Barth's day the standard rate of exchange in Hausaland was 2,500 cowries

to the Austrian or Spanish silver dollar. The value of the cowry can be better gauged by examining the prices of various items (taken from Johnston 1967: 163):

a needle	1 cowry
a small onion	1 cowry
a good razor	1,000 cowries
a sword blade	1,000 cowries
a bull	7,000 cowries
a pack-ox	9,000 cowries
a slave lad	33,000 cowries

11   *Tuwo* is the Hausa term for the staple food of northern Nigeria. It is made from guinea corn, millet, or rice and is served with butter and/or sauce.

12   The Hausa term *bature* originally referred to an Arab and by extension to any European, i.e. any non-African. For the original meaning of the term, Hausas now generally use *balarabe,* which specifically means "Arab."

13   In previous times Kanem was an extensive kingdom that included Bornu. It now refers to the geographic region north and east of Lake Chad.

14   *Tabib,* the Arabic word for "doctor," is the name by which Overweg was known in Bornu.

15   Barth started out for Kanem on September 11, 1851. Overweg and Dorugu followed a few days later.

CHAPTER III

1   This is the name Barth went by in Africa. It means "son of the merciful one."

2   Europeans (and Americans) have no objection to bivouacking in uninhabited countryside. Hausas (and other northern Nigerians) who travel make every effort to plan their journey so that every night they reach a town where they can sleep. To their way of thinking, the bush is for wild animals; men and other domesticated animals properly belong in towns. This contrast appears in many African folktales.

3 Overweg arrived at Yo on September 18 and departed with Barth four days later.

4 The Kanem expedition was undertaken in the company of a band of Arabs of the Awlad Sulyman who were going in search of booty. The Awlad Sulyman had migrated to the Kanem area from Fezzan about 1843, after the occupation of Tripoli and Fezzan by the forces of the Sultan of Turkey. "From the time of their arrival in the basin of the Chad, [the Awlad Sulyman] earned their living solely by plundering and raiding all and sundry" (Boahen 1962: 352). "They were almost annihilated in 1850 by a coalition of Tuareg ... and Kanem was in anarchy from this time" (Trimingham 1962: 213*n*). For a brief historical sketch of the Awlad Sulyman, see Urvoy (1949: 162–63). Dorugu's comment about a chance meeting with traveling companions in Yo is inaccurate. The arrangement for Barth and Overweg to accompany the Awlad Sulyman had already been made in Kukawa. "Their kind host, the Sheikh of Bornu, considerately equipped twenty Arabs expressly for the purpose of conducting them safe to the Arab [Awlad Sulyman] encampment" (Petermann 1854: 9).

5 "On the 1st of October they reached the encampment of the Uelad Soliman near Bir-el-Korno" (Petermann 1854: 9).

6 Many Kanembu, a people closely related to the Kanuri, are pastoral nomads.

7 "Tubu" is a general name for a group of peoples speaking closely related languages who "inhabit a vast area of the Eastern Sahara from the Libyan desert in the east to the Haggar in the west, and from Fezzan in the north to the Chad region in the south" (Trimingham 1959: 11). Those of the north are also known as "Teda," and those of the south as "Daza."

8 Barth notes that heavy things were left in the base camp and everyone traveled lightly since "the Arabs had conceived the hope of plunder" (II: 285). *Note:* All references to Barth's *Travels* are to volume and page number in the

three-volume American edition (1857–59), reprinted in 1965.

9 This event occurred on October 17, 1851. "We chose, about sunset, an open place for our encampment, where we were told we should rest till the moon had risen. Strict orders were given not to light a fire, in order that the enemy might not become aware of our approach" (Barth II: 295). However, the enemy had already heard of their approach.

10 "The horsemen galloped on in advance, while Overweg and I remained with the train, consisting of from sixty to seventy camels mounted by young men, and boys not more than ten years old" (Barth II: 296). Dorugu could not have been much older than that himself.

11 Mao, capital of Kanem.

12 Barth does not mention this particular stratagem. In general, Dorugu's account of the raid reads like a romantic movie scenario whereas Barth found the whole affair sordid and not to his liking.

13 The Tubus were defeated at first but then succeeded in raising all their neighbors to stop the Arabs' progress. The Arabs were a few hours from Mao when "with an overwhelming force the enemy made an attack upon their camp, which proved as unexpected as it was decisive. The Uelad Soliman were defeated and put to flight so suddenly, that Barth and Overweg saved their lives and instruments only by a quick retreat" (Petermann 1854: 9).

14 According to Barth the total number of fatalities was four Arabs and thirty-four enemy.

15 Barth observed after the earlier raids and before the counterattack that "all of the empty bags which they had taken with them on the expedition were now full of corn from the magazines of the enemy" (II: 303). According to Barth, the counterattack was not nearly as destructive as Dorugu makes it out to be.

16 When Barth and Overweg returned to camp, "we were rather surprised to find that not only all our luggage was

gone, but that not even a vestige of my tent was left" (II: 305). It is not clear how long Barth and Overweg had to sit in the sun, but it seems that their Arab band did pursue the enemy and succeeded in retrieving most of Barth and Overweg's luggage, including the tent.

17   Kukawa consisted of two towns separated by about half a mile. The Shehu and other important persons lived in the eastern town. The "English house" in which Barth resided was in the western town.

18   This price does not seem out of line. Johnston (1967: 163) gives the cost of a "slave lad" as 33,000 cowries, which converts to a little over thirteen Austrian or Maria Theresa silver dollars. These silver dollars are still found in Bornu, where they are now worth close to $2.00 each.

19   El Haj Bashir ben Ahmed Tirab was the chief adviser to Shehu Umar, over whom he had considerable influence. Haj Bashir was very much interested in the activities of the European visitors and acted as their protector until he was killed in an abortive coup in 1853. "Mohammed el Beshir, being the son of the most influential man in Bornu after the sheikh, enjoyed all the advantages which such a position could offer for the cultivation of his mind, which was by nature of a superior cast. . . . [He was] extremely fond of the fair sex, and had a harím of from three to four hundred female slaves. In assembling this immense number of female companions for the entertainment of his leisure hours, he adopted a scientific principle; in fact, a credulous person might suppose that he regarded his harím only from a scientific point of view;—as a sort of ethnological museum —doubtless of a peculiarly interesting kind—which he had brought together in order to impress upon his memory the distinguishing features of each tribe" (Barth II: 40–42).

20   The reference is to Fugo Ali, who conducted Overweg on his navigation round the islands of Lake Chad. Fugo Ali lived in Maduwari, a Kanembu town about eight miles from Kukawa.

21   Gujba is a town in the extreme southwestern part of

Bornu, about 160 miles southwest of Kukawa. The town had been controlled by Bornu only since 1847 when it was conquered by a combined army of the Shehu and the Awlad Sulyman. It served as headquarters for Bornu Province for a short period after the British established control at the turn of the century. Overweg left Kukawa on March 24, 1852, and arrived in Gujba on April 1. Sketchy information on Overweg's trip to southwestern Bornu is found in Petermann (1854) and reprinted in Benton (1912).

22   They left Gujba on April 9 and traveled southwest to the walled city of Fika.

23   "[Fika] lies at the opening of a valley, extending to the west into mountains, and is abundantly supplied with date-trees and water" (Petermann 1854: 10 and Benton 1912: 221).

24   "On the morning after his arrival, Dr. Overweg induced some of the inhabitants to ascend with him the hill which overlooks the town. . . . He was about to ascend a higher hill farther west, when messengers from the Sultan arrived to command his immediate return to the town. At the gate, the comers were greeted by an immense assemblage of the people, by no means in a friendly manner: the Fika men who had conducted the stranger to the top of the hill, were unceremoniously taken hold of and led away, and doleful cries and lamentations were uttered by the multitude, sounding 'La, la, ai, ai, yai, yai!' Dr. Overweg pressed forward through the crowd, and reached his habitation without any violence being offered to him. It was afterwards explained to him, that this scene arose from his ascending the hill, which affords so complete a view over their town, that the inhabitants feared this knowledge obtained by a stranger could not but be productive of evil. And such was the excitement, that one person had proposed that the stranger should at once be killed, in order to prevent the apprehended ill consequences" (Petermann 1854: 10 and Benton 1912: 221).

25 Dorugu is incorrect. The people of Fika are Bolewa.

26 The problem was not one of illness but of ill will. Overweg was politely advised to leave town because of the hill incident.

27 According to Islamic law, the meat of an animal that has not been slaughtered is *haram* (unclean) and cannot be eaten. It is thus important to slaughter an animal properly before it dies so that the meat will be *halal* (ritually clean).

28 "Apart from deaths due to eating poisonous plants . . . the highest mortality among camels in Air [a region northwest of Bornu] comes from a disease known locally as 'blood of the head.' It is a form of pernicious apoplexy or congestion of blood in the head. . . . If they [camels] are left in the Southland for the whole year, the rich feeding there aggravates the incidence of the disease. . . . When the disease is more advanced, resort has to be had to blood letting; the jugular artery is cut a span below the left ear and blood is drawn to an amount which will fill three cup-shaped hollows in the ground made by removing a double handful of sand or earth from each" (Rodd 1926: 200).

29 Dorugu referred to Overweg as "master" just as if he were still a slave.

30 This is Dorugu's first mention of Abbega, his close companion during his travels in Africa and Europe.

31 In Chapter XII, Dorugu contrasts the African method of finding lodging with the European use of inns.

32 Barth's diary entry of September 20, 1852: "Mr. Overweg thought himself strong enough to go about shooting, and was so imprudent as to enter deep water in pursuit of some water-fowl, and to remain in his wet clothes all the day" (II: 577). Dorugu implies that Overweg's sickness was caused by the wet clothes. Actually, Barth found Overweg to be in bad health when he (Barth) arrived in Kukawa from Bagirmi on August 20.

33 "[A few days later, Overweg] informed me that in the town [Kukawa] he should never recover, that it was absolutely

necessary for him to get a change of air, and that he entertained the hope that, if I could take him to Máduwári, he might speedily regain his health in the house of our friend, the kashélla Fúgo 'Alí" (II: 577).

34 Barth had taken Overweg the eight miles to Maduwari [on Friday, September 25] and then returned to Kukawa to settle some business affairs. The same evening, Barth was summoned by a servant to say that Overweg was worse. On Saturday, Overweg seemed better, so Barth returned to Kukawa.

35 "At an early hour on Sunday morning Mr. Overweg's chief servant came to me with the sad news that the state of my friend was very alarming, and that since I had left him he had not spoken a word, but was lying motionless. I mounted immediately on horseback; but, before I reached the place, I was met by a brother of Fúgo 'Alí, who, with tears in his eyes, told me that our friend was gone" (Barth II: 578). Overweg was thirty years old at the time of his death on Sunday, September 27, 1852.

36 "The servants of his unfortunate companion, Dr. Overweg, he [Barth] subsequently retained in the service of the expedition" (Petermann 1854: 12).

37 "Many of the inhabitants of the place, who had known him well during his repeated visits to the village, bitterly lamented his death, and no doubt the 'tabíb,' as he was called, will long be remembered by them" (Barth II: 579). "His [Overweg's] kind and cheerful deportment and his amiable disposition made him beloved by all who were personally acquainted with him. The inhabitants of Kuka [Kukawa] and the surrounding regions, among whom he had resided for a considerable period, and made himself a universal favourite, showed much grief on the occasion of his death" (Petermann 1854: 11).

38 The death and burial of Overweg, and the locating of his grave some fifty years later, are described by Kirk-Greene (1959) and by Maimaina (see Part II, pp. 160–61).

39 These people accurately sensed the difference in personality
    between the warm, friendly Overweg and the more austere
    Barth. Relations between Barth and Overweg were not
    particularly cordial, as seems evident from a careful read-
    ing of Barth's *Travels,* although it is never explicitly stated
    there.

40 Barth's only mention of Dorugu in his entire journal occurs
    when he is describing his entourage some time after the
    death of Overweg: "Besides these freemen [a list of his
    servants], I had in my service two liberated slaves, Dýrregu,
    a Haúsa boy, and Ábbega, a Marghí lad, who had been
    set free by the late Mr. Overweg" (III: 22). Interestingly,
    Barth records the exact amount of salary he was paying his
    servants ("freemen") but makes no mention of salaries for
    Dorugu and Abbega.

CHAPTER IV

1 "In order to get everything in readiness, and to be sure of
   having neglected no precaution to secure full success to
   my enterprise, I followed my old principle, and pitched
   my tent for the first day only a couple of miles distant from
   the gate" (Barth III: 23). Barth fails to mention that he
   borrowed the practice from the people he was visiting (see
   Dorugu's comments later on in this chapter).

2 Barth's party arrived in Zinder on December 25, 1852.

3 The trip actually took thirty days, Barth's party having left
   Kukawa on November 25. The calculation of the trip by
   horseback as fifteen days, or one-half the time actually
   taken on foot, is consistent with Dorugu's assertion in
   Chapter II that the distance from Zinder to Kukawa is
   twenty days by foot and ten by horse.

4 "The situation of Zinder is peculiar and interesting. A
   large mass of rocks starts forth from the area of the town
   on the west side, while others are scattered in ridges round
   about the town, so that a rich supply of water collects at
   a short depth below the surface, fertilizing a good number

of tobacco fields, and giving to the vegetation around a richer character" (Barth III: 73).

5   They departed from Zinder on January 30, 1853.

6   A large thorny acacia. It has foliage during the dry season only.

7   As mentioned earlier, Dorugu's fatalistic interpretation of his failure to be reunited with his father must be ex post facto. Barth was not a particularly warm type of person, but if Dorugu had strongly requested that he be taken home to his father by one of Barth's responsible servants I doubt that he would have refused. Dorugu himself stated that Barth offered to return him to his father. We can only conclude that, filial bonds notwithstanding, Dorugu preferred staying with Barth's party to returning to his father and the monotonous life in a small Hausa village.

8   Katsina was for centuries the major terminus of trans-Saharan trade routes in Hausaland. By the nineteenth century, it had been eclipsed by Kano in size and importance, a disadvantage that remains to this day. They reached Katsina on February 4, 1853. "I staid [sic] outside the town until the following morning, while my quarters in the town were preparing" (Barth III: 83).

9   "The most striking characteristic of the towns of the Sudan [e.g. Kano and Katsina] . . . is the mode of construction of the dwellings. There are two types of houses . . . . The first type is the circular hut with a low vertical wall carrying a conical roof . . . .The second type of house is many-roomed and formless. The whole building, including the roof, is made of mud and often has one or more stories" (Rodd 1926: 87–88).

10 Barth, who was obsessed with financial dealings and preservation of property during his travels (for understandable reasons), does not mention the burial but only that after the sharif had died of dysentery, the Emir of Katsina "seized upon what little property he [the sharif] had left, notwithstanding that person had placed himself, in some respects under my protection" (III: 88).

11 "Monday, March 21st. The whole town was in motion when we left; for the governor himself was to accompany us for some days' journey, as the whole country was exposed to the most imminent danger" (Barth III: 88).

12 Barth carried a large supply of needles that he used as currency, which gave rise to one of his nicknames, "The Prince of Needles."

13 On March 31, Barth's party reached the village of Fawasir, in the adjoining fields of which the Sultan "had taken up his camping ground, and was preparing himself for setting out upon an expedition against the Góber people" (III: 104). The Sultan at the time was Aliyu Babba, the third Sultan of Sokoto (1842–59). For a detailed historical account of the founding and early history of the Sokoto Empire, see Johnston (1967).

14 As mentioned earlier, Barth borrowed this procedure for his own departures.

15 Wurno, about four miles from Sokoto, was the Sultan's informal residence.

16 Barth's stay in the Sokoto vicinity lasted from March 31 to May 14, 1853.

17 The Hausa words in this section are written as in Schön's original transcription. Dorugu's dialect ("Northern Hausa") differs not only from Sokoto Hausa, as Dorugu observed, but also from present-day standard Kano Hausa. Consequently the entire Hausa text of Dorugu's *Travels* represents an invaluable document for the study of Hausa dialects. See appendix A for sample pages of the original text illustrating Dorugu's dialect.

18 Barth identifies a vassal district west of Zinder by the name "Tumtúmma." The district must have taken its name from (or given its name to) the founder of Zinder, Sulaiman dan Tintuma (Trimingham 1962: 202*n*).

19 Schön observed: "I discovered very soon that Abbega spoke Hausa like a foreigner, being a Margi by birth. . . . Dorugu is a real Hausa, speaks the language fluently and beautifully" (1862: viii).

20 "It is singular how the idea that the Europeans are fond of
    raw eggs (a most disgusting article to a Mohammedan), . . .
    has spread over the whole of Negroland" (Barth III: 402).

CHAPTER V

1   After the death in 1817 of Usuman dan Fodio, the founder
    of the Fulani empire, his territory was divided into two
    unequal parts. Mohammed Bello succeeded his father and
    retained most of the empire with the capital at Sokoto,
    while Usuman's brother Abdullahi wrested control of an
    independent emirate of Gwandu and set up the western
    empire of the Fulani.

2   The stay in Gwandu lasted from May 17 to June 4.

3   Say, on the River Niger.

4   According to Barth, the canoes were about forty feet long
    and four to five feet wide. The largest was able to carry
    three camels.

5   Dorugu is partially in error. Say is primarily Songhay-
    speaking, although many Fulani are found there.

6   Barth does not relate this episode. He does, however, de-
    scribe escaping from a hostile crowd by pretending to be a
    sharif and blessing people, "although it was by no means
    a pleasant matter to lay my hands on all these dirty heads"
    (III: 210).

7   On August 31, 1853, at Saryamo, Barth and company
    boarded a boat for Timbuktu and slept on it that night.

8   "But a storm that had been gathering induced us with the
    approach of night to moor the boat in a wide grassy creek
    of the eastern shore" (Barth III: 260).

9   This was Kabara, the Niger River port for Timbuktu.

10 Before his African travels, Barth knew nothing of the
    manatee (or Atlantic sea-cow), the strange riverine mammal
    called *ayu* by the Hausa. Barth affirmed its existence and
    Vogel, the naturalist who joined the expedition in 1854,
    provided a detailed zoological description of it.

11 These poles are about 18 feet long.

12 This is an error. Dorugu must have meant Kabara.

13 The Arab sheikh, Sid el Bakay, was Barth's protector during his stay in Timbuktu. According to Hourst (1898: 75) it was "thanks to him [Sid el Bakay] that Barth was able to stop six months at Timbuktu, pursue his voyage in safety, and go down the river by Say to Sokoto, whence he had started eighteen months before." During his entire stay, from September 7, 1853 until May 17, 1854, Barth's presence in Timbuktu was vigorously opposed by the Fulani in the town. It is not clear whether they sincerely objected to the presence of the Christian foreigner or whether Barth was simply caught in a power struggle between Fulani factions on the one hand and Arab-Tuareg factions on the other.

14 This was in the Sankore district, right across from El Bakay's town residence.

15 Mohammed el Gatroni, a Tubu man from Fezzan, accompanied Barth on the original journey across the Sahara in 1850 and served with him faithfully until their return to North Africa in 1855. He was the chief servant. He traveled on horseback and received a salary of four dollars a month, with a fifty-dollar bonus upon completion of the expedition.

16 "In the beginning of my stay I had consumed a great many young pigeons, which form a favorite dainty in this city" (Barth III: 348).

17 Barth estimated a permanent population of thirteen thousand and a transient population of five to ten thousand. He continued: "Although of only small size, Timbúktu may well be called a city . . . in comparison with the frail dwelling-places all over Negroland" (III: 325). For a firsthand description of Timbuktu in the early nineteenth century, see the recently reprinted journals of the remarkable Frenchman Réné Caillié (1830). Also of considerable interest is the somewhat later account by Dubois (1897).

18 Dorugu is describing the famous Sankore mosque, which

had only recently been restored by El Bakay. It was located
in the north sector of town where Barth was residing.

19 *Alkali* means "judge." The muezzin is called *ladan* in
Hausa. Dorugu's error must have been a slip of the tongue.

20 Meaning "God is great."

21 Barth had faced similar religious pressure among the
Fulani of Yola the previous year. "I had a visit from two
very handsome and amiable young Fúlbe [Fulani], and . . .
refused their urgent request, made in the most simple and
confidential way, to say the 'fat-ha,' or the opening prayer
of the Kurán, with them. I have always regretted my refusal,
as it estranged from me a great many people" (II: 186).
Compare this to Barth's statement in the preface to his
Travels (I: xxx): "I say that I have always avowed my religion and defended the pure principles of Christianity
against those of Islám."

22 I.e. Tuareg from the region of Air (Asben).

23 "With the Songhay people, smoking, although forbidden by
the present ruler of the western part of the former territory
of their empire, the fanatical [Fulani] prince . . . , is, next
to dancing, the chief enjoyment of their existence" (Barth
III: 204).

24 "When the Songhay were driven out of Taghaza by the
Moors in the sixteenth century they opened the now famous
mines at Taodeni [in the Sahara], which then became, and
to some extent still remain, the principal source of supply
for the countries of the middle Niger. It was carried as far
upstream as Bamako which [Mungo] Park found being
supplied from Taodeni" (Bovill 1958: 236).

25 As usual, independent accounts confirm the accuracy of
Dorugu's descriptions. For example, Rodd (1926: 220)
writes, "The [salt] loaves are made up in conical form . . .
standing some 18–24″ high by 9–12″ at the base," while
Petermann (1854: 5) describes "the *canto* [as] a kind of
pillar or pedestal, about 16 inches high."

26 "The valuable trade in kola nuts, most of which came

from Gwanja in the hinterland of the Gold Coast, was largely controlled by the people of Kano. This nut . . . had been in use in the Western Sudan since very early times. . . . Although the heavy cost of transport always kept the price high and for long it was a luxury only the rich could afford, it became, and still remains, a necessity to a large part of the population" (Bovill 1958: 240).

27 Barth tried the drink but did not find it to his liking: "Of býrgu they have an unlimited supply; and I tasted here the honey-water which they prepare from it, but found it insipid, besides being slightly purgative" (III: 449).

28 According to Barth (III: 367), the Timbuktu market did not match the Kano market in the quantity of merchandise available but surpassed it in quality.

29 Barth once observed a caravan of 750 slaves leaving Bornu (II: 78).

30 El Bakay moved to a camp some five to seven miles outside of Timbuktu because of his conflict with the Fulani. During his stay Barth shifted back and forth between the camp and his town residence.

31 According to Barth, Bábá Ahmed was five and Zen el Abidín was four years old (III: 315).

32 These children must have been unusually charming for, like the two Fulani youths of Yola, they even managed to win Barth's affection. Barth makes numerous comments in his *Travels* about Sid el Bakay's attachment to his family as well as to his own emotional ties with the young sons.

33 The text actually reads "two *dani*," which I have converted into feet in accordance with Abraham's definition of the term as a "unit of measurement from thumb to middle finger," i.e. about six inches (1962: 188). Dorugu must have slipped and used the wrong term here, for it is unlikely that Barth's "big boxes" would have been only one foot square.

34 Barth's allies were the Tuareg, Songhay, and Arabs. The Fulani constituted the enemy.

35 Although Barth gives a detailed account of the evening's events, he does not mention the Abbega incident.

36 "One of [the Fulani horsemen] was dismounted against his inclination. His horse received a wound either from the stump of a tree or from a spear, and thus he remained the sole victim of this glorious and memorable night's campaign" (Barth III: 390).

37 Mohammed el Gatroni, Barth's chief servant, had been sent to the house in town in order to get Barth's luggage.

38 The major confrontation between the Fulani troops and Barth's supporters located outside the town occurred during the night of March 17, 1854. The terms of the settlement that prevented an open battle were as follows: Barth would remain outside the town; El Bakay could enter the town at will; and Barth's house and goods would be left untouched.

CHAPTER VI

1 They departed on May 17, 1854, after a stay of eight months, as Dorugu says. Notwithstanding the conflict and tension that characterized Barth's sojourn in Timbuktu, he made many friends and left such a lasting impression on people throughout the area that Lieutenant Hourst, traveling through the same area forty years later, saw fit to pass himself off as the nephew of Abdul Karim (Hourst 1898).

2 "To be a real beauty with them [the Tuareg], a woman must have such a degree of obesity as will render her unable to walk without two assistants" (Caillié 1830, II: 68). "As they grow older the women of good family and wealth become fat . . . for fatness is a sign of affluence" (Rodd 1926: 172). "I am obliged to own that I cannot admire their figure, which resembles that of a Durham cow ready for a prize show, or of a moulting goose more than anything else . . . they are just one mass of fat; their arms are like the jellies exposed for sale in porkbutchers' shops, and the less said about the rest of their bodies the better" (Hourst 1898: 221).

3 Barth concurred that he "did not observe one [Asben] distinguished in any manner by her beauty or becoming manners" (III: 410).

4 This was Gao (or Gago), the ancient capital of the Songhay
   Empire on the River Niger.

5 During his stay in England Dorugu was baptized and
   adopted Christianity with great enthusiasm. In 1862 Schön
   could report: "Dorugu is still with us, reading and studying,
   and by God's blessing, preparing himself for still greater
   usefulness" (1862: x). Nevertheless, this is the only point
   in the entire narrative where evidence of his new-found
   religion is so conspicuous.

6 This translated passage is copied directly from Schön
   (1885: 44).

7 "The river at this point was frequented by several hippo-
   potami, one of which, in its pursuit of good pasturage in
   the dusk of the evening, left the shore far behind it, and
   was pursued by my companions, who fired at it, without,
   however, hurting it or preventing its reaching the water"
   (Barth III: 497).

8 The original house had been destroyed by a fire in the
   town, resulting in the loss of Barth's book collection, which
   he had left behind.

9 They arrived in Sokoto on August 29. The height of the
   rainy season in northern Nigeria occurs between mid-July
   and mid-September.

10 Barth commented on the fact that the Sokoto River was
   then a "powerful torrent."

11 "Here [at Wurno] we were lodged in our old quarters,
   where, however, the frail building of the hut had disap-
   peared, and nothing remained but the clay house" (Barth
   III: 558).

12 The survival of pre-Islamic beliefs in the heart of the
   Islamic Fulani Empire is not really surprising.

13 "A most disgraceful affair happened at this time. A caravan
   of unoffensive traders who had encamped in Gáwasú were
   surprised by [the Sultan's men] . . . and . . . deprived of

almost all of their property. These people had been reported to be hostile pagans . . . ; but after this cruel act of
injustice had been committed, it was ascertained that they
were peaceable traders on their way to Kano" (Barth III:
563). Barth does not confirm Dorugu's happy ending!

14 At Gandi, it was necessary for Barth to hire a guide to lead
them through the dense forest that began there.

15 Ten days later, according to Barth, on October 17, 1854.

CHAPTER VII

1 The Hausa word *lemu* "lime/lemon" was not borrowed
from English but is an Arabic loan, as is the English word.

2 Either Dorugu made a slip of the tongue or Schön made an
error in transcription. The hill is Dala, located in a northern quarter of Kano also called Dala. The steep rocky hill
is about 120 feet high. On Barth's first approach to Kano,
he was excited when someone spotted the top of Dala in
the distance and "we all strained our eyes to get a first
glimpse of this hill, which is the real landmark of Kanó"
(I: 488).

3 When Clapperton visited Kano in 1824, a rumor spread
that "by reading in my book, I could at any time turn a
handful of earth into gold" (Denham et al. 1828, II: 290).

4 "During the wet season it [the lunged mudfish] secretes fat
in its tail sufficient to supply itself with nourishment during
the five or six months of the dry season. At the approach of
the dry season it buries itself, forming a regular chamber in
the mud, which it lines with a protecting coat of hardened
mucus. . . . The use which it makes of its tail is analogous to
the use which the camel is said to make of its hump during
its long marches across the deserts" (Robinson 1900: 85).

5 In the nineteenth century Kano was the most important
commercial center in the Western Sudan. It had a resident
population of thirty thousand (Barth's estimate) over half
of which were slaves (according to Clapperton). During
the dry season the population might double due to the

influx of merchants and traders. Barth's description of the Kano market is particularly informative and noteworthy.

6   Actually, vessels made of skin or hide.

7   These loincloths are normally worn by men, except in Daura, Dorugu's home region, where they are also worn by girls up to the time of marriage.

8   Visitors to Kano a hundred years after Dorugu are still struck by the large number of blind people in the city. Concerted effort has been exerted in recent years to prevent blindness, the major causes of which are filariasis and trachoma.

9   The pond is called Jakara.

10 "A great part of the market-place during [the rainy season] is even inundated by the waters of the pond Jákara" (Barth I: 507).

11 "The principal commerce of Kanó consists in native produce, namely, the cotton cloth woven and dyed here or in the neighboring towns" (I: 510). "[Kano] owed its prosperity chiefly to the industry and extraordinary skill of its Hausa craftsmen, especially the weavers and dyers, whose wares were in demand all over northern and western Africa" (Bovill 1958: 239).

12 "A classic example of the combined entrepôt and market type of terminus was Kano . . . [where could be found] traders from towns as far apart as Tripoli to the north and Salaga in modern Ghana to the south, and from In Salah in Tuat to the northwest and Masena, the capital of Bagirmi, to the southeast" (Boahen 1962: 356).

13 In recent years, brightly colored enamel bowls have begun to replace calabashes as room decorations.

14 The split stick, the *dan majemi* (or "little majemi") is used as a scraping knife and thus forms the counterpart to the *majemi,* the tanning block itself.

15 This is the Egyptian Mimosa, called *gabaruwa* in standard Hausa.

16 The chief articles made from leather were sandals. "The

sandals are made with great neatness, and . . . are exported to an immense distance" (Barth I: 513).

17 In addition to the items of leather manufactured in Kano, "tanned hides . . . are not unimportant, being sent in great quantities even as far as Tripoli" (Barth I: 514). Much "Moroccan leather" was originally of Kano provenance, cf. "Panama hats" (from Ecuador), "Irish potatoes" (from Peru), etc. Interestingly, both in the case of cloth and leather, Dorugu focuses on the techniques involved in their production, while Barth was more interested in the nature of their trade and their economic importance.

18 Robinson (1899) gives this word to mean "hide already tanned"; Abraham (1962) and Bargery (1934) define *kirgi* as "untanned oxhide."

CHAPTER VIII

1 They departed from Kano on November 23, 1854 and arrived in Kukawa on December 11. On November 29, while en route, Barth met Edward Vogel, the German naturalist who had been sent out to follow up the Barth expedition. At the end of December, Barth and Vogel spent twenty days together in Kukawa. Surprisingly, Dorugu makes no mention of Vogel or of the two British soldiers who accompanied him to Kukawa.

2 Barth's financial troubles in Kano, which for a while made it impossible to outfit the journey from there to Kukawa, were partly due to the fact that he had already been written off as dead. The rumor of Barth's death had already been reported as fact by the British Consul at Tripoli. A premature obituary appeared in Germany in 1855 in a professional journal (Kirk-Greene 1962: 43*n*).

3 Barth, unlike the more avid abolitionist travelers of the nineteenth century, makes scant mention in his *Travels* of the evils and horror of slavery. Domestic slavery among Africans he actually found to be benign: "The quiet course of domestic slavery has very little to offend the mind of

the traveler; the slave is generally well treated, is not over-worked, and is very often considered as a member of the family" (I: 527). By contrast, the Arabs treated their slaves severely and sold even those they had had for a long time, whenever they could make some gain by doing so.

4 Kukawa was actually two distinct towns, Kuka Futebe (the western town) and Kuka Gedibe (the eastern town), separated by a distance of about half a mile. The great market, held every Monday, was located outside the town walls to the west of Kuka Futebe. It is interesting to note that in Maiduguri today the main market is held on Mondays, thus continuing the tradition of the Kukawa *kasugu lətəlinbe* or "Monday market." The term *duria* refers to the little daily markets that were open every afternoon. Barth specifically mentions only one of these, located just inside the west gate of Kuka Futebe. Dorugu places another daily market in the area between the two towns.

5 Thirty years earlier Clapperton reported that the practice of coloring the teeth with the flowers of the tobacco plant was "comparatively rare in Bornou" (Denham et al. 1828, II: 302).

6 "Circular bangles and bracelets with an opening between knobs such as are worn in the north are affected by the Tuareg women; they are made of brass and copper and in some cases of silver" (Rodd 1926: 283).

CHAPTER IX

1 They left Kukawa on May 4, 1855.

2 Barth does not mention buying provisions right in Yo, but he reports spending a full day buying dried fish for the journey in a town named Bárruwa a little further on.

3 Barth mentions traveling with the Tubu merchant, named Kolo, but he does not mention the twenty slaves. Surprisingly, Dorugu makes no mention of Corporal Church, the British sapper who accompanied Barth on this crossing of the desert.

4 The Senegal hartebeest.

5 On July 3, 1855 they "passed . . . with considerable difficulty and long delay, the rugged sandy passage called
   'Thníye el kebíra' " (Barth III: 623).

6 Bilma, the town Dorugu was describing, was an important
   way-station on the Bornu-Tripoli trans-Saharan route as
   well as a major salt-mining town, having "perhaps the
   finest salt deposits in Africa" (Rodd 1926: 218).

7 After leaving Kolo behind, Barth proceeded without a
   guide other than his faithful servant Mohammed el Gatroni.

8 Gatron consisted "of narrow groups lying closely together,
   and by the fringe of its date-grove, contrasting very prettily
   with the sandy waste around" (Barth III: 625).

9 This was Mr. Frederick Warrington, who met Barth on
   July 13, 1855 at Yese a few miles from Murzuk.

10 Dorugu apparently did not distinguish between Arabs and
   Turks.

11 They stayed only a week, departing on July 20.

12 They arrived in Sokna on August 2, 1855 and stayed until
   August 12.

13 Barth reported the average 2 P. M. temperature there as
   110 to 112 degrees.

14 Barth had just hired fresh camels before reaching Sokna
   but, because of the dangerous state of the road, was forced
   to raise the wages of his new camel drivers before leaving
   there. The trip from Murzuk to Tripoli, which should have
   been (deservedly) easy and devoid of dangers and diffi-
   culties, posed further hazards because of the revolution that
   had erupted against the Turkish government by independent Arab tribes.

CHAPTER X

1 Tripoli was full of European soldiers because of the Arab
   revolt against the Turks.

2 Barth was met outside Tripoli by the acting consul Mr.

Reade. On August 29, 1855, Mr. Reade wrote to Lord Clarendon: "My Lord, I have the honor to report the arrival yesterday of Dr. Barth accompanied by Corporal Church and 2 servants, all in tolerably good health" (Benton 1912: 242).

3 Most of these had been brought to North Africa as slaves, although a few had come on their own and were stranded there. For a description of Hausas in North Africa around 1900, see Tremearne ([1914]).

4 See the picture of Dorugu and Abbega included in this volume.

5 Dorugu obviously had some Moslem upbringing as a young boy but the nature and extent of it is unclear.

6 It was a Turkish steamer, the *Feizi Bahri*.

7 Note that Dorugu blames the sea's smell rather than its motion for his seasickness.

8 Ritually forbidden/ritually permissible.

9 Although Dorugu had seen European men, this may have been his first close look at a European woman.

CHAPTER XI

1 They disembarked at Marseilles and took a train from there via Paris directly to London.

2 Years later Dorugu's companion Abbega remarked that "each lady he shook hands with [while in Europe] left 2s. 6d. or 5s. in his palm" (Macleod 1912: 9).

3 What he was hearing was the sound of escaping steam.

4 After leaving Barth, Dorugu stayed with Schön, while Abbega lived for a time with T. F. Buxton, one of the leaders of the antislavery movement in England.

CHAPTER XII

1 The quotes are in English in the original Hausa text.

2 Excluding ornamental beads, mirrors were the major glass items found in pre-European Nigeria.

3 A kind of flute made from cornstalk or bamboo.
4 The quotes are in English in the Hausa text.
5 This paragraph, which Schön fortunately and surprisingly did not edit out, provides just a glimpse of Dorugu's perception of Schön and of his own attitude toward being a linguistic informant.
6 The sauce or gravy that goes with *tuwo,* the staple boiled grain.
7 Dorugu sensed the deprecatory attitude of Europeans toward things African.
8 Balls of cooked flour, usually eaten in sour milk.
9 The quotes are in English in the Hausa text.
10 This is still standard practice in rural northern Nigeria.

CHAPTER XIII

1 In October 1855. Barth's father, Johann Christoph Heinrich Barth, was a Hanseatic merchant.
2 The picture published in Barth (III: 22) fits this description exactly. Cf. the picture in this volume in which the pose is identical to Barth's picture but in which the boys are dressed in Turkish-style clothes.
3 "I could not induce this not very high-spirited and noble-minded prince [the Sultan] to make a sacrifice of a handsome horse, and he gave me an animal which, although it did not prove to be a bad traveling horse, was of small size, had a very bad walk, was not able to gallop at all, and, altogether, was more like an ass than a horse" (Barth III: 562).
4 The well-known geographer of the time, August Petermann.
5 Barth later caustically remarked that "Petermann had become so obsessed with his role in the Africa expedition that he was in danger of deluding himself that it was he and not Barth who had actually crossed the Sahara!" (Kirk-Greene 1962: 40).
6 During his stay in England, Dorugu became literate in both Hausa and English.

7   This was the Kaiser Frederick Wilhelm. A traveler who
    met Abbega in Nigeria some fifty years later related the
    following anecdote: "He [Abbega] told me that Dr. Barth
    also took him to Berlin and introduced him to the Emperor
    William I (then simply King of Prussia) who, noticing
    Abigah's strong and healthy appearance, tapped him on
    the chest and declared he was 'a piece of black mahogany' "
    (Raphael n.d.: 327).

PART II

The Story of Maimaina of Jega
Chief of Askira
as told by himself

TRANSLATED AND ANNOTATED

by Anthony Kirk-Greene

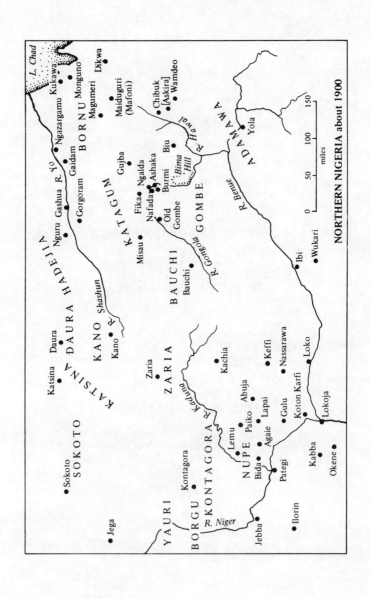

L. Chad

Dikwa
Kukawa Monguno
Ngazargamu Magumeri
BORNU
Maiduguri
Chibuk [Askira]
(Mafoni) Wamdeo

Gaidam
Gorgoram
Nguru Gashua R. Yo
Gujba
Biu
ADAMAWA
Katsina Daura Yola
KATAGUM Ngalda Ashaka Bima
Fika Burmi Hill
DAURA HADEJIA Nafada
Misau Old GOMBE
KANO Shashun Gombe
Zaria Kano R. R. Benue
SOKOTO ZARIA Bauchi BAUCHI R. Gongola
Sokoto KATSINA Ibi Wukari
Kachia Loko
Kaduna R. Keffi Nassarawa
YAURI NUPE Abuja
Kontagora Lemu Paiko Lapai Gulu Koton Karfi Lokoja
Jega BORGU Bida Agaie Pategi
KONTAGORA Kabba
R. Niger Okene
Jebba Ilorin

miles
0 50 100 150

NORTHERN NIGERIA about 1900

Chapter I
At Lokoja (1875–1897)

I was born in the year 1874. My father, Yerima Abdu, came from Jega in Sokoto.[1] He was the grandson of Abdussalam, the chief of Gimbana.[2] My mother was the daughter of a man from the Margi tribe,[3] called Abbega (that is to say, Bukar),[4] and it was he who became the servant of Dr. Barth and went with him to England.[5]

On Abbega's return from England,[6] the Royal Niger Company[7] made him chief of Lokoja. My father Yerima Abdu went to Lokoja where he married Salamatu, the daughter of Abbega.[8] When she became pregnant, my parents returned to Jega where I was born. A few months later my father took my mother and me back to his in-laws at Lokoja. He died there a short time afterward. And so I, Maimaina[9] of Jega, grew up in the care of my grandfather, the Chief of Lokoja.

In the year 1894 I was taken on as a servant by one of the military officers of the Royal Niger Company. This was the time when some people from the Ibo country, the tribes from Brass, attacked the company's establishment at Akassa.[10]

Next I worked for Major Arnold.[11] It was during this

period that Major Moloney was wounded in the thigh. He it was who, as commandant of the Royal Niger Constabulary, was killed by the Magaji, Dan Yamusa, at Keffi in 1900.[12] At that time there were no Northerners[13] employed as personal servants by the company officials apart from me and my friend Audu Dan Umaru. Audu was killed by the Brass people when they attacked Akassa. All the other servants[14] and cooks of the Europeans were soldiers in the constabulary,[15] except for a few Ijaws from Asaba and Onitsha.[16] The soldiers were mostly either from the Gold Coast or were Krumen and Yorubas, with some Sierra Leoneans as well.[17] At the time I am describing there was no store or important market at Onitsha,[18] only some missionaries living there.[19] The company warehouse was then situated at Abuchi, which was the main trading center, while the huge prison and the barracks were located in Asaba.[20] People sentenced at Lokoja or even as far up the Benue as Ibi were sent to the Asaba jail. I know this because I saw Zanna Gana, a Kanuri from Birni Ngazargamu[21] living in Wukari,[22] and Duna, the chief of Jibu, when they were prisoners at Asaba.

During that time, the people along the banks of the River Niger, especially those in the Koton Karfe district,[23] lived in constant fear of enemy attack. When the Nupe forces from Bida captured Koton Karfe they built a town and settled there. They appointed as their chief Bakango, a Gwari man, but one who had grown up in Abuja.[24] They maintained a garrison there which carried out a series of slave raids throughout the area. I remember the day, late in the afternoon about four o'clock, when a famous warrior from Koton Karfe named Aluku gathered together a large group of his followers and fell upon Bakango's war-camp. In the battle that followed they were routed and very many

of their men were killed, among them the leader of the com-
mando, Aluku. The Nupe cut off the heads of Aluku and
thirty-two of his followers. They then erected a special stall
in the marketplace and displayed the heads there, with
Aluku's in the middle.[25]

Also, a certain chief of Patiagoja, called Ajeto, died
about this time and left an enormous amount of wealth. Yet
very little of it ever reached his heirs, for the Benu of Bida[26]
hastened down to Patiagoja to take charge of things. The
same Benu also used to send his warriors at night right into
Lokoja, to raid and put people to the sword. On one occasion when they slipped into the town they hacked off the
hand of a Yoruba man called Baba Akwa, and on another
occasion they cut off the arm of a Sokoto woman known as
Bagobira.[27] These attacks prompted the Europeans to build
a sort of watchtower with an electric light on it that shone
in all directions and could be seen from a long way off.[28]
So Benu eventually withdrew from Patiagoja and crossed
the Niger to Koton Karfe. There he left in charge one of his
senior warriors, called Canyai, and returned home to Bida.

The people living on the banks of the Niger used to suffer
very severely. When the river was in flood you would see
them take refuge in the forest out of fear of the Bida raiders.
There they built a large shelter, plastering it over with mud
and thereby raising an improvised hut above the ground.[29]
A man and his wives and his children would stay right up in
the air, with their boat tied up in readiness underneath the
platform. They lived in this wretched state up until the year
1897 when the Royal Niger Company captured Bida and
the war-camp at Koton Karfe was broken up. Then at last
the local people were freed from this intolerable situation
and could live in peace.

The company now appointed as chief of Koton Karfe Ali,

the son of a former chief called Angefu. A man called Kimba and I were among those who escorted him from Lokoja to Koton Karfe on the instructions of the chief of Lokoja.

Chapter II
The Campaign Against Bida (1897)

In 1897, I left Lokoja together with Dr. Drill[1] and Major Festing, an officer of the Royal Niger Constabulary. We followed the way to Okene where we came across Maiyaki Nda Jiya,[2] the general of the Bida forces encamped at a town called Gidi, a little to the south of Kabba. He was engaged in slave forays. When we left Okene we stopped at a small village on the edge of a forest. When Maiyaki Nda Jiya heard of our approach, he sent one of the leading warriors of Bida, called Dokoyiringi,[3] to us, accompanied by a strong force of cavalry and foot soldiers armed with rifles. They surrounded our camp during the hours of darkness. Then at about six o'clock in the morning Dokoyiringi dispatched a mounted messenger who came and found me resting on the ground.

He asked me, "Where is the white man?"[4]

I said, "What is it you want?"

He replied, "I have been sent with a message."

So I went and told Major Festing and Dr. Drill, and they told me to bring the messenger. When he came before them he informed them that he had been sent by Dokoyiringi to come and summon them to a parley in a small wood nearby. The two Europeans left their escort of soldiers and the carriers in the camp and went out to meet Dokoyiringi. When we reached the place, Dokoyiringi said that Maiyaki Nda

Jiya had sent him to lead them back to the Nupe war-camp. The Europeans replied that first they would return to camp and make ready, but Dokoyiringi insisted that they send someone else instead. So our[5] Europeans sent Sergeant Baban Fali and Headman[6] Dari back to our camp and they fetched all our men. Then Dokoyiringi mounted his horse. Immediately three or four shots were fired,[7] large numbers of riflemen and cavalry came streaming out of the woods, and we all set off on the path to the camp at Gidi where we met the general, Nda Jiya.

This general intended to betray us, but Makun[8] (who later became Etsu Nupe Muhammad),[9] together with a handful of sensible people, refused to allow it. We were taken to lodge in the house of Etswan, the son of the Ndeji.[10] Maiyaki Nda Jiya's plan was to take away our rifles, arrest our European officers, and send them off to Etsu Abubakar[11] at Bida. We had forty-one soldiers in our party, but three of them had deserted when we marched out of our resting-place. This made Makun and some of the war captains suspicious, so they decided to drop the idea of dispatching only the Europeans to the Etsu at Bida and instead agreed to send the whole lot of us there together. Our host Etswan was put in charge of the party. He was an honest man who treated us well. We set forth from the camp and came to Kabba. When we reached the outskirts of the town, where there is a large fig tree[12] standing by the edge of the path, Major Festing suggested to Etswan that we should dismount and drink some water. Our party then dismounted. Our escort also dismounted a little way away from us, by the edge of Kabba forest. They had a formidable number of horsemen and riflemen, while we were only thirty-eight soldiers, but fortunately our commanding officer had already managed to send a message back to Lokoja from the camp as soon as he had learned that we were to be taken to Bida.

As soon as the Europeans at Lokoja heard what had happened to our party, they ordered two companies of soldiers to hurry to Alkwara and intercept us on the road. However, Major Festing acted before we reached Alkwara, for as early as Kabba he told Etswan, who was in charge of our escort, that he refused to go to Bida. There is a small rise in the ground to the east of the fig tree there. We all climbed up to this rising ground, where Major Festing arranged his soldiers in a line ready for battle. But Etswan had no heart for a fight and so withdrew into the town of Kabba. Thereupon we heaped up a sort of rampart of protective stones; but until sunset nobody came to disturb us. When darkness came we set out, taking neither the route to Lokoja nor the one to Bida, but heading instead for Patiagoja. We marched through thick forest until daybreak, when we came upon the path to Lokoja. This we followed, and reached Lokoja safely.

A short time after this affair the Royal Niger Company decided to make war on Bida. This was the first campaign undertaken by the Europeans against the Fulani emirs of Northern Nigeria.[13] It took place in the year 1897.[14] There was fighting all the way from Lokoja up to Bida. When we reached Bida, Etsu Nupe Abubakar came out with his army in front of the town and battle was joined. A younger brother of his, Lakpene Yusufu, bore down on us from the east with a mighty force of riflemen. On our side they killed one of the Europeans, Lieutenant Thomson.[15] But as soon as we began to open fire with our artillery and other heavy weapons, the Nupe army withdrew at once.[16] Etsu Abubakar fled to Lemu.[17]

From Bida the war moved to Ilorin, ruled at that time by

the Emir Suleiman,[18] who had just come to the throne. He came out and proposed a treaty,[19] so there was no fighting[20] and we all returned to Lokoja. During this campaign I acted as the company's interpreter.[21]

Chapter III
Lugard Assumes Command (1900–1901)

In 1900 Governor Lugard came to Lokoja with two regiments of troops, the First and the Second Battalions.[1] The First he stationed at Lokoja and the Second was sent to Jebba. The officer commanding the First Battalion was Colonel Pilcher;[2] the Second was commanded by Colonel Willcocks.[3] Governor Lugard made his headquarters at Lokoja.[4] His first act was to draw up all the company's constabulary and the government troops on the parade ground, while he himself stood by the flagpole. The Union Jack was hoisted and the flag of the Royal Niger Company lowered.[5] The constabulary was now amalgamated with the government troops.[6] A proclamation followed, ruling that from that day on there would be no more slavery.

Soon afterwards news reached us that the Emir of Lapai, Abdulkadiri,[7] had encamped at Gulu and was engaged in slave raiding. A military force assembled at once and marched to Gulu. I went with it as interpreter. As soon as we reached the enemy's camp they retreated without staying to give us a proper fight. We followed them right up to the gates of Lapai, which was completely deserted. We passed on to Agaie, at that time ruled by Nuhu.[8] He did not wish to fight either, and sent one of his palace officials, Nda Turaki, to meet us at the town gate and to welcome us warm-

ly on behalf of the Emir. Our commanding officer told him
to go back and invite the Emir to come out himself. When
the messenger reached the palace, the Emir became frightened and refused to come. Instead he fled to Paiko.[9] So
half a company of soldiers was left at Agaie under Captain
Skinner, together with Dr. Adams and myself as their interpreter, with orders to try and find Emir Nuhu. We sent a
message to him that he should come back from Paiko and
that nothing would happen to him, but he refused. The
people in town all remained happily with us. They were not
worried.

One day, a man named Dan Wanzan came and told me
that he knew where the Emir of Lapai was hiding. I passed
this information on to Captain Skinner. We marched out of
Agaie in the middle of the night, taking this man with us,
and made for the spot where he had seen the Emir. Dawn
was breaking as we reached a small village called Gobi. Now
it happened that one of the Emir's sons, Lukwan, was living there. As soon as he heard our approach, he came out
of his hut, sword in hand, ready to fight us. One of our soldiers, Gbadamosi, was just approaching the hut. Lukwan
struck him a blow with his sword, and Gbadamosi hit him
back with his rifle butt. When Lukwan slashed at the butt,
Gbadamosi threw himself at the man and knocked him to
the ground. One of the other soldiers, Asaryi, came to his
aid and shot Lukwan dead with his rifle. Although Gbadamosi had been slashed on the calf, it was not a serious
wound. We then returned to Agaie.

While we were there our lodgings were constantly being
raided by infiltrators from Bida, and at nighttime they used
to try to actually attack us. One night I wanted to go outside
my hut, but I suspected that these raiders might be around.

So I placed a small pot on a stick and, gently opening the door, thrust it out. Pushing it forward with difficulty, I suddenly felt the pot struck by a blow. I shouted for help, but the man was over the compound wall and away in a flash. After several attempts to discover where the Emir of Agaie was hiding had failed, we gave up and returned to Lokoja.[10]

This was the first campaign by the government Europeans in 1900. In 1901 a military expedition against Yauri was organized from Jebba. Captain Carr and a party of Mounted Infantry penetrated as far as Jega, but there was no battle and we returned to Jebba. Less than two weeks after our return I was attached to an army officer, Mr. Kincaid-Smith, with whom I went to Kaiama in Borgu country. At that time the French were in Kaiama, but when they heard that we were on the way they withdrew and made for Nikki.[11] It was here that the Mounted Infantry was first raised.[12] Six months later I returned to Lokoja.

Chapter IV
A Mission to Kano (1901)

The military authorities at that time asked my grandfather Abbega, Chief of Lokoja, to recommend a reliable man whom they could send north up to Kano in order to obtain some secret information for them.[1] Although I was quite young, my grandfather selected me for this undertaking. I was set up and dressed as if I were an itinerant trader and joined a trading-caravan bound for Kano. Consider our route in those days. We took a canoe from Lokoja to Loko. From there we went overland to Nasarawa and on to Keffi.

It was at Keffi that I first saw slaves for sale in a market—men, women, and children too—all seated with their legs stretched out. The trading for slaves was just the same as today's bargaining for buying a horse or a cow or a donkey.

When we set out from Keffi we joined a bigger caravan for Zaria, taking the route through Kacia.[2] This was because at that period only a sizable caravan would pass through the forest of Aduma to reach the banks of the river Kaduna, such was the fear of the Kaje pagans. These people were well known for their head-hunting. They used to split open a human head and clean it out, and from this calabash fashioned from a skull the groom and his bride would drink beer at their wedding.[3] From Kacia we made for the banks of the Kaduna, where the route split into two directions, for Zaria or Bauchi. The Zaria branch led to Girku,[4] that for Bauchi passed through Ririwai. We took the one for Girku and from there reached Zaria safely. The Emir of Zaria at this time was Kwassau.[5] In those days the emirs were still quarreling among themselves. For instance, when I reached Zaria, the Emir of Kontagora, Ibrahim, was not on friendly terms with Kwassau. He was living in a town called Kaya and was trying to seize some Zaria-controlled territory for himself. From Zaria we passed through Gimi, Dan Soshiya, and Madobi, and so came to Kano.

When I reached Kano I found that the Emir of Kano, Aliyu,[6] and the Emir of Hadejia, Muhammadu,[7] were at war.[8] The Galadima of Hadejia had recently killed Gadawur, the chief of Dutse, a town that was under Kano. The Emir of Kano sent the chief of Gaya, called Kolo, together with the chief of Kumci, by name Dano, to the boundary between Kano and Hadejia, ready for action. If any man came into Kano territory from Hadejia and was beyond doubt a Hadejia man, he was to be killed forthwith. Similarly, if any Kano man were to make for Hadejia, he was to be instantly slain. I even saw with my own eyes two men, alleged to be from Hadejia, being beheaded in Kano.

On my arrival in Kano I lodged in the compound of Muhammadu Mailiyari,[9] who lived in the Dagarda ward. He had at one time resided in Lokoja and had been a friend of mine, so I was certain that he could be trusted with the secret of my mission. He introduced me to the Wambai[10] of Kano, Mahmuda, who was a younger brother of the Emir by the same father and mother.[11] I sold some of my wares to him, taking along a few amusing small umbrellas and clocks. A banjo player bought these from me for the Wambai.

A little later the clock stopped, so the Wambai sent for me. When I reached his compound he told me the clock had broken. I said it was not broken and showed him how to wind it, and it began to go again. Then he brought out his gun, which he said would not work. There was nothing badly wrong with it, just a small screw had come loose. I tightened the screw, and cleaned and oiled the gun. He promptly loaded it and fired off a round. In this way I gradually became an intimate friend of the Wambai. Why, of course, I had come to Kano was to find out and report back to Lokoja whether the rumor was true that the Emir had a well-disciplined army. I was also to discover whether, as was said, he had sent some of his slaves to Lokoja to join the army there who, after their training, had returned to Kano and were now instructing the Emir's men in the arts of European warfare. The Emir was also said to possess immense supplies of rifles and ammunition, which he had bought from Tripoli merchants.[12] I found out that he certainly had a lot of rifles but no disciplined army.

Chapter V
Early Days in Bornu (1901–1902)

I now prepared to return to Lokoja. At Zaria, however, I received a message from my grandfather, the Chief of Lokoja, telling me that I should try and reach Bornu and get in touch with "the wager of war"[1] who was on his way to meet Fad-el-Allah, the son of Rabeh.[2] So I retraced my steps to Kano and set out on the road to Bornu through Nguru. At that time the Galadima of Nguru, Ibrahim, had his headquarters at Kacallari. From there we passed through Alanuirori and on to Gaidam. From Gaidam, however, we had to travel for two whole days through uninhabited bush before reaching Ngubula on the third. This sparsity of population was due to the way Rabeh had scattered the people of this area. So we came to Rinaskuri, or Ardoram. In those days there were important markets in Magumeri and Gubewa districts. There was also a certain Shuwa woman, called Adama, who was fighting to capture the plains of Maiduguri. She was a sort of chief there.

Before I reached Bornu I learned that "the wager of war" had already arrived. He had met Fad-el-Allah at Burgumma. Fad-el-Allah had given him his principal courtier, called Sururu, and together they had gone back to Lokoja.[3] So I now made my way back to Kano, where I found Bukar, a servant of my grandfather's, sent to tell me that I should go to Dikwa and meet Colonel Morland[4] who was making his way to Bornu through Bauchi. I attached myself to a caravan of Manga[5] traders, which took us through Babura, Danciwo, Sheri, Maini, and Keffi, and right on to Monguno. While I was at Monguno a French army officer, Captain

Dangeville, penetrated as far as Gujba, where he killed Rabeh's son, Fad-el-Allah, and captured his younger brother, Muhamman Nyabbe, along with some of his followers.[6] He then took Fad-el-Allah's head to Dikwa and set it up in the marketplace.

I was already in Dikwa by the time Colonel Morland arrived from Bauchi. The Emir of Bauchi at this time was Umaru,[7] who had prevented him from advancing beyond Burmi. Now the chief of Burmi was Mallam Zayi, better known as Mallam Jibrilla. This Mallam Jibrilla marched out to do battle with Colonel Morland, but within less than twenty minutes his forces had been scattered and he himself had taken flight. Musa Dedare, who had been one of Mallam Jibrilla's followers, was made chief of Burmi in his stead.

While Colonel Morland was advancing to Gujba, Mallam Jibrilla secretly made his way back to Burmi. Musa Dedare sent a message to the colonel telling him of Mallam Jibrilla's return. On receiving this information, Colonel Morland at once dispatched an officer[8] and twelve soldiers on horseback to Burmi, where they seized Mallam Jibrilla and brought him to Gujba. The colonel then left Gujba for Mafoni.[9]

On arrival he sent one of his officers, Captain Macarthy-Morrogh, to Shehu Garbai[10] at Dikwa. The Shehu accompanied the captain back to Mafoni to meet Colonel Morland. At that time there was a French army officer in Dikwa, the same Captain Dangeville, and I was there myself. One morning, one of our English army officers, a Captain Moses,[11] with whom I was already acquainted at Lokoja, came to Dikwa. He said my grandfather had told him that he would probably find me in Dikwa. He was making enquiries whether anyone knew of me, when Madugu Karagama came and told me about it. So I went to where he was lodging, in Rabeh's former house,[12] and he told me to go and prepare for a journey to Mafoni. I went and made ready, and we departed together for Mafoni. When we reached the town we found Shehu Garbai there. Colonel Morland read out to him the instructions of Queen Victoria, who was Queen of England at this period. The instructions given to the Shehu were that there was to be no more selling or buying of slaves, no more raiding, no more brutal justice such as the cutting off of people's limbs, and so on. The Shehu promised he would obey these rules.

Colonel Morland now departed for Yola,[13] leaving behind two companies of soldiers under the command of Captain Macarthy-Morrogh, the officer who had brought Shehu Garbai from Dikwa. The captain and his soldiers escorted Shehu Garbai from Mafoni to Monguno, where the Shehu set up his headquarters first before he returned to the original capital of Kukawa.[14] After seeing the Shehu safely established at Monguno, Captain Macarthy-Morrogh rode off and followed Colonel Morland to Yola. Captain Dunne next took one company of troops to Gujba,[15] which he made his headquarters. This left only me and one company, under a color-sergeant, at Mafoni. Colonel Morland had already told the Shehu to send some of his people to help us lay out a small cantonment there. The Shehu attached to us his personal representative, Kacalla Jajiwaji, together with his two assistants, Grema Ahmadu Shuwa and Grema Muhammadu Kawo. We moved the town of Mafoni to a site slightly to the south of the old one, and the inhabitants built a new settlement there. Where the Residency stands in Maiduguri today [1957] we built a fort.[16] It was really a walled enclosure, with four corners, about a hundred yards square. We also built two large houses inside the fort, on the rising ground where the G.R.A.[17] has now been built. This was the settlement known as Mafoni.

Some days later Captain Cochrane, who was in command of the single company we were with, came to inspect us at Mafoni. Soon after this Mr. Hewby,[18] Captain Mundy, and Mr. Burdett reached Mafoni. They were the first political officers in Bornu. All these events took place in 1902.

Chapter VI
"Mista Ibi" Arrives in Bornu (1902)

When Mr. Hewby came to Mafoni, he attached me to Captain Mundy. Together we trekked along the boundary between our land and the German part of Bornu,[1] right up to the shores of Lake Chad. From there we turned towards Monguno, where we met up with Mr. Hewby and the company of soldiers under Captain Cochrane, who had already made their way there from Mafoni.

Now, Shehu Garbai had in his possession at this time a very large number of guns, which he had got from Rabeh.[2] Mr. Hewby ordered the Shehu to collect all these weapons and surrender them to him. The Shehu agreed to do this, but some of his palace officials such as Kacalla Afuno[3] and Mallam Bukar, urged the Shehu not to carry out this order and said they would refuse to give up their own arms. When I heard of this, I immediately went to Yerima Aji, Abba Gana, and Shehu Umarmi, and told them I knew exactly what Kacalla Afuno and Mallam Bukar had told the Shehu. I added that I wanted them to remember that these guns had belonged to Rabeh. Only after Rabeh had been killed by the French had the Shehu come into possession of this arsenal. If they now refused to surrender them, I argued, might not the English take them by force? Since they were

aware that even Rabeh had not been able to oppose the
Europeans, did they expect that they could drive them
away? I advised them to point out the truth to the Shehu and
urge him to pay no attention to what his slaves were saying,
for they spoke like madmen. Then I went off and told Mr.
Hewby about the problem and also of my talk with Yerima
Aji and Abba Gana, who at that time were the nearest con-
fidants of the Shehu.

Eventually the Shehu did collect all his guns and surrender them to Mr. Hewby. Mr. Hewby handed back to the
Shehu one hundred gunpowder muskets and twelve rifles
that fire bullets. The rest were gathered up and burned.
Finally, Mr. Hewby built a courthouse[4] at Monguno.

I and the Shehu's representative, Mallam Bukar, were
now attached to Captain Cochrane for a tour of inspection
along our boundary with the French to the north. We went
through Kukawa as far north as Gashagar on the River Yo.[5]
When we arrived there, Mallam Bukar asked me to tell Captain Cochrane that he wanted permission to make a side
trip to see Grema Adamu, who was collecting taxes in Kabi.
Captain Cochrane agreed but told him to hurry and catch
up with us. However, he had not overtaken us even by the
time we reached Nguru. At that time the Galadima of Nguru
was Ibrahim, who resided at Kacallari.

Chapter VII
Trouble in Bedde (1902)

From Nguru we sent a message to the chief of Gorgoram,
Mai Sale, saying that we were coming to his town. He sent
one of his servants to meet us, a man called Gaji. Leaving

Nguru we stopped at Dumsai. We had sent word earlier telling them to prepare lodging and food for us, but when we reached Dumsai nothing had been made ready. I went on into the town in order to find out from the chief why they had made no preparations at all for our coming. As soon as I entered the town, the chief ordered his people to shoot at me. Grema, the representative of the Galadima of Nguru, advised us to turn back without further ado. We quickly withdrew from the town, but the people kept on following and firing at us, right up to our camp. Captain Cochrane at once ordered the soldiers to open fire. This dispersed the crowd, and we left Dumsai for Tagari.

As we approached Tagari, we found the people of the town, amounting to some three hundred bowmen and about thirty horsemen, drawn up in a line across the town gate, waiting for us. Captain Cochrane ordered me and the representative of the chief of Gorgoram to go and tell these people that we had not come to fight them but that we only wanted to pass on to Gorgoram. We also sent somebody into town to bring out some food and water for us, while I went and explained this to the Tagari people. Their village-head was a sensible man and he told his people to go back into town. They did so.

For our part, we now withdrew and made camp at the foot of a tall silk-cotton tree situated west of town. Earlier we had sent ahead two men, Audu and Yalema, but unfortunately they had been seized and bound with ropes. By about five o'clock in the evening they had not returned, nor had the people of Tagari brought anything out to us. Worse still, their bowmen had again taken up position along the town wall. When we sent scouts round to the north side, they found that the women and children were being led out of town under a well-armed escort of young warriors and taken away to a safe hiding-place. Their plan was obviously to evacuate their families and then come back when it was dark and attack our camp. I had already heard that this was the strategy these people had used against the Shehu of Bornu, Bukar,[1] when he had sent an expedition against Bedde. On that occasion the chief of Gorgoram, Alhaji Dan Babuje,[2] had assembled about a hundred thousand[3] bowmen for a surprise night attack on the Shehu's camp.

Knowing this, I warned Captain Cochrane of their method of fighting. Now we had spotted one of their lookouts watching us from a tall tree that stood in the middle of town. Captain Cochrane took a rifle and fired at him, and he fell to the ground. At once the fighting began, but we soon beat off the assault. Our two men who had been tied up managed to free themselves and escaped to us. Although the enemy continued to harass us during the night, we drove them off, and at dawn we set off for Gorgoram.

The chief of Gorgoram, Mai Sale,[4] came out himself and gave us a warm welcome. This was because Captain Cochrane was the first European the people of Bedde had ever set eyes on. The chief promised that he would do whatever the Europeans told him to do. This all happened in the year 1901–02.

From Gorgoram we followed the route through Jawa, Garin Dole, and Gabai Karama to Gujba. At that time there was no settlement the whole way from Gabai to Gujba. We met Captain Mundy, who was the administrator in charge of Gujba. From here we traveled through Burgumma and Marguba, and so back to Mafoni.[5] We had heard nothing more of Mallam Bukar, the man whom the Shehu had attached to us when we started and who had left us at Gashagar to go and see Grema Adamu, the tax collector at Kabi. Later we learned that he had stirred up a war in Kabi and many people had been killed. Just about that time Mr.

Hewby arrived in Gaidam from Monguno and arrested Bukar for the murder of three people. These had been the followers of Sururu whom Rabeh's son Fad-el-Allah had attached to Major McClintock, "the war horse." When the case came up before Governor Lugard in Lokoja, Bukar was found guilty of murder and was hanged at Mafoni. He was the first man to be sentenced to death by a British court in Bornu.

Shortly after this, Lieutenant Brandon arrived in Mafoni. At that time a tyrannical slave of the Shehu, Kacalla Ranasku, by name, was residing in the Busuguwa district. Lieutenant Brandon and I were sent to Busuguwa. We found this Kacalla in a town called Kufti. When we entered it, one of Kacalla's men, Grema Ali, attacked us, but Lieutenant Brandon promptly shot him dead. We arrested Kacalla Ranasku and took him back to Mafoni.

Some time later Captain Ross arrived in Mafoni to take over from Captain Cochrane, who went back to Lokoja through Yola. In those days there was no other way of getting to Bornu except through Yola, and everything, supplies and mail included, had to be brought up by that route. Wamdeo was designated as the halfway point.[6] Carriers from Yola would leave their loads at Wamdeo, then our own carriers would go down to Wamdeo and headload the supplies back to Bornu.

Chapter VIII
More Travels in Bornu (1903)

I was at Mafoni with Captain Ross when Captain Mundy, Lieutenant Lawrence, and forty-five soldiers left Gujba

for Biu. At that time Mai Garga was chief of Biu,[1] and he
greeted them in a peaceful fashion. This was the first appearance of any European in Biu. From Biu they marched
to Chibuk,[2] but here the people had made ready to resist
them. They wounded Captain Mundy just above his hip with
an arrow, but it was only slight and he soon recovered.[3]
From Chibuk Captain Mundy sent a note to Captain Ross
asking that I should be sent to meet him at Kopchi. I went
through Mulgwai[4] to Kopchi but I did not find him until I
got to Mudube. From here we went back to Mulgwai. At
this time the people of Mulgwai, Mudube, and Chibuk were
notorious as highway robbers on the route between Bornu
and Adamawa. As soon as we reached Mulgwai, the local
people ran off into the woods, but we went after them and
soon caught up with them. After a short fight they scattered.
I was given seven soldiers and sent to Ngrabego to capture
their chiefs, Mai Garisa and Mai Nyanya. I arrested Mai
Garisa but Mai Nyanya escaped. I brought Mai Garisa back
to our camp and we then left Mude for Mafoni. Mr. Lawrence now took his soldiers back to Gujba while we proceeded to Monguno with Captain Mundy. From Monguno
we went on to Gaidam and thence to Gashua.

At this time the chief of Gashua was Yerima Bolami,
famous ringleader of the brigands who infested the Kano-
Bornu route running to the east of Gorgoram. I myself was
once in a caravan traveling from Garin Role to Gorgoram
when Yerima Bolami came up to the cultivated farms near
Rinokuno, planning to ambush the caravan. The people of
Rinokuno had prevented him from attacking us, not only
because they feared for their crops but also because they
were subjects of the chief of Gorgoram, Mai Sale, and he
had ordered them not to allow anyone to molest any caravan

making for Gorgoram. Anyhow, fighting had broken out
between them, and Yerima Bolami had stabbed a Rinokuno
man with his spear. Therefore, this time, knowing his evil
reputation, as soon as we reached Gashua we arrested Yerima Bolami and took him along with us. We went on to
Albanjirori and thence to Daja. It was there that Yerima
Bolami managed to escape during the night. I took three
soldiers and went after him, and recaptured him after a
long search. Just when we were nearly at Captain Mundy's
camp, Yerima suddenly collapsed, muttering to himself,
without any physical harm or abuse having been done to
him. He simply fell down dead.

From Daja we followed the route through Sheri, Maini,
and Kabi, and so reached the banks of the River Yo at
Gashagar. When we arrived at a town called Lamawana, we
came on a camp of the Tubu,[5] a tribe who, along with Karekare,[6] practiced a lot of banditry in the northern parts of
Bornu. No sooner had they caught sight of us than they
took to their heels. The names of their leaders were Kedala
Aserti and Kedala Guwod. We left Lamawana and made
for Yo; from there we kept to the shore of Lake Chad until
we reached Monguno.

Chapter IX
The Battle of Burmi (1903)

It was while we were at Monguno that we heard the Sultan
of Sokoto, Attahiru son of Ahmadu, had fled from Sokoto
and had reached Bima.[1] Captain Browne,[2] with the com-

pany of troops stationed at Gujba, had stopped him from continuing eastwards and had forced him to return to Burmi. They had then followed behind the Sultan and camped at Ashaka to check any other of his movements. We now moved on to Ashaka, where we learned that the Sultan had a great number of horsemen with him. We waited at Ashaka until Major Marsh, in command of the reinforcements sent from the west, reached Burmi and camped outside the town wall. Then we marched out of Ashaka. We joined up with Major Marsh at about half past nine in the morning, and the fighting started.[3] When the battle had reached its height, about five o'clock in the afternoon, we forced our way into the town and pressed on through the middle of the shooting until we reached the gate of the compound where the Sultan was lodged. Some of the people ran into the Sultan's house, others took refuge in the mosque. The fighting continued until eight o'clock in the evening.

About noon Major Marsh was hit by an arrow. Within a short while he was dead. Captain Browne was also wounded but he recovered.[4] These are the names of the important chiefs who were with the Sultan of Sokoto at the battle of Burmi: the Etsu Nupe, Abubakar;[5] the Emir of Misau, Ahmadu;[6] Chief Tijjani Bashir from Futa, who had taken refuge in Sokoto when the French drove him out; the Madaki[7] of Kano, Kwairanga; and Dan Yamusa, Magaji of Keffi. The Etsu Nupe and Tijjani Bashir were taken prisoner. Both the Emir of Misau and the Magaji of Keffi escaped and reached Mecca.[8] The Madaki of Kano was killed in the fighting.

Now I want to tell you the story of how Attahiru, the Sultan of Sokoto, met his death. We had already left Burmi, the scene of the battle, and returned to Ashaka, when

Mr. Temple,[9] the Resident of Bauchi Province, Captain
Mundy[10] from Bornu, and the military commander who
had taken the place of Major Marsh, started to look for any
local people who might have known the Sultan.[11] They
found three such men from Burmi, so together with them
we went back to the battlefield. There was a dried-up bor-
row-pit beside the town wall to the southeast of the market.
It was there that Sultan Attahiru had been killed along with
almost a hundred of his followers.[12] When we reached this
spot, we left two men a short distance away and took the
other one to walk among the corpses and help us find the
Sultan. He had been wearing blue trousers, a white gown
and turban, and rubber-soled shoes. He was also wearing
an amulet and charms tied around the upper part of his arm.
The other two men were called in turn and they both singled
out the same corpse. All three of them testified that this
really was the body of the Sultan.

Now there was also a wounded man lying near the Sultan.
He had had both his thighs broken by bullets and was in a
very pitiful condition. When we came up to him we stopped,
for we could see that he was still alive. So I greeted him and
asked him about the Sultan. Pointing to a body lying in
front of him, he said to me: "I was with this man, my
brother, over there at the foot of the wall when we suddenly
heard that the Sultan had been hit. We rushed over here,
and when we got here we were struck by bullets. I was hit
in my thighs and my brother was killed." He added that, if
among the bodies we found one with blue trousers and a
white gown, that would be the body of the Sultan. This is the
story of how Sultan Attahiru was killed at Burmi and of
how his death was confirmed. God is great, may God rest
his soul in peace, amen, amen.

Chapter X
The Incident at Fika (1903)

Then we left for Nafada.[1] At Nafada we assembled more soldiers and set out for Fika.[2] This was because on an earlier occasion, when we had camped at Ashaka, we had sent one Maina Barna to the Emir of Fika, Sule,[3] asking him to send us some food; but he had refused and had driven away our messenger. This Maina Barna was the man the French had appointed chief of Damagaram. He had then declared that there could never be peace between him and us. It was because of this incident that, immediately after the battle of Burmi, we set out for Damagaram.

When we crossed the river at Nafada and reached Ngalda, we met two of the Emir's sons, Maina Kura and Maina Gana. They stopped us and said they wanted to talk to our leader. So I took them to Captain Mundy. Maina Kura, then known as Mai Disa, later became the Emir of Fika.[4] He was the father of the present emir.[5] He now explained that his father had been foolish in his behavior and that neither they nor the elders of the town had any wish to fight. That was why they had come to submit to the white man. Captain Mundy told them to lead us to their town.

When we reached the gate of Fika, the captain told the two princes to go and summon the Emir. They went off to the palace but soon returned, saying we should be patient while they tried to persuade the Emir to come out, because they were truly anxious to avoid any fighting. So our party withdrew to a slight rise to the southeast of the town and there made camp.

But when about four o'clock in the afternoon the Emir had still not appeared, Captain Mundy told me to go and call the two princes back. When they arrived, he took half of

the soldiers in his company and entered the town together
with Mai Disa, the eldest son of the Emir. We reached the
palace gate and Captain Mundy ordered me to go in and
summon the Emir. As I went in, the Emir was just coming
out, so I told him the white man was waiting for him outside
at the palace entrance. When we got to Captain Mundy he
told the Emir that he must accompany us back to our camp.
The Emir started to turn back into his compound, but Captain Mundy ordered us to stop him. So we seized him. When
we had gone part of the way toward our camp, the Emir
suddenly threw himself to the ground and called on his
people to shoot us. But his two sons, Maina Gana and
Maina Kura, were close beside us and so nobody dared to
shoot their arrows. We released the Emir anyway and returned to camp.

The Emir's eldest son, Maina Kura, again begged us to
remain patient, promising that he would try his best to bring
the Emir to us. First of all, however, he wanted to bring
Tunja Mama and Mallam Alhaji to me so that I could talk
to them and persuade them to help him in bringing the Emir
out to our camp. These men were the leading elders of the
town and also had no wish to fight. So he went and brought
them back to the camp, and I spoke to them and told them
they should do their utmost to bring the Emir back with
them so that he might make a treaty with the Europeans. I
told them to ask the Emir whether he had heard about how
the Emir of Gombe, Umaru,[6] had made a treaty with the
Europeans and how everything was now quiet and peaceful
in his district. But if he decided on war, how could he think
he would win when the Sultan himself had failed? I told them
to go and fetch the Emir. So they went and brought the Emir
to our camp. Now twenty-five soldiers had already been detailed off. They immediately placed him under escort and
took him away to Gujba. Then we appointed his son Maina

Kura, also known as Disa, to be Emir of Fika. He was the
father of the present emir. All these events happened in
1902–03. When this expedition was over, we returned to
Monguno with Captain Mundy.

Chapter XI

Events in Bornu (1903–1907)

It was in 1903 that Shehu Garbai moved his capital from
Monguno back to Kukawa.[1] In this year, too, Mr. Hewby
went on leave to England and Mr. Howard moved the Residency from Monguno to Magumeri. Six months later, when
Mr. Hewby returned from leave, Mr. Howard was transferred to Bauchi as Resident. He died there shortly afterwards.[2]

In 1904 Governor Lugard visited Bornu.[3] From Bauchi
he passed through Nafada to Magumeri and thence to Mafoni to inspect the company of soldiers there. From Mafoni
he toured Misau and Kukawa. It was on this occasion that
he confirmed Garbai's appointment as Shehu, giving him a
staff of office, a sword, a royal umbrella, and a bed.[4] While
he was on tour in Kukawa, an army officer called Major
Cubitt[5] and a troop of cavalry followed the river Yo all the
way from Kano to come and meet Lugard there. Lugard
now rode to Gaidam by way of Yo. It was then that the
settlement at Gaidam Ballara was moved to Damageri.[6]
From Gaidam the governor set out for Kano.[7] On this
tour of Bornu the governor was accompanied by his younger
brother, Major Lugard.[8]

It was during this year also that the Residency was moved from Magumeri to Kukawa, where Mr. Hewby selected a site for his headquarters at Gonge, some two miles to the east of Kukawa. This was also the year when a tax was imposed on the export of potash along the shores of Lake Chad.[9] Every cone had to have an official seal stamped on it The tax was set at 116 cowrie shells for every cone of potash exported.[10]

During the same year Mr. Hewby sent for the chief of Biu, Mai Garga, grandfather of the present emir of Biu,[11] and ordered him to come to Magumeri. On receiving this summons the chief fled from Biu to Pelamulta, for he was frightened by being sent for like this by the Europeans. Then I sent a man named Mallam Mustafa to accompany the messenger. He had once spent some time with the chief of Biu. These two went to Biu and explained things to the chief, so he agreed to accompany them to Magumeri, where he was given a staff of office. At one time the people of Biu believed that if their chief ever left his land for another district he would never return alive but would die there.[12] But now the chief had visited Magumeri and had come back to Biu safe and sound. As soon as he reached his land, the chief refused to stop in his new capital of Pelamulta but instead passed straight through to the old settlement where his father had lived. This place is the site of the modern town of Biu.

It was during the same year that the Tubu attacked Kaigama Kakami between Gashagar and Yo.[13] They inflicted heavy casualties on him, killing about fifty-three of his horses and a large number of his men.

In the same year Bornu was divided into districts for the first time, under district headmen.[14] These were called *ajiyas* and each one was given a staff of office according to his grade. There were first, second, third and fourth class district heads, just like our emirs and chiefs are graded today.[15] Village headmen were also appointed. They were called *lawans* and were placed in the fifth grade.

About this time a European by the name of Boyd Alexander came to Bornu, together with his servant, one Mr. Lopez. Their intention was to trek from Bornu across to Khartoum.[16] While they were in the Margi country, Boyd Alexander ordered the district head, Kacalla Mammadu Kaku, to be laid down and whipped for being slow in having food sent along for his carriers.[17] Kacalla reported this incident to the Resident of Bornu Province, Mr. Hewby, who summoned Boyd Alexander before him and sentenced him in his provincial court. This affair made the people of Bornu begin to realize the Europeans' sense of justice and fair play; they saw that their law was impartial since it favored nobody.

This Boyd Alexander succeeded in crossing Lake Chad and got just beyond Wadai in French territory. In Wadai there is a small tribe known as the Masalit. These people attacked Boyd Alexander and killed him.[18] Lopez, however, escaped and made his way back to Maiduguri. Mr. Hewby gave him a letter to the French officials at Fort Lamy. They sent out a search party to the place where Boyd Alexander had been killed, and they gathered up his bones and brought them back to bury him here. Today his grave can be seen in Maiduguri.[19]

There was also another European who had visited Bornu as a companion to Dr. Barth, more than a hundred years ago now. He too had died in Bornu, in a town called Maduwari, in Kanembu district on the shore of Lake Chad. His name was Mr. Overweg. Mr. Hewby ordered me to find out exactly where Overweg had been buried. I came across an old woman, about eighty years old, who showed me his grave. I reported this to Mr. Hewby, and he came to see for himself. We dug up the ground and found his bones. We collected them and brought them back to Maiduguri, where we reburied him. Today Overweg's grave can also be seen in Maiduguri.

It was the same in the case of Mr. Burdett, the first district officer to come to Bornu along with Mr. Hewby in 1902. He died at Monguno. We also dug up his remains and brought them to Maiduguri for reburial. Today his grave, too, is in Maiduguri.

Between 1902 and 1906 Tubu from the north continued to harass Bornu Province with their raiding, carrying away cattle and camels. These incursions took place mostly to the north and west of Kukawa. Because of this, Kacalla Kakami, who was stationed at Yo on the frontier, was given twenty-five mounted infantry to help him guard the area against such raids. It was at this time that a remarkable and very amusing incident occurred. A certain Tubu man, called Hindimi, was being pursued by Kacalla's men over the border. Just as he realized that he had no hope of escaping from them he spotted an anteater's hole. Dropping from his horse he crept into this hole. Along came Kacalla Kakami. He stopped by the hole and ordered his men to start digging. They dug and they dug and they dug until they were exhausted, but they could not find the man. Later he was reported to be alive, having somehow got out of the hole, albeit with a sorely abraded back.

By 1907 it was realized that Kukawa was not a suitable town for the capital of Bornu because of a continual water shortage and also because it lay too far to one side of the province. So Mr. Hewby consulted the Shehu, and they decided it would be best to abandon Kukawa and move the capital to Maiduguri, which was almost in the middle of Bornu.[20] Furthermore, there was excellent land for farming nearby, and the town was already a well-established commercial center, through which the main caravan route passed from west to east. There was also an ample water supply there. These were the reasons why the capital was moved from Kukawa and transferred to Maiduguri in 1907.[21] Mr. Hewby now built a Residency in Mafoni, about two miles away from the new capital of Maiduguri.[22] When the Shehu set up his palace at a place called Kalwa, quite close to Maiduguri, Mr. Hewby suggested that he should call the whole area Maiduguri, since this was already the name of a town widely known outside. The Shehu replied that he intended to call his part of the town Yerwa.[23] That was how the twin names Maiduguri and Yerwa, used today, came into being.

Chapter XII
The Chibuk Expedition 1906–07

In 1906 the pagans of Chibuk still enjoyed a widespread reputation for their daring highway robberies on the route from Bornu to Adamawa. They used to kill merchants and plunder their goods. One day about this time they killed a government clerk, a native of Sierra Leone called Mr. Cook,[1] who was being transferred from Maiduguri to Yola. It was now realized that their wicked behavior had gone too far, so a strong military patrol was sent out against them, consisting of mounted infantry as well as ordinary troops. Nevertheless, it took almost three months to subdue the people of Chibuk. This was because there was a large hill there, and prior to this expedition most of the people lived on the hilltop. This hill, moreover, had vast caves inside it. The people always kept an abundant supply of fresh water and plenty of food inside the caves.[2]

Now when the fighting reached its fiercest, the chief of Chibuk, Yahi Ganama, led his people into these caves. The European officers placed soldiers to guard the entrance to the main cave, but the Chibuk warriors would creep out at night and shoot their arrows at the soldiers. One day I went to the mouth of the cave with Mr. Hewby. On this occasion I had a very lucky escape. Mr. Hewby had told me to call inside to Yahi Ganama that he should come out by this exit so that they might discuss terms to end the fighting. I stooped down by the mouth of the cave and called out to Yahi Ganama. He said he was listening. I was just about to shout Mr. Hewby's message to him when somebody shot an arrow at me. I was indeed fortunate that it just missed me. We besieged the Chibuk people in their cave until their food was exhausted. Then they came out and surrendered. This was the end of the expedition.[3]

NOTES TO MAIMAINA'S STORY

CHAPTER I

1 Jega is in Gwandu emirate and was at one time a major market of the Western Sudan. Barth found that "the town of Jega has not yet lost . . . the whole of its former importance, and is still the great entrepôt for that coarse kind of coloured silk which is imported from the north, and which, notwithstanding its very inferior character, is nevertheless so greatly sought after by the natives for adorning their leatherwork" (III: 147; cf. III: 552). The reason for its subsequent decline has not yet been fully examined. Cf. E. W. Bovill: "In Northern Nigeria there is an obscure town called Jega, once an important market. Barth . . . mentions that it is the place which had caused a very considerable interest in Europe some years before. I have endeavoured for a great number of years to discover how this obscure little town had aroused interest in Europe some time in the first half of the nineteenth century, and nobody has been able to help me" (Discussion at the Royal Geographical Society, London, 25 November 1957).

2 See also the genealogical note on pp. 184–85. Benton refers to Maimaina as Abbega's nephew (1912: 253*n*).

3 The Margi, today numbering about two hundred and fifty thousand, are concentrated in the northern districts of the former Sardauna and Adamawa provinces and in the adjoining Margi district of Bornu emirate. Their principal towns today include Gulak, Damboa, and Mulgwe. For anthropological studies, see Meek 1931, II: 213–51; Vaug-

164

han 1964a, 1964b, 1965; and Kirk-Greene 1958b. For a detailed analysis of their language, see Hoffmann 1963.

4 Abbega is a corruption of the Hausa name Abubakar, Kanuri variant Bukar. There is a story told by his son in Lokoja that, when he was presented to royalty in Europe, "Abbega" was the nearest the imperial lips could come to pronouncing "Abubakar" (Pedraza 1960: 61). In fact, Barth had already employed this form in his text.

5 This was in September 1855. For an account of their sojourn in England, see Introduction and Part One of this book, and Kirk-Greene 1956.

6 In late 1857, some seven years before Dorugu's return. Ostensibly he was to evangelize the Nupe in Lokoja, building on the pioneer work of Consul Baikie and Bishop Samuel Crowther. "As events turned out, however, they [Abbega and Dorugu] soon discovered that the knowledge of the world which they had acquired might be turned to more profitable account by trading than by preaching and consequently they forsook Christianity and embraced Islam" (Mockler-Ferryman 1902: 44).

7 The Royal Niger Company, derived from the amalgamation of a number of merchant firms trading on the lower Niger into the United African Company in 1879 and reorganized as the National African Company in 1882, received its royal charter in July 1886. Under the dynamic leadership of its founder, Sir George Goldie, it played an important role in the administration as well as the trade of the Oil Rivers during the last two decades of the nineteenth century. For the definitive biography of Goldie, see Flint 1960.

8 Abbega's wife's name was Fatima.

9 The name Maimaina (or Mai Maina) derives from the Kanuri words for "king" and "prince" (see Introduction). His Islamic name was Muhammadu.

10 A dramatic contemporary account of this major uprising against the company is to be found in Bindloss (1898: 78–

114). It was followed in February 1895 by a punitive expedition by two gunboats and the sacking of the town of
Nimbe. A year later an official investigation into the Brass
disturbances was carried out by Sir John Kirk (Parliamen-
tary Papers 1896, 59: 361, C. 7977).

11 Major A. J. Arnold (1866–1933), Third King's Own Hus-
sars, joined the Royal Niger Constabulary in 1894 and
commanded the force from 1895 to 1898. In 1897 he
commanded the Bida-Ilorin expedition under Sir George
Goldie (see Flint 1960: 243–63; Vandeleur 1898: 159–234;
and Kirk-Greene 1968).

12 Maimaina is in error here. Not only did the incident take
place in 1902, but at the time of his murder Captain (not
Major) Moloney was no longer in the company's service
but was a Resident in the Northern Nigerian Political
Service. His murder is described in the *Annual Report for
Northern Nigeria 1902*, para. 13 ff., and in Orr (1911: 110–
11). See also Hogben and Kirk-Greene (1966: 533–34).
The fullest account is that given in Muffett (1964: 62–68),
which comprises the valuable eyewitness testimony of
Hassan Keffi, recorded when he was eighty-four. Moloney
was buried on top of a hill outside the town, his grave
inscribed "Sacred to the Memory of Captain Gustavus
William Moloney, Resident of the Nassarawa Province,
who was murdered in the fearless execution of his duty,
October 3rd 1902. Requiescat in pace." The affair was by
no means forgotten at Keffi, even fifty years later.

13 The term used by Maimaina here, *'yan arewa*, is very much
a product of the time the autobiography was written, for
by the late 1950s the policy of organizing the civil service
on a regional basis had developed a parochial ethnicity
and a deliberate awareness of being a "Northerner."

14 Maimaina here uses the anglicized *boyi*, which has a greater
domestic connotation than *yaro*, servant or follower. In
colonial francophone Hausa areas, this was feminized as
la boyesse!

15 Maimaina naturally describes them as *soja*, but apart from

the specific military recruitment for the 1897 campaign against Bida (see p. 136), the company's charter permitted only the raising of a constabulary. This force was, however, of a marked paramilitary nature and included artillery and machine-gun units. For organizational details of the Royal Niger Constabulary, see Flint 1960: 142–44.

16 The Holy Ghost Fathers (established 1885) ran a successful cookery school in Onitsha, the male products of which were much sought after by early Coasters. The Hausa text has "Ijaws [Ijo], that is to say people from Asaba and Onitsha," but as these are not Ijaw towns it may be a misprint for Ibo. On the other hand, Ijaws have remained popular as stewards and house servants.

17 It is interesting that Maimaina makes no mention of Hausa troops, so highly thought of from the very raising of "Glover's Hausas" and their own militia in Lagos thirty years earlier, and again in the First Ashanti War (1872). Shortly after this, the constabulary was reorganized into three companies: Hausa (No. 1), Yoruba (No. 2), and Fanti, Igala, Borgu, Krumen, etc. (No. 3).

18 The market built at Onitsha during the 1950s was one of the largest covered markets in West Africa. It was reduced to rubble during the prolonged battle for the town during the civil war of 1967–70.

19 Onitsha was one of the earliest major stations of the Church Missionary Society, established by the Ibo clergyman J. C. Taylor during Crowther's evangelizing expedition of 1857 (see Ajayi 1965).

20 Opposite Onitsha, on the right bank of the Niger. The marine workshops were at Akassa, in the Delta. Major trading stations upriver, subsidiary to the Asaba headquarters, included Lokoja, Loko, and Ibi.

21 The ancient capital of the Sef dynasty of Bornu, founded ca. 1470 and destroyed by the Fulani in 1808 (see Hogben and Kirk-Greene 1966: 313–20).

22 Wukari is a major Jukun town in the lower Benue region.

Historical ties between the Kanuri and the Jukun are of a long-standing, two-way nature.

23 The modern administrative district of Koton Karfe runs along the north bank of the Niger to the west of the river's confluence with the Benue, and includes within its boundary the urban area of Lokoja.

24 Though the majority of the inhabitants of Abuja emirate are Gwari, the governing classes are essentially Hausa, being the direct successors to the original Habe ruling dynasty of Zaria who were driven out by the Fulani at the beginning of the jihad. The Emir of Abuja is still referred to locally as Sarkin Zazzau, "Chief of Zaria." See Hassan and Shu'aibu 1952.

25 The practice was a common one in nineteenth-century Northern Nigeria, serving to convince an illiterate population that the local terror had indeed been exterminated. Cf. the Fad-el-Allah incident on p. 145.

26 One of the important Nupe titleholders. The office is retained in Bida society today, and is traditionally held in the Etsu Masaba dynastic house. In the nineteenth century his fief included Lokoja.

27 This is the feminine form of the Hausa word for a man from Gobir, *bagobiri.*

28 This is one of the earliest recorded uses of a searchlight in Nigeria.

29 A similar device, known as *rudu,* was used by the Sokoto people, but there it was principally to escape the mosquitoes. Barth accompanies his description of these huts with a sketch (III: 102).

CHAPTER II

1 The Royal Niger Company carried a number of medical doctors on its establishment, primarily for service with the constabulary.

2 *Maiyaki* was a common Hausa war-title, signifying "field commander" in charge of the reserve troops behind the

battle. *Nda* is the Nupe equivalent of the Hausa *dan,*
"son of," or "the small [one]"

3   In fact, this was his title. Dokoyiringi was one of the two
major Nupe military titles of the *ena maiyaki* or army
command. Along with the *Uban Dawaki,* he was a cavalry
general. (Nadel 1942: 108–14.)

4   The Hausa word *bature,* pl. *turawa,* literally means "a
man from Ture." Although the identification of an assumed
Ture is obscure, the term was generally applied to the
lighter-skinned Arab traders resident in Hausaland long
before the Europeans came. From the turn of the century
it began to take on the specific meaning of "European." In
modern usage it can also signify "a senior Government
official," e.g. *baturen makaranta* ("education officer"),
baturen gona ("agricultural superintendent").

5   It is interesting to note how throughout his autobiography
Maimaina identifies himself with the Europeans and con-
sistently uses the we/our form, *mu/-mu.*

6   The rank of *heluman* ("headman") was adopted by the man
in charge of a group of porters or carriers, typically known
as *leburori* (sing. *lebura,* "laborer"). Later it also became
used for the overseer in charge of a gang of roadworkers.

7   Not in anger but, in accordance with Moslem practice, as a
feu de joie.

8   Another senior Nupe title, still found in Bida and traditionally held in the Umaru Majigi royal family. His fief in
precolonial days was Kacha. For the Makun's subsequent
collaborations with the Royal Niger Company, see Nadel
1942: 83, 93*n*, and Hogben and Kirk-Greene 1966: 275–
76.

9   *Etsu* is the Nupe word for "king" or "emir," equivalent to
the Hausa *sarki.* Muhammadu, son of Umaru Majigi (1873–
84) and great-grandson of the founder of the Nupe emirate,
Mallam Dendo (d. 1832), was the sixth ruler and reigned
from 1901 to 1906. Today Etsu Nupe is the correct pro-
tocol title of the Emir of Bida.

10 The Ndeji, "Father of the Town," was the head of the Nupe nobility and, in his official duties as confidant to the Etsu, corresponded to the *waziri* or "prime minister" of the Hausa courts.

11 Son of Mallam Dendo's second son, Masaba (1841–47; 1859–73), and fifth emir of Bida (1895–1901).

12 The genus *ficus gnaphalocarpa,* renowned in Nigeria for its ample shade.

13 The implicit reference here is to the major campaign against the Fulani emirs by the British government after it had assumed control of the Protectorate in 1900, which was directed primarily against the powerful emirates of Kano and Sokoto. They submitted in 1903. For a detailed account of this campaign, see Muffett 1964; Orr 1911; and Crozier 1932.

14 For accounts of the campaign, see Vandeleur 1898: 159–234; Flint 1960, Chap. 11; and Kirk-Greene 1968. In 1966 the *Nigerian Citizen* reported that D. J. Muffett was working on a full-scale study of the campaign.

15 He was transport officer to the expedition. His grave is still visible.

16 In addition to the campaign narratives listed in note 13, this engagement has been described by Etsu Ndayako, *In ji Etsu Nupe*. This is a vernacular account by the grandson of Etsu Muhammadu, who was installed by the company when Etsu Abubakar fled.

17 A Nupe town about sixty miles to the north of Bida.

18 Sixth emir of Ilorin (1896–1915).

19 The treaty, still extant, reads as follows:

> This Treaty is made on the 18th February 1897 of the Christian Era, and the 15th day of Ramadan, in the year 1314 since the Hegira. The Treaty is between Sir George Goldie, Governor for the Royal Niger Company, and the Emir Suliman, son of the former Emir Alihiu, for his chiefs and people for ever.

1. The Company will recognize Suliman as Emir of Ilorin.

2. The Emir Suliman recognizes that Ilorin is entirely under the protection and power of the Company.

3. He will obey all such directions in respect of his Government as the Company may give him from time to time.

4. The Emir Suliman agrees to make no war without the consent of the Company, and to accept such frontier line between Ilorin and Lagos as the Company may decide.

5. The Emir Suliman agrees to take every step in his power to prevent the further introduction of gin and rum into his country from Lagos, and to destroy all the gin and rum that may be found in his country.

All previous Treaties are abrogated, but Ilorin remains under the protection of Her Majesty, the Queen of Great Britain and Ireland, and Empress of India.

7. I, Suliman, Emir of Ilorin, hereby accept this Treaty, and I, George Taubman Goldie, Governor of the Royal Niger Company, also hereby accept it.

[Signed] SULIMAN [in Arabic]
"   GEORGE TAUBMAN GOLDIE

20 Maimaina's memory is not quite accurate here. The palace was shelled and the Fulani quarter of the town was fired, but there was no pitched battle as had been the case at Bida.

21 His knowledge of English, Nupe, and Hausa must have been invaluable in those early days of administration. Later he was to become equally fluent in Kanuri.

CHAPTER III

1 The West African Frontier Force was raised by Colonel Lugard in 1897 and comprised two battalions of infantry with ancillary units. For Lugard's diary of this commission, see Perham and Bull 1963: 321–419. The standard history of the regiment is that by Haywood and Clarke 1965. For

a survey of the literature and unpublished documents on the history of the RWAFF, including the battalion standing orders for the years 1897–99 now in the Military Museum at Zaria, see Kirk-Greene 1965.

2 Colonel T. D. Pilcher (1858–1928), Fifth Fusiliers. "While Lugard took to him personally, he was a man who had never seen active service, a Staff College Officer, and an expert on the German Army. . . . He was a wealthy man and much interested in the sartorial side of the force, down to the design of buttons" (Perham 1956: 643). He later became a major-general.

3 Later General Sir James Willcocks (1857–1926). He had served with Lugard in India, and was then invited to join his chief in raising the West African Frontier Force in 1897 and succeeded him as commandant in 1899. See Perham 1956 and his own narrative (Willcocks 1904).

4 The capital of the new Protectorate of Northern Nigeria was only temporarily here. Lugard soon abandoned his search for a site in the Lokoja area and transferred his headquarters to Jebba, before moving to Zungeru in 1902 and finally to Kaduna in 1917.

5 Cf. the opening words of Lugard's first annual report to the Colonial Office: "Arriving at the end of December, 1899, I took over the administration from the Royal Niger Company, and the Union Flag was hoisted in place of the Company's at 7.20 A.M. at Lokoja on January 1st 1900, in presence of a parade of all arms, at which civilians were present in uniform." A fuller account, drawing on the records of two persons present at the ceremony, is to be found in Perham 1960: 23–26.

6 Lugard gives details of the incorporation in his *Annual Report for Northern Nigeria, 1900,* para. 2.

7 Grandson of Jaura, the founder of the emirate, and seventh emir of Lapai (1893–1907).

8 Grandson of Attahiru, founder of the emirate, and fourth emir of Agaie (1877–1900).

9 A Gwari town about thirty-five miles away.

10 The Agaie elders had disregarded the counsel of their emir
     and had given active support to Bida when the Royal
     Niger Company attacked it in 1897. Agaie was then oc-
     cupied and Lapai burnt. There was further resistance in
     this whole Middle Niger area during the first years of the
     British occupation, and a stern letter sent by Lugard to the
     Chief of Zuba in May 1900, after he had boldly shut the
     gates of his town in the face of the British, is preserved to
     this day. It reads:

          The Fourth Day of May in the Year 1900.
          This letter comes from Governor Lugard:
              Greetings and more honour to Mahamman, the
          Chief of Zuba, together with the expression of my
          confidence.
          After this:—
              I let you know that I have seen the messenger whom
          you sent, and I have heard your message and under-
          stood all that you have said.
          After this:—
              I tell you that you have done wrong; but since you
          realize this, I will forgive you and pardon your fault.
          After this:—
              I tell you to watch your actions carefully. I have
          heard what you have to say and I have also heard all
          the white man's report.
          After this:—
              I warn you with the utmost seriousness to take heed
          of your conduct and to pass on this warning to your
          people. Also you shall take care of this flag; do not
          treat it lightly. Every town which possesses a flag such
          as this becomes thereby a place of importance, for
          this flag is the flag of our Queen and not to be treated
          lightly. Should you hold it cheap, it is your own honour
          and authority which you cheapen.
          After this:—
              I notify you that I am clearing a road from the bank

of the Niger to your town, and from there to the
banks of the Kaduna river, so that even a woman
travelling alone with her load may pass in safety, or a
child. This is my intention. As to the road from
Kurmin Giwa to Zaria, all is well; with the road from
Lafiya to Wukari, all is well as far as the Birnin Gwari
road; every man, woman, and child, the old and the
young, may pass in safety.

After this:—

I tell you that we are the rulers of the world. If a man
does aught by night, we know of it by morning; if by
day, we know of it by night, you may be sure of that.
Therefore take heed of your behaviour. I have accepted your explanation and forgiven you for what is
past, but for the future take care that nothing shall
happen to harm our mutual confidence and respect.

    That is all.

11 Nikki was the goal of the great international "Borgu
Steeplechase" of 1894, when Lugard beat the Frenchman
Decoeur by a short head to secure a treaty with the chiefs
of Nikki and Kaiama. In 1897 the French occupied
Kaiama, later withdrawing to Nikki and Illo. For Lugard's
own diary of the undertaking, see Perham and Bull 1963:
47–318. The treaty with Nikki is reproduced on pp. 185–
87. See also Perham 1956: 473–557.

12 Lieutenant Kincaid-Smith was the founder of the celebrated
Mounted Infantry units of the West African Frontier
Force. Subsequently expanded to battalion strength, they
were finally disbanded between the wars.

CHAPTER IV

1 Kano was not occupied by the British administration until
the beginning of 1903. This episode of Maimaina's visit to
Kano remained something of a mystery until the publication of his autobiography in 1958 explained his cover story.

An entry on the provincial files in Maiduguri, dated 1937, notes how Maimaina resigned his interpretership in Lokoja and then went to Zaria and Kano trading, "though precisely what attracted him to this place he is not prepared to state" (author's personal field notes, Bornu, 1957).

2   Still an important staging-point on the main road running south from Kaduna to link up with the Keffi trunk road. It is about a hundred miles from Zaria.

3   The Kajes' reputation for wildness is substantiated in the records of the early political officers who toured the hill tribes of southern Zaria. Today mission education and natural alertness have placed such peoples as the Kagoro, Kaje, Kagarko, Kajuru, and Katab in a very favorable position. One of the first administrators of the area described Jema'an Dororo as "the centre of the country where head-hunting is seen in its most flourishing state" (Tremearne 1912: 92).

4   Situated some forty miles south of Zaria, this became the first northern center of the Church Missionary Society under Dr. Walter Miller, until he moved to Zaria city itself in 1905. See Miller 1936, 1950.

5   Twelfth emir of Zaria (1897–1902). The raiding of even his own subjects by his notorious bands of armed men, 'yan bindigogi, is still vividly recalled. There are accounts in Miller 1936, 1950; in Smith 1960; and in Hogben and Kirk-Greene 1966.

6   Seventh emir of Kano (1894–1903).

7   Tenth emir of Hadejia (1885–1906).

8   There had been a running war between Hadejia and Gumel up to 1872, and another major war with Kano in 1893. Kano itself was almost crippled by internecine conflict between 1893 and 1895, when Muhamman Tukur's appointment as emir plunged the country into civil war.

9   I.e. a money-changer. *Liyari* is the Hausa word for the Maria Theresa dollar, simultaneously current with the cowrie shells. This dollar is still in use, especially in the

northeast, but as an ornament instead of as currency. Its
present value is about two American dollars.

10 An important Hausa titleholder, and in the Kano of that
time an intimate of the emir.

11 Because of polygamy, the description *uba daya uwa daya*
("one father, one mother") acquires an added element of
kinship determination.

12 The trade across the Sahara to Tripoli was an important
part of Kano's economy. Today many descendants of mixed
Tripolitanian and Hausa/Fulani marriages live in Kano.
The trade was finally killed by the advent of the railway in
1911, which obliged Kano to turn away from the Mediter-
ranean and face the southern seaports for the import and
the export of its merchandise. Compare the groundnut
export figures for the years either side of the completion
of the vital Kano-Lagos railway line:

Value of crop, 1910:   £8,150
Value of crop, 1914:   £179,219
Quinquennial average tonnage, 1910–1914:   8,200 tons
Quinquennial average tonnage, 1915–1919: 41,300 tons

CHAPTER V

1 This was the nickname of Major Augustus McClintock,
an early political officer in Bornu. His British colleagues
gave him the affectionate sobriquet of "The General." One
of them described him as "a delightful Irishman, with a
slight lisp and an inexhaustible supply of blarney . . . big
both in mind and body. While he could mete out, if occasion demanded, a telling off which made itself felt, he
was not above doing some real spade work; and I have
known him at tax time sit at my table for seven successive
days helping to count thousands of pounds' worth of three-
pences and sixpences" (Langa-Langa 1922: 32). He died
at Ngubala, Bornu, in June 1912.

2 Rabeh was a client of the famous Sudanese slave-raider

Zubeir Pasha. After Zubeir had been defeated and impris-
oned by the Egyptians, Rabeh gradually made his way
westward across Africa with an army of some seven hundred formidably armed men, raiding and pillaging everything in his path. In 1893 he occupied Bornu, after defeat-
ing and executing the Kanuri emir Shehu Kiari, and established himself at Dikwa, which he turned into a military
camp. In Dikwa his force was estimated by contemporary
accounts to have swollen to twenty thousand men, nearly
five thousand of whom were equipped with firearms. He
was killed by the French at the battle of Kusseri in 1900,
though not before he had personally slain the French commandant, Lamy. For further details see Hogben and Kirk-
Greene (1966: 334–37, 345–50); and Gentil (1902). There
is as yet no adequate biography in English of this "African
Napoleon." His son Fad-el-Allah then retired to Dikwa,
but was driven out by the French column and withdrew to
the Kilba district of Adamawa. For his death, see pp. 145.

3   At this time (1900–01), Bornu was still unoccupied territory
and the governor had, as Maimaina relates, sent Major
McClintock up north to contact Fad-el-Allah. "He was
received with acclamation as a friend and treated with
great hospitality, and he himself formed a high opinion of
Fad-el-Allah, who appears to have been a most gallant
soldier and a capable and determined ruler—Major Mc-
Clintock's report was wholly in favour of recognising Fad-
el-Allah as Emir of Bornu." Lugard was, however, far from
pleased with the behavior of McClintock, who had "in-
judiciously presented Fad-el-Allah with a shot-gun of his
own," from which courtesy there sprang a rumor, "incred-
ible and absolutely untrue," that the British were supply-
ing Fad-el-Allah with arms to fight the French. (Quotations
from Lugard's *Annual Report for Northern Nigeria, 1901*.)

4   Later General Sir Thomas Morland (1865–1925). He was
one of the founding officers of the West African Frontier
Force, and served in Nigeria again from 1901–03. His
command of the Kano-Sokoto campaign has been described

by Muffett (1964). He subsequently became inspector-general of the regiment.

5 The Manga were located in the Hausa-Bornu marches, and during the nineteenth century enjoyed a reputation as audacious warriors (Barth III: 36, 549). Today they make up part of the population of Bedde emirate.

6 This was in 1901. Fad-el-Allah made his last stand in a grove of baobab trees which can still be identified to the southwest of Gujba. When he was shot through the chest, one of his followers, Yerima Lama, lifted him onto his own horse and rode away to safety; however, Fad-el-Allah died within a matter of hours. He was buried in the nearby swamp at Mutwe, but the French dug up his body and carried his head to Dikwa, Rabeh's former capital, where it was publicly displayed.

7 Fourth emir of Bauchi (1883–1902).

8 Lieutenant Dyer.

9 The story has not quite the same sequence in Lugard's official report:

> Leaving a company as garrison at Bautshi, Colonel Morland advanced through Gombe towards Gujba in Bornu. The country to be crossed has long been the scene of constant warfare. A certain Mallam (Mullah) Jibrella arose some years ago and gathered round him a band of fanatics.* He defeated the King of Gombe
>
> *In 1887 the Mallam was expelled from Messau for witchcraft. He went to Kano and was again expelled. He settled in Dukul in Gombe territory, and was given some lands and farms, but began to intrigue and formed a war-camp at Bajoga in 1894. He was attacked by the King of Gombe, who was killed. The Mallam then took most of Gombe's territory—Rabeh quarrelled with him, but Fad-el-Allah was not strong enough to attack him. He continued harassing the country round until he was defeated and captured, as here related.

and annexed a part of his country, and threatened
Bautshi, which there is little doubt would have fallen
before his troops had not the British expedition happened to intervene. For many years he had led a career
of unbroken conquest, defying even the armies of
Rabeh and Fad-el-Allah, and at the time of Colonel
Morland's arrival he was the most dreaded power in
the east. He had lately declared himself to be the
Mahdi, and dressed his followers in the "jibbeh" of
the Dervish. While advancing in the open, the scouts
reported the presence of a body of some 600 foot and
100 horsemen behind a fold in the ground, and Colonel Morland had barely time to form square with the
advance guard to cover the long column before he
was charged in a most determined fashion by these
fanatics, with the Mallam at their head. They reached
within 50 yards of the small square (consisting of 100
men with a maxim and a gun) before they were
checked by the fire, when they swept round, making a
turning movement. They were, however, beaten off
and fled in disorder, having 60 killed and a large
number of wounded. Our casualties were only two
wounded, since the enemy fired little, but tried to close
with the sword and spear. Colonel Morland pursued
for two days and then sent out several flying columns
who captured many horses, men, and banners, but
the credit of the capture of the Mahdi himself fell to
Lieutenant Dyer, who rode 70 miles in 17 hours to
effect it. Jibrella was a white-haired old man of a fine
type. The dash and pluck shown by him had won the
admiration of our officers, and he was well looked
after till his arrival in Lokoja, where I placed him in
charge of the local chief [Abbega] with a small subsidy
for his maintenance. He is very feeble, and no longer a
danger.

10 Bukar Garbai, Emir of French Bornu at Dikwa 1901–02
    and, after fleeing from Dikwa and accepting Morland's

offer of recognition, Shehu of British Bornu from 1902 to 1922. The French had made his life impossible by imposing a huge indemnity to be collected from his impoverished kingdom for having delivered him from the "scourge" of Fad-el-Allah. Maimaina's account tallies with Lugard's as given in his *Annual Report for Northern Nigeria, 1902,* para. 9:

> The expedition reached Gujba on March 11th, and leaving a company there as garrison proceeded thence to Maiduguri. Colonel Morland himself made a rapid trip to the ancient capital of Bornu at Kuka on Lake Chad. The situation as he found it was as follows:— After the death of Rabeh, Fad-el-Allah, his son, had taken command of the remnant of the forces and had retired westwards into British territory pursued by the French. Some fighting had taken place before the French gave up the chase and returned to their headquarters at Dikwa. Fad-el-Allah now sent one of his generals to return to the neighbourhood of Dikwa in order, I believe, to dig up some buried ammunition. The French officer, Captain Dangeville, was away and the general marched as far as Ngala and attacked the French post there, but was repulsed. Captain Dangeville, returning, collected his forces and marched by forced marches upon Fad-el-Allah's camp at Gujba. Taking that chief by surprise he defeated him and annihilated his army, and Fad-el-Allah himself was killed. In addition to their own troops employed on this raid, the French raised levies in British territory. A great number of prisoners were taken in the battle and much loot. In return for delivering the Sultan of Bornu from his enemy Fad-el-Allah the French imposed a war indemnity of $50,000 upon this chief, in addition to the balance of $21,000, which Sanda

had failed to pay, and detained him at Dikwa till it should be paid. Prior to this they had placed on the throne of Kuka the second son of the late Sheikh (Sanda), on condition that he should pay them $30,000, and they deported to Kanem (East of Chad) the elder and legitimate heir on account of his refusal to pay;—Sanda had paid $9,000 only. The total indemnity claimed was thus $80,000, of which $73,500 had been paid up, and the Sheikh Shefu Garbai was now in Dikwa awaiting the arrival of his messengers who were ransacking the impoverished and destitute country to obtain the balance ($6,500) required. Colonel Morland sent messages to Shefu Garbai telling him that he would recognise him as Sultan of British Bornu if he came to reside in the country, and at the same time he put a stop to the collection of any further payment to the French. Garbai accepted our offers with alacrity, returned with a large following, and took up his residence at Mongonu on Chad, pending the rebuilding of Kuka. The French, who were waiting at Dikwa for the balance of their impost, nominated the third brother, Sanda, as Sultan of the very small part of Bornu which lies to the east of the British boundary, with his capital at Dikwa. The advent of a large German expedition, however, at this moment caused the French to evacuate Dikwa and German territory, and retire beyond the Shari. The situation created by the French action was one which naturally gave rise to constant friction, the followers of each of the rival Sultans attempting to raise tribute and interfering with the towns of the other, and especially, as might be expected, on the part of Sanda, whose residence was on the frontier line, and who had but little territory to the east. This again caused mutual "protests" between the representatives of the two European

Powers, and much valuable time was spent in attempting to lay down a temporary frontier.

11 He was quartermaster of the Northern Nigeria Regiment.
12 The ruins of this rambling palace, now scheduled as a
historical monument, still manage to emanate an effective
impression of what it must have been like in Rabeh's day.
For many years it remained the residence of the district
officer in charge of Dikwa division, and as late as 1957 it
was still being used as a rest-house for officers on tour in
Bornu.
13 The capital of Adamawa, captured by the British only a
few months before. He reached there on April 18, 1902,
having left Bornu ten days earlier.
14 "At present Kukawa is one large cornfield," noted the
Resident on the provincial files. The Shehu therefore continued to live in Monguno until the former capital, sacked
by Rabeh, could be rebuilt (author's personal field notes,
Bornu, 1956).
15 Gujba for a while became the provincial headquarters of
western Bornu when the province was made into a double
one.
16 The outline of the fort can still be traced on the ground,
and the old magazine is also identifiable in the compound
of what for many years became the senior district officer's
house. There is a photograph of the fort in its heyday in
Boyd Alexander 1907, I: 241.
17 Government Residential Area. This was the term by which
the "European" residential part of each principal town in
Northern Nigeria was known up to the time of indepen-
dence. For the distinction between Mafoni, Maiduguri, and
Yerwa, see p. 162.
18 W. P. Hewby, C.M.G., is well remembered in Bornu as
"Mista Ibi." Transferred from being senior agent of the
Royal Niger Company, he became one of Lugard's out-
standing Residents, going first to Kano and then remain-

ing in charge of Bornu from 1902 until his retirement in 1913. Captain J. Cochrane was Military Resident for the first few months of 1902 until a civilian administrator took over.

CHAPTER VI

1 Soon after Shehu Garbai fled to British Bornu in 1902 (see p. 181), the French withdrew to Kusseri, which they renamed Fort Foureau, and the Germans assumed control of the Dikwa region. It remained in their hands until 1916. A mandate over the former Cameroons was granted to Britain and France in 1922. Dikwa was then included in the administration of Bornu Province.

2 An estimate of arms held by Rabeh in 1895 showed over three thousand rifles and forty-four pieces of artillery, making his the best-armed force in the West Africa of the time. See chap. V, note 2.

3 Kacalla is an important Kanuri title, formerly a military, slave one. *Afuno* is the Kanuri word for the Hausa people.

4 Justice in the Provincial Court, exercised by a political officer vested with considerable judicial powers, was one of the early manifestations of the British colonial presence in Africa and Asia.

5 For some 120 miles, from Bosso westwards to Damasak, the River Yo marks the northern frontier between Nigeria and the Republic of Niger.

CHAPTER VII

1 Bukar Kura (1880–84), fourth shehu and grandson of the dynastic founder El Kanemi (d. 1835).

2 Fourth emir of Bedde (1842–93). Gorgoram, whose fortifications can still be seen, was built in ca. 1825 as the capital of the Bedde people. Today the Emir resides at Gashua.

3 *Sic;* but doubtless the phrase is intended to convey an impression of countless magnitude rather than an actual figure.

184 Anthony Kirk-Greene

4 Sixth emir of Bedde (1897–1919), and grandfather of Umar Suleiman, the present emir (1945–   ).

5 If one starts to add up the miles covered by Maimaina as he accompanied these political officers on their tours of inspection, one cannot fail to be impressed by the great distances involved in those days of ceaseless trekking. This tour alone would have involved over five hundred miles of horseback riding. One recalls Lugard's dispatch to the Colonial Office reporting on events of the year 1904, which included an account of his "inspection of provinces covering a distance of over 2,000 miles by land [horse or foot] and over 1,600 miles by water, and dealing with the fifteen provinces whose capitals I have visited during this tour" [Northern Nigeria, no. 476 of 1905].

6 Supplies came up the Benue from Lokoja as far as Yola in the shipping season (June–September) and were then transferred overland to Bornu during the dry months. Wamdeo was roughly halfway between the two administrative headquarters, being about 110 miles each way. The 217 miles were done in eighteen marches. For many years the route enjoyed a bad reputation for highway robbery, especially on the stretches either side of Wamdeo itself.

CHAPTER VIII

1 Garga Kwomting (1891–1908), the twenty-third chief of Biu.

2 The area took its name from the Chibuk tribe living there.

3 The official report gives three soldiers wounded, with enemy losses of ninety killed. The Chibuk people were to prove a thorn in the flesh of the Bornu administration (see pp. 162 ff.).

4 Among the provincial archives in Bornu, there is a pedigree attributing to Maimaina an ancient connection with the royal family of Mulgwai. This had been an important Margi center at the beginning of the nineteenth century. The genealogy shows Maimaina's grandfather, Abbega, as

the great-grandson of the chief of Mulgwai, Mai Nere, and
grandson of one Maina Biri. By the time Abbega's father,
Wulaji Ari, succeeded to the title, the chieftainship of
Mulgwai had been reduced to that of a *bulama* or village
headman. There is also extant, in Maiduguri, a minute by
H. R. Palmer, Resident of Bornu and a deep student of
Nigerian history, declaring Maimaina to be "the grandson
of Abigai, a Marghi slave, and a son of Chato (a natural-
ised Nupe) and a Hausa woman from Jegga" (author's personal field notes, Bornu, 1956).

5 A tough, nomadic people from the rocky fastness of Tibesti
   in the Sahara.

6 A major tribe in the Misau-Potiskum area.

CHAPTER IX

1 Muhammadu Attahiru I (1902–03), eleventh sultan of
   Sokoto and son of the fourth sultan Ahmadu Atiku, Mai
   Cimola (1859–66). Defeated after a heroic stand by the
   Fulani cavalry at Sokoto on March 15, 1903, he fled first
   to Gusau and thence to Bima, the hill beside the River
   Gongola which by tradition has a certain mystique for
   Moslem resistance movements. Accompanied by a large
   following of Fulani notables, the Sultan was aiming to reach
   asylum in Mecca. This movement of religious dynamism is
   known in Fulani history as the *perol*.

2 Fully, W. Hamilton-Browne.

3 The account of this major battle and the events leading
   up to it, as given in Lugard's official reports to the Colonel
   Office reads thus:

   The ex-Sultan [Attahiru], contrary to my expectation,
   did not accept my conciliatory offers. It would probably have been easy to have captured or driven him
   out of the country, but I hoped that he would settle
   down peaceably. Probably he could not believe in
   the genuineness of such proposals to the head of an

army which had recently opposed us, and supposed it
to be merely a ruse to capture him, and he was in all
probability encouraged in this belief by the Magaji of
Keffi, who it appears had joined him, and who knew
that for him there was no pardon. There were also
with him, Abu Bekr, ex-Emir of Bida, Belo, who had
neglected his chances of being Emir of Kontagora, the
Galadema and other irreconcilable chiefs of Kano,
with the implacable Lapini of Bida, etc. The ex-Sultan
established himself at Gusao with a small following.
This village being near Sokoto, the garrison of that
place drove him out. He found no following in his
own territory, and the Sokoto chiefs remained loyal.
He then passed eastwards between Kano and Zaria,
giving out that he was about to proceed on a pilgrimage
to Mecca, and ordering all the people to follow him.
Not a chief or man of any sort left Kano, but the
villagers of the districts he passed through, appealed
to on religious grounds, and misunderstanding his
intentions, flocked to him by thousands. A party of
mounted infantry from Zaria attacked him, and inflicted some loss upon him (two of our men being
killed), whereupon many of the villagers returned to
their homes. The ex-Sultan fled eastward into the only
portion of the Protectorate still untraversed by our
troops and to which no Resident had as yet been appointed. The people of this district, which consists of
a number of small but ancient Emirates lying between
Kano and Bornu, could only have received the usual
exaggerated and often wholly untrue reports of the
events which had been taking place, which in Nigeria
are circulated with magical rapidity. Probably under
the impression that the British had ousted the head of
their religion and declared war against "the Faith,"
enormous numbers joined in the so-called pilgrimage.
These consisted largely of unarmed peasantry and

women. "From all I can gather," writes the Acting High Commissioner, "the movement was not against us; the Sultan wished to establish himself in some region remote from our influence, and simply called upon the people to follow him." During his flight, writes another officer, he scrupulously avoided our posts, and had even passed close to the Resident of Kano, who had only a tiny escort with him, without attempting to molest him. Captain Sword, from Kano, joining forces with the Bautshi garrison, pursued the ex-Sultan, and after a series of skirmishes, in all of which he was successful, arrived at the town of Burmi, on the confines of Bornu. Here was a colony of aliens, who coming from the north and probably of Tuareg origin, had settled here, and had received the remnants of the Mallam Jibrella's army after his defeat by Colonel Morland in March, 1902. One of the sons of that chief had been elected "Mahdi" in his place. Captain Sword attacked the town and severe fighting took place, for these people were of a very valiant race. An officer and a British noncommissioned officer and 60 rank and file were wounded, while four were killed. Captain Sword, having no big gun to breach the walls, which were very strong, was unable to storm the town, and retired on Bautshi with his wounded unmolested during the night. The loss inflicted on the enemy appears to have been very great, and this, combined with a defeat which a party of mounted infantry from Kano inflicted upon a separate section of the ex-Sultan's adherents, broke up the hostile gathering. Meanwhile steps had been taken to concentrate a powerful force at Bautshi with the object of capturing the ex-Sultan and his principal chiefs, including the Magaji, but before it could take the field messages were received from him saying that he had no desire for further fighting, and that his adherents were starving. It appears probable that very many of the misled peasantry must have died in this way. A reply was sent to the effect that the Sultan must surrender unconditionally, and meanwhile the expedition pushed on. On reaching Burmi it was opposed (on July 27th) with great determination and fanaticism. . . .

[Our] force was composed of about 500 men of the Northern Nigeria regiments; sixty mounted infantry under Major Barlow; one millimetre, one seven-pounder and two maxim guns under Captain Henvey; the whole under the command of Major Marsh. Meanwhile, the defences of Burmi had been strengthened, all the seven gates having been barricaded save that on the south side, where a second trench had been dug in addition to the one that ran all round the walls. At the foot of the latter, holes had been made to enable the defenders to escape within the town. The construction of double trenches revealed a degree of ingenuity unexpected in the natives, and leads one to believe that there must have been some ex-soldiers of our own or of the French forces in the service of the Sultan. Previous to the attack all the women and children had been sent away, and it is said that there were at least 10,000 men in the town. The majority of the defenders were armed with bows and many of the arrows were poisoned; some used throwing spears and others "dane" guns and rifles.

The attack was made at eleven o'clock on the morning of July 27. The troops formed square 300 yards from the town and the millimetre opened fire on the southern gate. It is a pity that this point had been chosen for the assault, as it was the only one at which an enfilading fire could be maintained from the trenches and walls. After a few rounds had been fired, making excellent practice, three half companies of infantry, supporting one another in column, delivered an assault upon the gate.

Within, the city seemed deserted, not the shadow of a living soul was seen and an ominous silence reigned. Then, as the troops neared the trenches and got within the angle of the walls, suddenly the air was benighted with clouds of arrows and shouts of "Allah! Allah!" arose upon a deafening alarum of drums. So tremendous was the surprise of the shock, that the leading column was forced to fall back on its supports, and the men refused to go on, for they said the place was full of "ju-ju." Thereupon Major Marsh, who had been directing the operations from the square, realising the critical position, went down at once to the fighting line to lead the assault; but he had no sooner come within the line of fire than he was struck in the thigh by a poisoned arrow and died within twenty minutes. Meanwhile, Captain Robinson, Chief Staff Officer, had sent Lieutenant Fox with a section to attack a hole in the wall about 150 yards to the left of the gate. The attack was successful and an entrance effected; when at the same moment Captain Lewis and Lieutenant Maud with a few picked men made a brilliant rush and captured the gate. Captain Lewis was twice wounded, but continued in action, and one of his native sergeants was shot through the heart. Once inside the walls, his men worked round on either side of the gate till they joined with those of Lieutenant Fox, and then there was no longer any doubt that the assault had been successful. The enemy fought with fanatical fury, defending themselves in the bukas (or round reed huts) that crowded the town by the southern gate. These were so tough that they resisted all attempts to fire them, and heavy losses resulted as a way was fought through them. Then for some reason unexplained the "retire" sounded, which

the men obeyed reluctantly, for they had now warmed
to their work. In the afternoon reinforcements came
up and the assault was again delivered, this time to
meet with a weakened resistance, and it was not long
before the ground was regained. But fighting continued with stubborn opposition till sunset, when the
enemy, refusing to surrender, made their final stand
at the Masalachi (or House of Prayer), where Captain Henvey, who had worked all round the town
with signal results, brought up his millimetre and fired
case shot. The body of Attahiru was found among
the dead by the gate. It is said that he was praying in
the mosque with his mallams when the attack was
made and hearing that the "white man" had carried
the gate, went down there with his personal followers
to attempt to save defeat.

An important and detailed collection of sources wrapped
round an exciting narrative is contained in Muffett 1964.

4   The British casualties were one officer and ten men killed,
three officers and sixty-nine men wounded. Enemy casualties were put at seven hundred killed.

5   Abubakar, fifth of the Fulani Etsuzhi Nupe (1895–1901).

6   Ahmadu, sixth emir of Misau (1900–03).

7   Madaki or Madawaki, "commander of the cavalry." After
the death of Waziri Gidado in 1937, this became the most
important title in Kano emirate, and the waziriship, never
an indigenous Kano office, was allowed to lapse.

8   Muffett infers that the Magaji, who had been "the enigmatic
cause of it all" by providing a *casus belli* through his
murder of Captain Moloney, was in fact killed at Burmi or
even Sokoto (1964: 210–11); but this is contradicted in a
footnote on p. 199, which states that the Magaji did reach
Mecca. Boyd Alexander, writing three years after the
battle, asserts that the Magaji was among those killed at
Burmi (p. 228). This was also Lugard's opinion.

9 C. L. Temple, who later became chief secretary (1910–13) and lieutenant-governor (1914–17) of Northern Nigeria. He is still remembered by his Hausa nickname of *Dogon Lamba,* "the tall mark." The fullest accounts of him are to be found in Perham 1960; Muffett 1964; and Hiskett's introduction to the reprint (1968) of Temple 1918.

10 It was Captain G. C. R. Mundy, later the first administrative officer to be posted to Bornu, who was said to have seized Dan Fodio's flag from the corpse of Sultan Attahiru on the battlefield. There is, however, a footnote to bring the story of Dan Fodio's flag up to date. For many years a torn, faded standard, believed to be the one found by the Sultan's side at Burmi was kept in the regimental museum of the old Royal West African Frontier Force. Its original inscription, datelined Burmi, July 27, 1903, read:

> This flag is the original Holy Standard raised by Othman dan Fodio, the founder of the Fulani Empire, in 1809. It has ever since remained in the hands of the Emirs of Sokoto. It was captured by the British Forces at the taking of Sokoto in April 1903, but stolen three days later by a native follower and restored to Aliyu, Emir of Sokoto. It was borne beside the Emir of Sokoto at the battle of Burmi and taken from beside his dead body by Captain G. C. R. Mundy. Presented to the Officers' Mess, 2nd Lancashire Regt., by Captain G. C. R. Mundy June 1904.

The incident of its capture and subsequent loss is told, in lighthearted vein, by Crozier 1932: 149–52. The original flag was green, but this one was officially described as white. Lugard considered it to have been lost in battle with the Kebbi in the 1890s. On November 6, 1960, the museum's flag was returned to the Sultan of Sokoto at a special military ceremony held near the site of the battle fought by Sultan Attahiru against the British outside the city on March 12, 1903. (For pictures, see Muffett 1964, facing

pp. 192–93, and his excellent map and chronology of the
Sultan's flight from Sokoto to Burmi on pp. 162 and 218–
20).

11 In view of the widespread allegiance throughout Northern
Nigeria to the Sultan as Sarkin Musulmi, or the spiritual
chief of the Moslems, it was clearly imperative to the con-
quering power that his death should be established beyond
doubt. In Nigeria's colonial period there were several instances when the death of an emir was denied, giving rise
to rumors of his continued existence. Typical was the re-
action of the Yola Fulani to Lamido Zubeiru's death in
1903 (Kirk-Greene 1958b: 63–64), which was followed by
the retention of the Lamido's gown and cloak for the next
twenty-four years against his expected return. Among the
Tera people who live at the foot of Bima Hill one can still
hear stories of Sultan Attahiru being seen on certain nights,
riding a white horse along the top of the hill and carrying
a green flag.

12 Cf. note 4, above. Probably Maimaina is referring to the
bodies actually lying around the Sultan, in which case his
estimate accords with Temple's "round his body were piled
the corpses of 90 of his followers" recorded in his dispatch
of August 8, which gave Lugard full details of the engagement (reproduced *in extenso* in Muffett 1964: 200–02.)

CHAPTER X

1 An important military post in the early days of the British
occupation, located on the strategic river Gongola, which
at that time provided a line of communication up the
Benue to Bornu as an alternative to the overland route of
Yola and Wamdeo (see p. 184, n. 6.).

2 Although the town still stands, its importance has declined
since 1924 when Potiskum, on the main road from Kano
or Jos to Bornu, began to be developed as the capital of the
emirate.

3 Thirty-third emir of Fika (1865–1902).

4 Thirty-fourth emir of Fika (1902–22). Disa is a local variant of Idrissa.
5 Muhammadu Ibn Idrissa, thirty-fifth emir of Fika (1922–).
6 Seventh emir of Gombe (1892–1922). With troubles on his hands first from Mallam Jibrilla (see p. 145 and Hogben and Kirk-Greene 1966: 468–70), and then from the aftermath of the battle of Burmi, Umaru—like Aliyu in Zaria—doubtless found collaboration with the British the least of the several threats to his security.

CHAPTER XI

1 This would be after the harvest, for at the end of the previous rains Kukawa had been hidden in an extensive cornfield. The court's sojourn in Monguno was only temporary while Kukawa, sacked by Rabeh in 1893, was being rebuilt.
2 In fact, not until 1907. A plaque in Bauchi commemorates his death.
3 A minutely itemized account of his "royal progress" through the Northern Provinces is given by Lugard in his *Annual Report for Northern Nigeria, 1904,* paragraphs 50–188. The grand tour of Bornu province is described in paragraphs 62–69.
4 Lugard's own description of the installation is as follows:

> Escorted by the Shehu and some 300 horsemen we reached Kuka on November 27th. I was very favourably impressed by the King, who is a remarkably intelligent man, with a frank and open manner and the bearing of a well-bred gentleman. According to my custom, I fully explained his Letter of Appointment and the conditions of British rule, and I discussed with him in the presence of his principal chiefs the questions of slavery, taxation, etc. He was fully satisfied to accept the prohibition against slave-dealing, while as regards the system of taxation he begged that the ancient capitation tax should remain. He expressed

a fear lest the district headmen should become too powerful—shewing in this his grasp of the subject, for it is indeed the vital point. He also desired that these headmen should reside at the capital, where of course they would become mere satellites of his Court, and could not be held responsible for the maintenance of order or the collection of taxes in their districts. The object of the suggestion was, in fact, to neutralise their power and influence. I could not concur in this proposal, but I desired that they should have houses at the capital, where they could reside for short periods at the King's summons.

Before leaving I presented the chief with his staff of office and the installation present I had brought with me. Many thousands assembled in the great open space before the King's residence, and a crier repeated my words to them. The Shehu took the Oath of Allegiance, and, himself holding the Koran, said before the assembled crowds that he understood that there was nothing in the oath which would interfere with his religion, and for the rest he accepted all the conditions and the policy I had described to him.

There is a good facsimile of the Arabic letter of appointment issued to emirs at this period in Macleod 1912, facing p. 244.

5 He was commander of the Mounted Infantry.
6 "In north-west Bornu the headquarters had been placed at Geidam, where a few mud huts had been built. It was situated on a sandy plain, swept by dust-storms, and two miles from the river, with a very inadequate water supply. After very careful examination of various sites, I decided to move this to Damjiri, six miles to the east, situated 33 feet above the river" (Lugard, "Report on tour to Bornu," 1904). This "far more pleasing site" was still in use as a base for a junior administrative officer (when staff permitted) from Maiduguri in the late 1950s.
7 Described in paragraphs 80–86 (see note 3, above).

8 Major Edward Lugard, who in 1903 had been appointed as chief clerk to the High Commissioner's Office with the rank of Second Class Resident, by this time held the special post of political assistant to the governor. When Sir Frederick returned to Lagos in 1913 with a commission to amalgamate the two protectorates, he took with him his *alter ego*, brother Ned, as his political secretary. There was a seven-year difference in age between them.

9 The value of potash brought by camel from over the Bornu border was nearly $12,000. in 1903/04.

10 The value of the cowrie fluctuated considerably, not only over the years but also in different areas of the North. At this time 14¢ would realize about 1000 cowries in Sokoto but up to 3000 in Lokoja. By 1906, 20,000 cowries were worth $1.70 in Kano and $2.00 in Katsina. For discussion of the cowrie and other currencies of Nigeria, see Hiskett 1966. Cowries came later to Bornu than to the Hausa emirates, and according to Barth started to replace the silver dollar only in the 1840s.

11 Muhammad Aliyu (Maidalla Madu), twenty-sixth emir of Biu (1951–59).

12 A common belief among many of the non-Moslem peoples of Northern Nigeria—notably, the Jukun, Tiv, and Idoma —who for many years refused to allow their chiefs to travel across the Benue and attend government conferences of chiefs in Kaduna lest ill befall them. Although the chiefs of Biu claim a long-standing Moslem ancestry, few of the common people in the area would have been Moslem at this earlier period.

13 Lugard, on his 1904 inspection of Bornu, had noted how the Gaidam "garrison of Mounted Infantry (the last of the frontier posts to the east) will hold in check the Tubus and other raiders from the north." But they were too far away from the Yo area to be of much help on those hit-and-run raids.

14 Bornu had largely been an exception to the pattern of the Hausa emirates where the principal titleholders and cour-

tiers had enjoyed the benefits of their country fiefs but had themselves preferred to live in the emir's city, leaving their estates to be ruled through an agent (H. *jekada,* Ful. *cima*). At the same time as this reform, Bornu's classification as a double province was revised to divide it into eastern (with stations at Mafoni and Kukawa) and western (stations at Geidam and Gujba) subprovinces instead of the earlier northern and southern division.

15 At the time of Maimaina's writing, there were in the Northern Provinces sixteen 1st class chiefs, thirty 2nd class, thirty-one 3rd class, seven 4th class, one 5th class, and thirty-seven ungraded chiefs. Maimaina himself, as the first chief of Askira, was an ungraded chief. Although the formal grading of the district headships has lapsed, the provincial titles of *ajiya* and *lawan* have been retained.

16 Lieutenant Boyd Alexander sailed from Liverpool in February 1904 and reached Port Sudan in January 1907. His expedition was composed of his brother, Captain Claud Alexander (who died in Mafoni in 1904); Captain G. Gosling (who died in the Congo Free State in 1906); Mr. P. A. Talbot, the celebrated Nigerian anthropologist (who left the expedition in Nigeria); and his majordomo, the Portuguese collector José Lopez. The expedition achieved considerable geographical and zoological results in its crossing of Africa, and the leader wrote up his account in two ample and well-entitled volumes, *From the Niger to the Nile,* 1907.

17 There is no record of the incident in Boyd Alexander's own narrative, but there are several indications of this kind of tempestuous behavior, e.g. his fining a village head in Bauchi fifteen goats for having switched two "consumptive-looking creatures" for the two goats that Alexander had had to buy off him earlier when he "omitted the customary 'dash'" (B. Alexander 1907, I: 218–19). In his unpublished diary of 1909, however, we find this entry: *"September 15.* Early this morning the Kachella, Bukar Karga, who is now posted at Chibuk, rode into the town

and saluted me. He is the same man I caused to be flogged at Maifoni in 1904. As we met the remembrance of this seemed to flash through both our minds, but the next moment it had gone and we were shaking hands" (H. Alexander 1912: 173).

18 This was not until Boyd Alexander's second expedition, in 1910. The murder has been described thus by his brother Herbert:

> At 5.30 in the evening they reached a little village called Ilarné, a mile from Nyeri, where they made their camp beneath a big tree by the roadside. Boyd sent at once to advise the Sultan of his presence, and to say he would visit him next morning. Accompanied by two Furians, the village people brought him the customary present, but they seemed so excited and unfriendly that José begged his master to take the money and papers on their horses and fly while there was yet time. But this Boyd would not do.
>
> In an hour's time the two Furians returned, together with some of Sultan Othman's men and a crowd of natives, all armed with clubs and rifles. They ordered Boyd to come with them to the Sultan. No white man could submit to such treatment, so he quietly refused, but at the same time repeated his intention of going next morning. Then some of them laid hold of him and attempted to drag him off, while others seized upon the camels and the baggage. Meantime José ran for his rifle. It was unloaded, and he could find no ammunition. But he pointed the weapon as it was at the men who were running up to seize himself, and pretended that he was about to fire.
>
> At this they fell back a moment, not daring to attack him, and he was thus able to gain cover in the bush by the roadside. At the same time he heard a shot, and saw Boyd surrounded by men who were striking him with clubs, while his master defended

himself with his fists, calling out all the time, "José!
José!"

Believing himself to be powerless to help, José succeeded in escaping, and luckily finding his horse rode
into Abechir on the 5th of April, where he made a
deposition before the Commandant.

On the 7th of April, five days after the murder,
Captain Chauvelot, in command of the French forces,
met and defeated the Furians at Guereda, and found
among the enemy's deserted baggage upon the battlefield a box belonging to Boyd. It had been broken
open, but the diary and a few papers were left in it.
This was the first hint Captain Chauvelot received of
the tragedy. Native rumour, however, soon supplied
details, but the French officer lost no time in pressing
forward in the hope of rendering assistance. At the
same time the Sultan of Wadai's messenger reported
to him that he had just come from Ali Dinar, who
had treated him with civility, and had given him letters, both to the Sultan Othman and to his general,
Abdul Rashid, with instructions that the utmost con-
sideration and assistance should be given to Boyd.
These letters arrived five days too late.

On his arrival at Ilarné Captain Chauvelot found
Boyd's remains half buried beneath a pile of stones.
Death was due to a rifle-shot and to blows from clubs
and stones. For fifty yards the ground bore marks of
resistance; then they ceased, and the track of the body
on the earth was even, showing that the struggle was
at an end.

Boyd Alexander's death led to Olive Macleod's brave journey, with Mr. and Mrs. P. Amaury Talbot, to Maiduguri
and on to Fort Lamy to learn what she could of his fate, an
undertaking she described in *Chiefs and Cities of Central
Africa,* 1912.

19 There are graves of both Boyd and Claud Alexander in the

historical little cemetery outside the Residency gates at Maiduguri.

20 This was contrary to Lugard's original assessment of Kukawa. Although he had, on his tour of Bornu in 1904, accepted the insalubrious site of the town and had moved his Resident's station south to Mafoni [Maiduguri], with its "advantage of being healthy, central, and near to the independent tribes in the south (Margi and Babur) over whom direct supervision is necessary, and only 45 miles from the German Station at Dikwa," he believed that, as the Shehu's traditional capital, Kukawa "must inevitably be the political centre of Bornu." However, it became apparent after the Shehu's reoccupation of Kukawa in 1904 that, owing to its commercial inaccessibility and its climatic disadvantages, the town was unlikely ever to regain its former glory, so glowingly depicted by early travelers such as Denham and Barth.

21 Additionally, Maiduguri lay 1000 feet above sea-level.

22 The name Maiduguri was (and still is) that of a small village northwest of the present shehu's palace. Mafoni is today the major residential area of the city. See the anniversary booklet [Hausa and English texts] by Kirk-Greene 1958a.

23 Said to be a corruption of an Arabic expression signifying great happiness.

CHAPTER XII

1 During the early years of the British administration, many of the clerks in the northern service were Sierra Leoneans. Some of these married, and right up to after World War II their progeny were to be found as factors for the large expatriate trading companies in the North. For an account of part of the contribution of Sierra Leone to Nigeria's administrative and intellectual development, see Kopytoff 1965 and Hair 1967.

2 The caves could be easily visited as late as 1957, but in recent years scholars working in the area have commented

on the local people's reluctance to admit to their existence.
3 Compare Maimaina's account with the official report of
the famous Chibuk Patrol of 1906–07:

> This was a punitive expedition carried out against
> the small Chibbuk tribe of savages—akin to the
> Marghis and Kilbas,—and has stood out prominently
> this year, as our troops met the most determined lot
> of fighters in the strongest position in the Protectorate.
> Works of bygone writers show that they have defied
> Bornu armies for generations. For the past four years
> they have been left alone, as breaking them, without
> occupation following, would have done harm rather
> than good. Year after year these people have been
> the chief marauders on the Yola-Bornu road, and
> their stronghold, some 20 miles west of the road, has
> been a refuge for other truculent pagans who have
> from time to time been punished by the Government.
> The increase of the Bornu Political Staff towards the
> end of the year rendered occupation of the Marghi
> Districts feasible, and at the end of November the
> Chibbuk rocks were attacked by a small force of 170
> men under Lieutenants Chapman and Chaytor.
>
> The assault was continued for 11 days, and every
> occasion on which the troops attacked they suffered
> some losses. At the end of this time the hills were
> considered taken, our casualties being two officers
> slightly wounded, 10 rank and file killed, and 40
> wounded; this was the end of the first phase of the
> operations. The bulk of the people had dispersed over
> the country, but many of them held their extraordinary
> network of impenetrable tunnels in the north-western
> part of the hills, and refused all submission. Before,
> during, and after these operations every effort was
> made to induce the Chibbuks to come in, but without
> success. The second phase of the operations began
> when Lieutenant Wolseley proceeded in mid-Decem-

ber with 80 men to systematically picket the hill. This officer is the only one, so far, who personally knows the wonderful internal formation of this hill. Lieutenant Wolseley, in an attempt to clear the tunnels, had one man killed and 12 wounded, and decided then that further attacks were futile and much too costly. By the most careful picketing and through the chance discovery of the natural water supply, deep down in the centre of the hill, this officer, now late in February, cleared the last man off the rocks. The hillsmen had unlimited food and sufficient water to last probably until the rains, and if, as with more combination might have happened, from 500 to 1,000 of these pagans had held to the tunnels and taken no risks, no force could have removed them. In most cases the arrows were shot at a range of from 5 to 20 yards through rocky apertures, from unseen foes, in passages to which daylight did not penetrate. After three months' operations this unique robbers' den was broken up and the tribe dispersed all over the country, mostly southward.

The following extract from the Resident's report is also of interest:

> Twice again before the Political Officer and the troops arrived at Chibbuk, the headmen were called upon to come in and submit, but no answer was returned, and the result was a series of the most stubborn fighting for 11 days, in which our troops met with such determined resistance as has seldom, if ever, been seen in the Protectorate; and I venture to state my deliberate opinion that no military operations have taken place during the last seven years in which the troops engaged had such genuine fighting to do under conditions extraordinarily difficult and nerve trying.

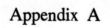

Appendix A

MAGÁNA HAUSA.

NATIVE LITERATURE,

OR

𝔓roberbs, 𝔗ales, 𝔉ables and 𝔥istorical 𝔉ragments in the 𝔥ausa 𝔏anguage.

TO WHICH IS ADDED

A TRANSLATION IN ENGLISH.

BY

J. F. SCHÖN, D.D., F.R.G.S.,

CHURCH MISSIONARY.

LONDON:

SOCIETY FOR PROMOTING CHRISTIAN KNOWLEDGE,

NORTHUMBERLAND AVENUE, CHARING CROSS.

1885.

gáni tana táfiāwa mun fāra žā da bāyā ; da ta
yi kúsa suka halbēta da bíndigā, ta sǫ ta ṭāya ta
yi fadá. Na žēfa sándāta na gúdu, ban ṭāya ba.
Ta šíga ga číkin rūa, muka dāwoí ga lēmamu. .

Muka tāši dagá wūri nán da dērę, kána muka
íssa ga garí ęnda muka šíga ga číkin žīrigī dafāri.
Da muka tāši dagá nán muka záka ga Saï (Saye)
garîn da muku šíga ga žīrigī dafāri. Dagá nán
na žī wǫni mútum šina sǫ ya kášsę́ Abd el Kęrim ;
wǫni Sármāyī ya čē máni, ší ya sáni magánān
Anasāra. Ba mútānę́ da yāwa muka žī suna yīn
magánān Anasāra, saí daía dagá číkin Timbúktu;
ši mállamī nę, ámmā ši mai rāgaïtu nę, ya čē ši
kāramī nę tun da ya tafí ga wǫšîēn Anasāra, šina
yīn magánānsu dafāri, ámmā yánzu ya mánčę, mútum nāgarī da kyaún gáni, ámmā mūgun hálli.

Da muka tāši dagá Saï muka kētārē gúlbi, muka
záka ga wǫni garí, ši kę kādan nēsa dagá Saï ; nán
muka kwāna. Da muka tāši dagá nán kuá kwānaki da yāwa, kána muka íssa ga Gǫ́ndu. Da mútānę́
wǫ́dānda suka sán'mu sun yi múrna, da mu kuá
muna yīn múrna, don mun záka ga īyākān Haúsa.
Dagá nán kuá, ína tamáha mun zámna kwānaki
fúdu. Gídān da suka sāmú ba gídā ba nāfāri da
muka šīda da muna zūa ga Timbúktu ; ámmā
wǫ́nan gídā da suka sāmú šina da dādi, da šina
da dándǎlī. Suna da itātuān Kūka dagá nán da
yāwa. Žīkīn itāčęn Kūka daía šina yīn mútānę́

*tālatin ; ámmā Kūka ba ta ṯāwo kámān Rīmi, sai
tana da gíriῐmā ; tofōnta mu kan yi mīā tana kẹ̄-
kašẹ̄ ko daínya. Diānta suna da gíriῐmā. En
ka daúka daía hānūnka biú ba su tábā žūna, ẹ́n
ka sāsu dagá ṯāka ; da ṯaínta kámān dámšin mútum. Ámmā wọ́dānsu sun fī da ṯāwo. En ka
tábá diānta, ẹ́n kaíkaí na bāyānta sun tábāka, ka
yi sūsān žīkīnka har ka gāži, ámmā ba ta yí
máka kọ̄mi. En ka pássa daía ka sāmú číkīnta
farí fẹt kámān nọ̄nọ, da ga číkīnta kuá akoí wọ́-
dānsú diā, su nẹ ka kẹ čī, ámmā da ṯāmi, wọ́dānsu
ba su da ṯāmi. Da muna da wọ́ni abú, sūnānsa
dánkalī, žīkīnsa ǰā da ṯāwọnsa dagá wῐ̄yān hānū
ga yāsāka maiṯāwo, da fádīnsa kámān yāsā úku,
kọ fúdu šina da zāki, kadán andáffa, da tápši kuā ;
ína sọ̄nsu kwaraí. Wọ́takīla Abd el Kẹ̄rim ya
dándănāsu, ko ba ši dándănā baᵢ, ban sáni ba.*

*Da muka tāši dagá nán muka záka ga wọ́ni
garí, nán muka šīda. Da kāsuān garí nán mútānẹ́
sun záka čīnta. Sīliān alharẹ̄ni da yāwa ; rígῐnā
da farí ; šānu, nọ̄nọ da maï ; itáčẹ ka sāyẹ ga fūra
wūta da yāwa. Kāramā kāsuā čẹ, ámmă ačīkẹ,
da itāčẹ da gíriῐmā dagá nán. Da muka fíta
dagá garẹ̄ta ban sáni ba wọ́ni garí muka záka,
da wọ́ni gārí mun bẹ́rši, da muka íssa ga
Sọ́kọtu.*

Íssa ga Sọ́kọtu fítowa dagá Timbúktu.

Da muka záka ga Sọ́kọtu kumá muka šīda ga

*wǫ́ni gídā ba nafāri ba. Ina gánin wūri ya sāwoyā,
dǫṅ dāmǎnā ta záka. Hāzi da čiāwa dúka suna
gírĭmā.* Wǭšį̄ę̄ ę́nda muka šīda dafāri ban sáni
ba ga wǫ́ni wǭsę̄ ši kę. *Da muka fíta ga Sǫ́kǫtu
muka gáṅgǎrā ga kálkāšin duāsa, bābu dádi ga
rākŭmā ga šīda ga kálkāšin túdu da su. Da muka
šīda ga kálkāšin duāsa kǫrámā ta hánamu wúčę̄-
wa, doṅ dafāri da muka wúčę ga číkin bāsara,
ámmā yánzu rāni. Muka šiḍę kāyā dagá bāyān
rākŭmā akasā su ga číkin žīrigī ; háka muka yi mu
dúka muka fíta. Da wūri nán ba ši da kyaú ga
rākŭmā.* Ę́u kāfān rākŭmī ta šiga ga číkin tābǫ́
dúka tana šíga, da ęn zāši fūsāta, kadán ta fíta ta
kan būgę kāfāsa daía, hákanán ya fādi da kāyā.
*Tún da muna zámnę dagá nán rūa ya záka bį̄sa
garę̄mu, ámmā ba mu kúlla ba da rūa, doṅ mun
sābę da ši kámān kīfi ga číkin gúlbi. Muka bę́r
wūri nán muna táfiā ga číkin házī da šínkāfa har
muka záka ga Wūrnu ga sǫfǫn gídāmu. Da mú-
tānę́ sun sāmę̄mu da mūrna dagá nán. Na sǭ ę́n
zámna ga číkin Wūrnu ya fī Sǫkǫtu. Da itāčę̄n
ábdugá sun čīka wūrārę dagá wǫ́ta kǫramá. Kúsa
ga Wūrnu suna da wǫ́ta kǫramá, nán mútānę́ su
kę kámā kīfayę̄, da mátā suna daúka rūa dagá
číkin tūlu su dǭra ga kā'nsu, su záka ga gídā.
Tún da muna nán na žī akáče : Káda kǫwa ya
tafí ga bākin rūa nán gǫbę da sāfę har ga šā(n) rūan
dǭki ; doṅ yāyān rūa suna wúčęwa ; hákanán kūa*

*bābu kǫwa da ya tafí har ga hánši (kǫ šā rūan dǫki,
rūnan ṭáka kẹ nán) na támbāyẹsu : Dǫmi mútānẹ
káda su tafí ? Suka čẹ : én ka gáni yāyān rūa ka
mútu : Suka čẹ : suna da ṭāwǫn gāši, ámmā su
gāšiẹru nẹ.*

*Tún da muna zámnẹ dagá číkin Wūrnu kumá
wǫdānsu suka kāwǫ labāri ga sārĭkī Alīyu,
kǫ sārĭkĭn Sǫkǫtu, suka čẹ : Ga fātakẹ sun šīda
kúsa ga Gawasu. Sārĭkī Alīyu ya aíkẹ yāyān-yā-
kĭnsa da galladīmānsu; ya čẹ másu; én su mútānẹ
na lāfiā nẹ, káda ku tábāsu, ámmā kadán mútānẹn
gábá nẹ, ku daúkẹ kāyānsu. Hákanán suka fíta da
dẹrẹ, wāta na bāda háskẹ. Da suka íssa garẹsu.
Wǫtakīla sun támbāyẹsu, kǫ ba su támbāyẹsu, bān
sáni ba, ámmā sun daúkẹ kāyānsu dúka, suka kāwǫ
ga Wūrnu. Da sāfiā ta yi kána suka sáni su mútānẹ da lāfia nẹ, fātakẹ māsutáfiā ga bịrnin Kānu.
Sārĭki, Alīyu, ya čẹ ga mútānẹnsa: kǫwānẹ da ya
daúkẹ kāyānsu ya kāwǫ ya bāsu ; hákanán suka
kāwǫ kāyānsu dúka, suka fíta dagá Wūrnu.*

*Da muka tāši dagá Wūrnu muka kẹtārĕ kǫramā
muka záka ga Góndi. Kīfi da yāwa dagá nán.
Nán muka yi gúzuri. Da muka tāši dagá Góndi
muka šiga ya číkin dāži ; mútānẹ da yāwa tārẹ da
mu, ámmā da kwānaki ša fúdu sun yi, muka íssa
ga bịrnin Kānu.*

VII. *Íssa ga bįrnin Kānu.*

Bįrnin Kānu garín yāyā yȩ (yȩ-nȩ). Ámmā wǫ́dānsu mútānȩ́ su kan čȩ̄ : Bįrnin Kānu garín ya-mátā, don diānsu suna da kyaú. Zákuāta tafāri kȩ nán ga číkin bįrnin Kānu.

Bįrnin Kānu kǫwǫ́čȩ sāfiā Abd el Kȩ̄rim da nī mu kan fíta ga wǫ́ta kǭfa muka gȩ̄woya, mu šígo dagá wǫ́ta kǭfa. Bāyām bįrnin Kānu suna da gǭ-nakī da yāwa, da suna da rūkukī, da suna da kǫramā da yāwa ga bāyām bįrni dagá wǫ́ni wǭšīȩ̄. Kǭfam bįrnin Kānu, īna tamáha ša fúdu. Da ginam bįrni šina da ṭāwo ; anginā̌ši da yímbu. Da suna da gǭndan mazar. Gǫ́ndan mazar tana da ṭāwǫ, ámmā ba ta da ṭāwǫ kwaraí ba ; diānta sun kúsa kaín mútum da gírīmā ; ȩ́n ta nīna ba jā ba ta kȩ, ámmā žīkīnta kámān wǫ́ta īrin kabȩ̄wa, ba čánwa ba ; ȩ́n ka pássāta tana dazāki da tápši ; fātānta ba ta da kābrí. Da akoí wǫ́ta īrin gǫnda kúá, ámmā bamu kírānta gǫnda mazar, saí gǫ́nda; itāčȩ̄nta kámān kaín mútum, tana gírĭmā-gírĭma ga číkin dāži ; ba ta kǫwǫ́nȩ ba ta kȩ ; ámmā wǫ́dānsu sun fì mútum ga ṭaí ; tǭfǫnta ba ta da gírĭmā ya fì hānūn mútum. Ȩ́n diānta suna kānănā čánwa su kȩ, ȩ́n su nīna jā ; ámmā wǫ́dānsu har suna nīna čánwa su kȩ ; ȩ́n zāka ka čīra diānta ka yi hánkalī da mačīžĭ, don mačīžĭ da kānsa šina sǫnta, háka-

nán kuá zūnsāye. Gīrĭmān diānta kámān čibirin kāsa ga hānū ; da ga čĭkīnta akoí diā babāku.

Da akoí wǫ́ni itāčę̄ sūnānsa lę̄mu šina da ṭāmi ; kǫwǫ́nę dān Haúsa šina sǫ lę̄mu ga číkin alzīfūnsa; suna sǫ šān lę̄mu ; wǫ́dānsu da gírĭmā kámān gǫn̄dan dāži, ámmā wǫ́dānsu-kānănā.

Bį́rnín Kānu daqá číki suna da wǫ́ni dūši sūnānsa Dāda. Tún da ba ka gáni ba bį́rnin Kānu ka na gánin kānsa. Ámmā ę́n ka zámna kúsa da ši, ę́n rīgānka fāra čę̄ tana sāwoyā kámān ka čī gōro ka zūba bį́sa garę̄ta. Da na žī ga mútānę́n Kānawa, mútumę́ daía, mútumę́n Inliz, ya záka nán, ya čę̄ ga sārĭkī šina sǫ ya fītásda sināria daqá číkin dūši nán, ámmā ę́n ya fūtás yuṅwa ta šíga ga garí nán. Sārĭki ya čę̄ : ę́n yuṅwa ta šíga ga garína, kadá ka tába dūši nán, ka bę́rši ya zámna. Kāria ko gáskiā nī bān sáni ba ; abin da na žī na čę̄ ; da ši nę makārᴉnsa.

Ga wōšĭę̄n Bala bābu gídāšę̄ saídaí fīli ; čiāwa ta fíta ga číkin garí ; rākŭmā, šānu da žākaí suna kᴉᴉwo daqá náṅ : da bāyi suna yę́nkan čiāwa su kāwǫ ga gídā. Rūa da yāwa ga wōšĭę̄ nán. Dagá číkin rūayę̄ kuá suna kámā gaíwa. Ę́n ka kámā gaíwa ka yę́nkę kānta, da abūbuā na číki dúka ka fūšĭę̄su, ka zūbas ; ka ṭīrę̄ta ga itāčę̄ maiṭīni, ka kaffāta kúsa ga wūta, ę́n ta žī wūta ka gę̄woyāta, ka zūba gīširi, bę́rkǫno kǫ taúši da dūsa ; ka zūba dúka garę̄ta ; tún da kana yīn zánčę̄ da abǫkīnka ita tana gássuā ; kadín ta gássu ka āzēta har gōbe da sāfe. Da sāfe en ka tāši ka ṭīra wōzēn wūziā, nán ne dādinta ši ke ; ámmā zīkīnta dúka da dádi ba kámān wūziā ba. Da bābu kašši dagá zīkīnta, sai daía ya ṭafi ga bāyānta, da en ban čē ba kāriā hákōrānta kámān na mútum. Sāo daía ta kắma yāsāta har ta kúsa pášše fārĭčina ; ámmā ba ta da káffa kámān kādo ko kīfī, saídaí wódānsu abú da ṭāwo kámān hāki ga zīkīnta biú ga zīkī, da ína tamáha kuá biú kuá kúsa ga kūnēnta. Ēn rāni ya yi ta kan šíga ga číkin tābo, da wūrin da ta kwānta ba īya ba kēkášewa. Tana nāde zīkīnta kámān ma- číži, da ba ta da abú da zāta čī sai ta čī wūziānta da tābo, abín da ta ke čī ke nán ga rāni har dāmănā ta záka. Ēn dāmănā ta záka ta fíta dagá číkin rāmi, ta kámā kānănān kīfayē ta čīsu ; hákanán ta ke čída kānta ; wódánsu da gírĭmā kámān kábrin mútum, em ba ta fī ba da gírĭmā ; da tana da ṭāwo ya fī šášin kāmu.

Da ga číkin rūa muna kášsēta da māži, ámmā ga číkin tābo muna gínānta da fántāriā. Wūrin da gaíwa ta ke, kana zín čīwūki, da wódānsu mútāne kuá, na zī, ga rāni, en suna wúčewa, kōda ba su zī ba čīwūkin gaíwa, suna gáni énda ta kwānta, ámmā ba mútāne da yāwa ba, sun sání háka ; kāsa tana sāwoyā énda ta kwānta.

Appendix B

LABARIN
MAI MAINA NA JEGA
SARKIN ASKIRA

KASHI NA FARKO

Shi ya faɗi da kansa

A. H. M. KIRK-GREENE, di'o
ya rubuta gabatarwa

Norla 1958

LABARIN MAI MAINA

An haife ni a cikin shekara ta 1874. Ubana mutumin Jega ne a ƙasar Sakkwato sunansa Yarima Abdu, shekara Abdussalam, sarkin Gimbana. Mahaifiyata 'yar Abiga ce, ko Bukar, wanda asalinsa Margi ne, kuma ya zama baran Likita Barth, har suka tafi ƙasar Turai tare da shi.

Daga bayan komowarsa daga Turai, ya zama sarkin Lakwaja, wanda Turawan ciniki suka naɗa, watau Neja Kamfani. Yarima Abdu ya zo Lakwaja ya auri 'yar Abiga, mai suna Salamatu. Suka tafi Jega tare da ita, a lokacin tana da cikina, aka haife ni nan Jega. Bayan 'yan watanni, babana ya koma Lakwaja wurin surukinsa, amma bai daɗe ba ya rasu a can Lakwaja. Ni kuma MAI MAINA NA JEGA na girma a hannun kakana sarkin Lakwaja. A cikin 1894 na shiga aikin boyin Baturen soja na Neja Kamfani sa'ad da mutanen ƙasar Ibo, waɗansu kabila na Buras suka faɗa wa Turawan kantin Akasa da yaƙi.

Sa'an nan ina tare da Manjo Anal, kuma a lokacin ne suka harbi Manjo Miliyo a cinya. Shi ne kwamandan sojan Kamfanin Nijeriya a cikin shekara 1900, wanda Magaji 'Danyamusa ya kashe a Kafi. A lokacin nan babu wani ɗan Arewa wanda ya ke aikin boyi a wurin Turawan Kamfani sai ni, da abokina Abdu ɗan Umaru, wanda mutanen Buras suka kashe a Akasa. Dukan boyi da kuku soja ne, sai yaran Ijo watau mutanen Asaba da Anaca kaɗan. Soja kuwa har da mutanen Golkwas, da Kurbayi da Yarbawa, da mutanen Saliyo a ciki. A lokacin nan babu kanti ko wata muhimmiyar kasuwa a Anaca, sai mishan.

Aboci ke da kanti. Nan ne wurin ciniki, Asaba kuwa shi ne babban gidan kurkuku, da barikin soja. Ko mutum ya yi laifi

daga Lakwaja, ko Ibi ta Benue, Asaba za a kai shi. Domin na ga
Zanna Gana, Babarbaren Wukari na Birnin Gazargamo da
Duna, sarkin Jibu a Asaba.

Kuma mutane mazauna a bakin Kwara, da ƙasar Kwatanƙarfe a lokacin nan suna cikin wahala ƙwarai da gaske. A sa'ad
da mutanen Bida suka ci Kwatanƙarfe sai suka kafa gari a
wurin. Suka naɗa sarki, sunansa Bakango. Bagwari ne, amma a
Abuja ya girma. Suka ajiye mayaƙa suka yi yaƙe-yaƙen ƙasar
suna kamun bayi. Na tuna wata rana da la'asar kamar ƙarfe
huɗu, akwai wani gago, sunansa Aluku, ya tara mutanen ƙasar
Kwatanƙarfe da yawa, ya zo ya faɗa wa sansanin Bakango
da yaƙi. Nan da nan aka watsa su, aka kashe mutane da yawa.
Duk da Aluku shugaban gayyar. Aka yanke kawunan mutane
talatin da uku duk da kan Aluku aka yi babbar rumfa a kasuwa,
aka zuba su, aka kafa kan Aluku a tsaka. Kuma akwai wani
sarki na Patiagwaja sunansa Ajeto, lokacin da ya mutu, sai benu
na Bida ya zo Patiagwaja. Dukiyar da sarkin nan ya mutu ya bari,
tana da yawan gaske. Amma sai kaɗan aka bar wa magada.
Kuma a lokacin ne benu ya riƙa tura dakarunsa suna zuwa Lakwaja da dare suna sarar mutane da takobi. A lokacin ne suka
sare hannun wani Bayarabe sunansa Baba Akwa, da wata mace
sunanta Bagobirə, a Lakwaja. Sai Turawan Kamfani suka kafa
wani burji na fitila, yana haskaka ko ina, daga nesa ana gani.

To, sai benu ya tashi daga Patiagwaja ya ƙetare Kwara ya zo
Kwatanƙarfe. A nan ne ya bar wani babban mayaƙinsa mai
suna Canyai, shi kuma ya koma Bida. A lokacin nan mutanen da ke kusa da Kwara sun matsu ainun. A lokacin cikowar
kogi sai ka ga mutum a cikin kurmi, don tsoron dakarun Bida,
ya yi babbar rumfa, ya yaɓe da taɓo ya yi ɗaki a kai. Da shi da
matansa da 'ya'yansa suna kai, ga jirginsa a ɗaure a ƙarƙashin
rumfarsa. Suna cikin wannan wahala har 1897, lokacin da
Turawan Kamfani suka ci Bida, sa'an nan sansanin Kwatanƙarfe ya watse. Sa'an nan ne kuma mutanen ƙasar suka sami
kansu daga irin wannan wahala. Turawan Kamfani suka naɗa
Ali ɗan sarkin Kwatanƙarfe na da, mai suna Angefu. Suka
kawo shi Kwatanƙarfe, ni ma ina cikin 'yan rakiyarsa, tare da
Kimba. Sarkin Lakwaja ya sa muka rako shi. A cikin 1897
muka tashi a Lakwaja tare da Likita Durul da Manjo Festi Baturen sojan Kamfani, muka bi hanyar Okene zuwa wurin Maiyaƙi Indajiya, sarkin yaƙin sarkin Bida, wanda ya yi sansani a

wani gari wai shi Gidi, kudu da Kaba, yana yaƙin kamun bayi. Da muka tashi a Okene muka sauka a wani ɗan ƙauye a bakin kurmi. Da Maiyaƙi Indajiya ya sami labarimmu, sai ya turo wani babban jarumin Bida sunansa Dokoyiringi da dawaki da masu bindigogi da yawa, suka zo suka kewaye mu da dare. Sai da sassafe kamar ƙarfe shida, Dokoyiringi ya turo wani mai doki ya zo ya same ni ina zaune.

Ya ce da ni, "Ina Bature?"

Na ce, "Me ka ke nema?"

Ya ce, "An aiko ni ne."

Sai na je na shaida wa Manjo Festi, da Likita Durul, suka ce ya zo. Sai ya zo ya ce da su Dokoyiringi ya aiko shi, ya zo ya yi kiransu, ga shi can a bayan kurmi. Suka bar soja da lebura a zango suka je wurinsa. Da zuwammu Dokoyiringi ya ce Maiyaƙi Indajiya ya aiko shi su tafi tare da shi a sansaninsa. Sai suka ce za su tafi zango su yi shiri. Sai ya ce sai a aiki mutum. Sai Turawammu suka tura Saje Baban Fali da Heluma Dari, suka tafi zango. Suka zo da mutanemmu. Sai Dokoyiringi ya hau dokinsa. Sai suka buga bindiga kamar uku. Sai dawaki da masu bindigogi suka yi ta fita daga cikin kurmi, muka kama hanyar sansanin Gidi muka zo wurin Maiyaƙi Indajiya.

Maiyaƙi ya yi niyyar ya yi mana mugun abu, amma Maku, wanda ya zama Etsu Nufe Muhammadu, da waɗansu mutane masu hankali ba su yarda ba. Sai aka kai mu gidan Ecuwa ɗan Indeji muka sauka. Amma Maiyaƙi Indajiya nufinsa ya ƙwace bindigogimmu ya kama Turawammu ya aika da su Bida, wurin Sarkin Nufe Abubakar. Muna da soja 41, amma uku sun gudu sa'ad da muka tashi daga zangommu. Maku da manyan mutane na sansanin ba su yarda ba. Suka tsai da shawarar aikawa da mu Bida wurin Sarkin Nufe Abubakar, sai suka ta da mu zuwa Bida. Mai gidammu Ecuwa shi ne uban tafiyar, shi kuma mutumin kirki ne. Sai muka fito daga sansanimmu muka zo Kaba. Da muka wuce bayan gari, akwai wani ɓaure kusa da hanya, sai Manjo Festi ya ce wa Ecuwa za mu sauka mu sha ruwa. Muka sauka. Su kuma suka sauka a bakin kurmin Kaba. Suna da dawaki da bindigogi da yawa, mu kuwa sojammu 38 ne, amma mun aike da takarda zuwa Lakwaja tun daga sansani a lokacin da muka samu labari za a aika da mu Bida. Sai Turawammu na Lakwaja tare da kamfanin soja biyu suka tafi Alkwara suka tsare hanya. Amma duk da haka

Manjo Festi bai yarda ya kai can ba, a nan Kaba ya ce wa Ecuwa uban rakiyarmu ba za shi Bida ba. Akwai wani tudu gabas da Bauren, sai muka hau kan tudun nan, Manjo Festi ya jera sojammu. Amma Ecuwa bai ta da faɗa ba, sai ya shiga cikin Kaba. Mu kuma nan da nan muka yi shingen dutse, babu wanda ya shigo wurimmu har rana ta faɗi.

Da dare muka tashi muka bar hanyar Lakwaja, muka bar hanyar Bida, sai muka nufi Patiagwaja. To, daji mu ke ratsewa har gari ya waye. Da haka har muka faɗa hanyar da ta fito daga Lakwaja. Sai muka komo Lakwaja lafiya. Bayan lokaci kaɗan sai Turawan Kamfani suka yi niyyar zuwa yaƙin Bida. Watau shi ne yaƙi na farko wanda Turawa suka fara yi da sarakunan Filani a Nijeriya ta Arewa a cikin 1897. Yaƙi ya tashi daga Lakwaja zuwa Bida. Da muka isa Bida sai Sarkin Nufe Abubakar ya tare mu da yaƙi a bayan gari, aka kama yaƙi. To, akwai ƙanen sarkin sunansa Lafene Yusufu, ya fito mana ta gabas. Shi kuwa yana da bindigogi da yawa. A sansanimmu ne suka kashe mana Bature guda, Laftana Tomsin. Amma da aka soma buga igwa da sauran muggan makamai, nan da nan sai Nufawa suka watse. Sarkin Bida Abubakar ya gudu ya tafi Lemu. Daga nan sai yaƙi ya zarce Ilori. A lokacin nan Sarkin Ilori Sulemana ne, bai daɗe da samun sarauta ba. Sai ya fito ya tari yaƙi da lumana, don haka ba a yi yaƙi ba, sai muka komo Lakwaja. A lokacin nan ni ina yin tafinta.

LABARIN GWAMNA LUGGA

A cikin 1900, Gwamna Lugga ya zo Lakwaja da rundunonin soja biyu, da bataliya ta ɗaya, da ta biyu. Sai ya ajiye bataliya ta ɗaya a Lakwaja, bataliya ta biyu kuma a Jaba. Sunan kwamandan bataliya ta ɗaya Kanar Pikchon, kwamandan bataliya ta biyu kuma Kanar Wulkok. Shi Gwamna Lugga kuwa mazauninsa a Lakwaja ya ke. Abin da ya fara yi sai aka jera sojan Kamfani, da kuma sojan gwamnati, sai gwamna ya tsaya a gindin tuta. Sai aka ɗaura tutar gwamnati aka saukad da tutar Turawan Neja Kamfani. Sai aka haɗa sojansu suka zama abu ɗaya. Aka yi shela aka ce babu bauta daga yau. A cikin lokaci kaɗan aka sami labari, Sarkin Lapai Abdulƙadiri ya yi sansani a Gulu, yana yaƙin kamun bayi. Nan da nan aka ta da rundunar soja, muka tafi Gulu, a lokacin ina tafinta, muka je sansaninsu. Nan da nan muka watsa su, ba su tsaya sun yi yaƙin kirki ba, suka gudu. Sai muka bi su har Lapai, garin ya fashe, muka wuce zuwa Agaye. A lokacin nan Nuhu shi ne sarki, shi kuwa bai tare mu da yaƙi ba. Sai ya turo wani bafa-densa wai shi Inda Turaki, ya tare mu a ƙofar gari, ya ce sarki ya aiko shi ya yi mana maraba. Sai uban yaƙimmu ya ce masa ya koma ya shaida wa sarki ya zo. Da ya koma sai sarki ya ji tsoro ya ƙi zuwa, ya gudu ya tafi Paiko. Sai aka bar rabin kamfanin soja da Kyaftin Sikina, da Likita Adam, da ni, ni ne tafinta, domin mu yi ƙoƙarin samun sarkin Agaye Nuhu. Muka aika masa da jawabi ya zo babu kome, amma shi bai yarda ba. Talakawa kuwa suna cikin gari tare da mu, ba su kula ba.

Wata rana sai wani mutum wai 'Danwanzan ya zo ya gaya mini ya san inda sarkin Lapai ya ke. Sai na shaida wa Kyaftin Sikina. Sai muka tashi daga Agaye da dare tare da mutumin, muka nufi wurin da ya ga sarkin Lapai. Sai gari ya waye mana a wani dan ƙauye sunansa Gobi. Ashe a nan ne wani dan sarkin Lapai sunansa Lukwa ya ke. Da jin motsimmu, sai ya fito da takobi a zare. Wani sojammu, Badamasi, yana kawowa bakin ƙofar gidan, sai ya kai masa sara, sai Badamasi ya tare da bin-diga. Ya sari bindigar, Badamasi ya kama shi ya ka da shi. Sai wani soja sunansa Asaryi ya kawo gudummawa, ya harbe shi da bindiga, ya kashe shi. Amma duk da haka ya sari Badamasi a ƙwauri, sai dai da sauƙi. Sai muka komo Agaye. Sa'ad da mu ke cikin Agaye sai dakarun Bida suka riƙa zuwa masaukimmu, da dare suna neman yi mana farmaki. Wata rana da dare zam fita daga daki, sai na yi shakka, sai na dauki 'yar tukunya na soka sanda, na bude ƙofa a hankali, na tura ta waje. Turawata ke da wuya, sai na ji sara a jikin tukunyar. Sai na yi kiran gudum-mawa, mutumin ya hau katanga ya tsere. Da muka yi ƙoƙari mu sami Sarkin Agaye Nuhu, abu ya gagara, sai muka koma Lakwaja.

To, wannan shi ne yaƙin Turawan mulki na farko a cikin shekarar 1900. Kuma a cikin shekarar 1901 aka fid da rundunar yaƙi daga Jaba zuwa Yawuri. Kyaftin Karo da wadansu so-jan dawaki, har sun kai Jega, amma ba a yi yaƙi ba, sai muka koma Jaba. Bayan komowarmu ba mu fi sati biyu ba, sai aka hada ni da wani Baturen soja sunansa Mista Kinked Smith, muka tafi Kayama a ƙasar Bargu. A lokacin nan Faransi suna zaune a Kayama. Da suka ji muna zuwa sai suka ƙaura suka tafi Nigaski. To, a nan aka fara sojan doki. Bayan wata shida sai na komo Lakwaja.

NA TAFI KANO BINCIKE

Turawan soja suka tambayi kakana Abiga sarkin Lakwaja, ya ba su amintaccen mutum ya je arewa, har Kano, ya binciko musu labari. To, ko da ya ke ni yaro ne, sai kakana ya zaɓe ni ga wannan tafiya. Aka yi mini shiri irin na fatake, na shiga ayarin fatake na zo har Kano. To, ga hanyarmu a lokacin nan: muka shiga jirgi daga Lakwaja muka zo Loko. Daga Loko, muka bi tudu zuwa Nasarawa. Daga Nasarawa sai Kafi. A Kafi ne na fara ganin bayi a kasuwa, mata da maza, da yara, duka suna zazzaune sun miƙe ƙafafuwansu, ana ciniki, kamar yadda a ke cinikin doki, ko sa, ko jaki, a yanzu.

Sai muka tashi daga Kafi muka shiga cikin babban ayari zuwa Zariya. Ta hanyar Kaciya muka bi. Gama a lokacin nan sai babban ayari zai iya shiga dajin Aduma har zuwa bakin Kogin Kaduna, domin tsoron fashin Arnan Kaje, waɗanda sun fi so su sami kan mutum. Su kan fafe kai su gyara, da ƙoƙon kan ne ango da amarya su ke shan giya. Daga Kaciya muka tashi muka zo bakin Kogin Kaduna. A nan ne hanyar Bauci da ta Zariya suka rabu. Ta Zariya ta nufi Girkum, ta Bauci kuma ta nufi Ririwai. Sai muka zo Gɪrkum lafiya. Daga Girkum sai Zariya, a lokacin nan kuwa Kwasau shi ne sarkin Zazzau. Amma a lokacin waɗansu sarakuna ba su jituwa. Gama a sa'ad da na zo Zariya Sarkin Kwantagora Ibrahim ba su jituwa da Kwasau. Shi yana zaune a wani gari sunansa Kaya, yana ƙoƙarin cin iyakar Zariya. Daga nan fa muka tashi muka bi hanyar Gimi, ta 'Dansoshiya, ta Madobi zuwa Kano.

Da na isa Kano sai na iske Sarkin Kano Aliyu, da Sarkin Haɗeja Muhammadu, suna yaƙi da juna. A lokacin nan ne galadiman Haɗeja ya kashe Sarkin Dutse Gadawur, ta Kano. Sarkin Kano ya tura Sarkin Gaya Kolo, da Sarkin Kumci Dano, suka tafi kan iyakar Kano da Haɗeja, suka tsare. Idan mutumin Haɗeja ya zo Kano aka tabbata lalle mutumin Haɗeja ne sai a kashe shi. Haka kuma im mutumin Kano ya je Haɗeja sai a kashe shi. Gama na gani da idanuna an sare kan mutane biyu a Kano, aka ce mutanen Haɗeja ne. To loka-

cin da na zo Kano, sai na sauka a gidan Muhammadu Mailiyari, a unguwar Dagarda. Shi kuwa ya taɓa zama a Lakwaja. Da
ma shi a bokina ne, na kuwa tabbata ba zai buɗe asirina ba. Sai ya
haɗa ni da Wamban Kano Mahmuda, ƙanen Sarkin Kano
Aliyu, wanda su ke uwa ɗaya uba ɗaya. Sai muka yi ciniki da
shi. Na kai waɗansu irin laimomi ƙanana masu ban sha'awa,
da agogai. Wani mai kaɗa molo ya saya masa su.
     Da agogon ya tsaya, sai wambai ya ce a kirawo ni. Da na zo
sai ya ce agogon ya ɓaci. Na ce bai ɓaci ba. Sai na nuna masa yadda a ke waninsa, ya kama aiki. Sai kuma ya kawo bindigarsa
babu abin da ya same ta, wata 'yar ƙusa ce ta yi lako-lako. Na
murɗa ta, na wanke bindigar da mai. Shi ke nan ya sa harsashi
ya buga. Sai na zama mutuminsa. To, da ma abin da ya kai ni
shi ne bincike don aŋ kai labari Lakwaja an ce wai sarkin Kano

yana da horarrun sojoji, wai bayinsa ne ya tura Lakwaja, suka
shiga soja, da suka ƙware suka koma Kano, suna koya wa sansaninsa aikin soja. Shi kuma yana da bindigogi da harsashi, da
yawa, waɗanda ya saya wurin Turabusawa. Akwai bindigogi
da yawa, amma babu horarrun soja.

To, sai na yi niyyar komawa Lakwaja. A Zariya ne na sami
takardar kakana sarkin Lakwaja, cewa in yi ƙoƙari in tafi Barno,
in gamu da 'Mai-Doron-Yaƙi', za shi Barno wurin Fataralla
ɗan Rabe. Sai na komo Kano, muka tashi daga Kano zuwa
Barno ta hanyar Nguru. A lokacin Galadiman Nguru Ibrahim
yana Kacallari, nan ne birninsa. Daga Kacallari sai Alanuirori, sai Gaidam. A lokacin nan idan ka tashi daga Gaidam

sai ka kwana biyu a daji, a na uku tukuna ka zo Ngubula don ƙarancin mutane. Rabe duk ya watsa su. Sai muka zo Rinaskuri, ko Ardoram. A lokacin nan akwai manyan kasuwoyi a ƙasar Magumeri da Gubewa. A lokacin nan akwai wata mace Shuwa, sunanta Adama, tana yaƙin karkarar Maiduguri. Ta zama kamar sarki.

Kafin in zo sai na iske 'Mai-Doron-Yaƙi' ya zo. Ya iske Fataralla a Burgumma. Fataralla ya haɗa shi da babban bafadensa sunansa Sururu suka koma Lakwaja. Daga nan fa sai na koma Kano, na gamu da yaron kakana mai suna Bukar, kakana ya aiko shi cewa idan mun gama in yi ƙoƙari in tafi Dikwa. Don mu gamu da Kanar Molon yana zuwa Barno, ta hanyar Bauci. Sai na bi ayarin Mangawa, ta hanyar 'Baɓura, ta 'Danciwo, ta Sheri, ta Maini, ta Kafi, sai na zo Monguno. Ina Monguno ne wani Baturen sojan Faransi wai shi Kyaftin Dansiwul ya tafi Gujiba, ya kashe Fataralla ɗan Rabe, ya kama ƙanensa Muhamman Nyabbe da sauran mutanensa, ya kuma ɗauki kan Fataralla ya kawo Dikwa. A nan ne aka kafe kan Fataralla a kasuwar Dikwa. To, ina Dikwa ne Kanar Molon ya biyo hanyar Bauci. A zamanin Umar shi ne sarkin Bauci, ya hana shi ya wuce Borni. Kuma a lokacin M. Zayi ko M. Jibirilla, shi ne sarkin Borni. To, Sarkin Borni Zayi ya fito ya tari Kanar Molon da yaƙi. Ba a yi minti ashirin ba aka watsa su, M. Zayi ya gudu. Sai aka ba Musa Dedare riƙon Borni. Shi kuwa bafaden M. Zayi ne.

Daga nan sai Kanar Molon ya je Gujiba, M. Zayi ya komo Borni. Sai Musa Dedare ya aiko wurin Kanar Molon cewa ga M. Zayi ya komo Borni. Da jin haka sai Kanar Molon ya tura wani hafsa da soja goma sha biyu, a kan dawaki suka tafi Borni, suka kama M. Zayi, suka zo da shi wurin Kanar Molon a Gujiba. Daga nan fa sai Kanar Molon ya tashi daga Gujiba ya nufi Mafoni. Da ya sauka a Mafoni sai ya tura wani kyaftin na soja, sunansa Kyaftin Makoptenmoro, zuwa Dikwa wurin Shehu Garbai. Sai suka zo Mafoni tare da shi wurin Kanar Molon. A lokacin akwai Baturen sojan Faransi a Dikwa, sunansa Kyaftin Dansiwul a lokacin ina Dikwa. Kashegari kuma sai wani Baturen sojammu ana ce masa Kyaftin Mosis ya zo Dikwa. Da ma mun saba da shi tun a Lakwaja. Kakana kuma ya gaya masa watakila ya gan ni a Dikwa. Yana tambayar mutane ko sun san ni, sai Madugu Karagama ya zo ya gaya mini. Na zo masaukinsa a gidan Rabe. Ya ce da ni in je in yi shiri mu tafi Mafoni. Na tafi na yi shiri na zo, muka tafi Mafoni. Muka iske Shehu Garbai a Mafoni. Kanar Molon ya gaya masa ƙa'idodin sarauniyar Ingila, watau *Queen Victoria*, don a lokacin nan ita ce ke sarautar Ingila. Abin da ya faɗa masa su ne : babu sayad da bayi, babu sayen bayi, babu yaƙi, babu muguwar shari'a, watau kamar yanke gaɓuɓɓan mutum, da sauransu.

Shehu kuma ya yi alkawari ya yarda. Shi ke nan, sai Kanar Molon ya tashi daga Mafoni ya nufi Yola. Ya bar kamfanin soja biyu, tare da Kyaftin Makoptenmoro, Baturen da ya kawo Shehu daga Dikwa, suka tafi tare da Shehu zuwa Monguno, watau a nan ne Shehu ya fara zama. Daga baya ne ya koma Kukawa. To, Kyaftin Makoptenmoro da ya raka Shehu zuwa Monguno, sai ya komo ya bi Kanar Molon zuwa Yola. Kyaftin Dan kuma ya tafi Gujiba, tare da kamfanin sojansa, ya kafa mazauninsa a nan Gujiba. To, kamfani ɗayan nan tare da kalasaje guda, da ni, aka bar mu a Mafoni. Kanar Molon ya gaya wa Shehu ya ba mu wakilansa waɗanda za mu yi aikace-aikacen gidaje tare da su. Sai Shehu ya haɗa mu da wakilinsa, Kacalla Jajiwaji. Mataimakansa su ne Girema Amadu Shuwa, da Girema Mammadu Kawo. To, sai muka ta da garin Mafoni suka koma can kudu, suka yi sabon garinsu. Watau a gidan razdan na Barno na yanzu, a nan ne suka fara gina matsara, watau gajeren garu mai kusurwa huɗu, taki ɗari ɗari. Muka gina ɗakuna manya guda biyu a kan tudun nan na unguwar Turawa ta yanzu. Shi ne Mafoni.

Bayan kwanaki kaɗan sai Kyaftin Kokeren ya zo. Shi ne kyaftin na kamfanin sojan nan wanda mu ke tare da su. Kuma bayan kwanaki kaɗan, sai Mista Yubi, da Kyaftin Monde, da Mista Bedat suka zo Mafoni. Su ne joji na farko a Barno. Waɗannan abubuwa duka a cikin shekara ta 1902 ne aka yi su.

Lokacin da Mista Yubi ya zo Mafoni, sai ya haɗa ni da Kyaftin Monde muka bi iyakar ƙasarmu ta Ingilishi, da ƙasar Jamus ta Dikwa, har bakin Cadi. Daga nan muka zo Monguno. Mista Yubi tare da Kyaftin Kokeren da kamfanin soja suka taso daga Mafoni suka zo Monguno. Shehu Garbai kuwa a lokacin nan yana da bindigogi da yawan gaske, waɗanda ya samu na Rabe. Sai Mista Yubi ya ce wa Shehu Garbai ya tara bindigoginsa duka ya kawo. Shehu kuwa ya yarda. Amma sai waɗansu bayin Shehu, da Kachalla Afuno, da Malam Bukar, suka ce kada Shehu ya yarda da wannan shawara, su ba za su ba da makamansu ba. Da samun wannan labari, sai na tafi wurin Yarima Aji da Abba Gana, da Shehu Umarmi, na ce da su na ji abin da Malam Bukar da Kacalla Ali Afuno suka gaya wa Shehu. Na ce musu, amma ina so su tuna bindigogin nan na Rabe ne. Turawan Faransi ne suka kashe Rabe suka samu waɗannan bindigogi. Idan suka hana, Turawa suka ce za su karɓa da ƙarfi fa ? Sun sani Rabe ma bai gagara ba, yaya su za su gagare su ? Sai su gaya wa Shehu gaskiya, ya rabu da maganar bayi, marasa hankali. Sai na tafi na shaida wa Mista Yubi wannan labari, da kuma maganar da na gaya wa Yarima Aji Abba Gana. Gama a lokacin nan su ne manyan mutanen Shehu. Shi ke nan sai Shehu ya tara bindigoginsa, ya kawo

wurin Mista Yubi. Sai Mista Yubi ya ba shi bindiga 100 na
albarushi, da bindiga 12 na harsashi. Aka tara sauran duka aka
kone su. Shi ke nan Mista Yubi ya gina gidan joji a Monguno.

Ni kuma aka hada ni da Kyaftin Kokeren, da wakilin
Shehu, Malam Bukar, domin mu bi iyakar kasarmu da Faransi
ta arewa. Sai muka bi ta Kukawa har zuwa Kogin Yo, ta
Gashagar. To, da muka zo Gashagar sai wakilin Shehu Malam
Bukar, ya ce in gaya wa Kyaftin Kokeren yana so ya ratse zuwa
wurin Girema Adam wanda ya ke karbar haraji a Kabi. Sai
Kyaftin Kokeren ya yarda, ya ce ya yi maza ya iske mu, amma
har muka zo Nguru bai iske mu ba.

A lokacin kuwa Galadima Ibrahim shi ne galadiman Nguru,
garinsa kuwa Kacallari. Daga Nguru sai muka aike wurin
Sarkin Gogaram Mai Sale, cewa muna zuwa garinsa. Sai ya
turo mana mutuminsa mai suna Gaji. Da muka tashi daga
Nguru sai muka sauka a Dumsai, da ma mun aike musu su yi
mana masauki da abinci. Sai muka iske ba su yi kome ba.
Na shiga cikin garin, domin in tambayi mai garin abin da ya sa
ba su yi mana masauki ba, kuma ba su kawo mana abinci ba.
Da shigata cikin garin, sai mai garin ya ce wa mutanensa su
harbe ni. Sai yaron galadiman Nguru, Girema ya ce mu fita.
Muka yiwo waje, su kuma suka biyo mu da harbi, har
masaukimmu. Nan da nan Kyaftin Kokeren ya ba soja oda.
Sai harbin bindigogi nan da nan muka watsa su, muka tashi
daga Dumsai zuwa Tagari. Da muka isa Tagari, sai muka iske
mutanen Tagari da bakankunansu dari uku, sun jeru a kofar
gari, da dawaki kamar talatin, suna jirammu. Sai Kyaftin Kokeren ya ce ni da mutumin sarkin Gogaram mu tafi wurinsu
mu gaya musu ba mu zo domin yaki ba, domin wucewa zuwa
Gogaram ne muka zo.

Sai muka shiga cikin garin, domin su kawo mana ruwa da
abinci. Muka tafi muka shaida musu. Akwai wani Bulamansu
mai hankali, sai ya ce wa jama'arsu su koma, sai suka koma
cikin gari. Mu kuma muka tafi muka sauka a gindin rimi yamma da gari. Da fari muka aiki mutane biyu, Audu da
Yalema. Ashe an kame su, an daure. Muka ga har
kamar karfe biyar na maraice ba su kawo mana kome ba,
yarammu wadanda muka aika kuma ba mu gan su ba. Ga shi

kuma sun jera 'yam baka a kan garu. Da muka duba arewa, sai
muka ga sun fid da iyalansu mata da yara, mazaje da makamai sun sa su gaba, za su kai su wurin ɓuya. Watau nufinsu
idan suka fita da iyalansu, su komo da darè su faɗa mana
da yaƙi. Da ma ina da labarinsu, haka suka yi wa Shehun
Barno, Shehu Bukar, a sa'ad da ya kawo yaƙi Bedde. Sai
Sarkin Gogaram Alhaji ɗam Babuje ya tara baka kamar dubu
ɗari, ya zo ya faɗa sansanin Shehu da dare. Sabo da haka sai
na shaida wa Kyaftin Kokeren.

Akwai wani ɗan gadinsu wanda ya hau wani dogon itace
a cikin garin. Sai Kyaftin Kokeren ya harbe shi da bindiga ya
faɗo. Shi ke nan sai yaƙi, nan da nan muka watsa su, mutanemmu biyu waɗanda aka ɗaure suka sami dama suka gudo,
suka zo wurimmu. Amma duk da haka sai da suka kawo mana
farmaki da dare, muka kore su.

Da gari ya waye muka tafi Gogaram. Sai Sarkin Gogaram
Mai Sale ya fito ya tare mu da murna. Watau Kyaftin Kokeren
shi ne Baturen da mutanen Bedde suka fara gani. Sarkin kuma
ya ce duka abin da Turawa suka gaya masa zai yi. Wannan duka
a cikin shekarar 1902 ne. Daga Gogaram sai muka bi hanyar
Jawa, ta Garun Dole, ta Gabai Karama zuwa Gujiba. A lokacin
nan idan ka tashi daga Gabai, babu gida sai Gujiba. Muna tare
da Kyaftin Monde. Shi ne joji a Gujiba. Sai muka bi hanyar
Burgumma, ta Marguba, muka zo Mafoni. Labarin wakilin
Shehu, Malam Bukar, wanda aka haɗa mu da shi, ya ratse daga
Gashagar zuwa wurin Girema Adam, mai tara haraji a Kabi,
bai iske mu ba. Ashe ya ta da yaƙi a Kabi, suka yi kashe-
kashen mutane. A lokacin nan Mista Yubi ya zo Gaidam daga
Monguno, sai ya kama shi. Da ma kuwa ya kashe mutane uku.
Watau mutanen Sururu waɗanda Fataralla ɗan Rabe ya haɗa
su da Manjo Maklintok 'Mai-Doron-Yaƙi'.

Da zuwa Lakwaja wurin Gwamna Lugga sai aka yi masa
shari'ar kisan kai, aka rataye shi a Mafoni. Wannan shi ne
mutumin da shari'ar Turawa ta fara kashewa a Barno. Bayan
lokaci kaɗan sai Mista Brandy, wani Laftana Hafsa, ya zo Mafoni. Akwai wani bawan Shehu sunansa Kacalla Ranasku, a
ƙasai Busuguwa, yana zalunci ainun. Sai aka haɗa ni da Mista
Brandy muka tafi Busuguwa, muka iske shi a wani gari wai shi

Kufti. Da muka isa garin akwai wani mutuminsa, mai suna
Girema Ali, sai ya taso mana, nan da nan Mista Brandy ya harbe
shi. Muka kama Kacalla Ranasku muka kawo shi Mafoni.
Kuma bayan lokaci kaɗan sai Kyaftin Ross ya zo Mafoni ya
yi canjin Kokeren. Kyaftin Kokeren kuma ya bi hanyar Yola,
zuwa Lakwaja. A lokacin kuwa babu wata hanyar zuwa Barno,
sai ta Yola, kayammu duka da mel, ta Yola a ke kawo mana su.

Aka tsai da mahaɗammu a Womdiyo. Leburan Yola su kowa.
Womdiyo su ajiye, na Barno kuma su je Womdiyo su ɗauko
Ni kuma ina Mafoni tare da Kyaftin Ross, sai kuma Kyaftin
Monde ya tashi daga Gujiba tare da Baturen Soja Mista Lorin,
da soja arba'in da biyar suka zo Biu. A lokacin nan Mai Garga
shi ne sarkin Biu. Sai ya tare su da lumana. Wannan shi
ne farkon ganin Turawa a Biu. Daga Biu sai Cibok. Da
zuwansu Cibok, sai mutanen Cibok suka ta da yaƙi,
suka harbi Kyaftin Monde da kibiya a kwiɓi, amma bai yi
masa kome ba, ya warke. A Cibok ya aike da takarda zuwa
wurin Kyaftin Ross, ya ce yana nemana mu gamu da shi a
Kobshi. Sai na bi hanyar Mulgwai, na je Kobshi ban same shi
ba, sai a Mudube. Daga Mudube muka tafi Mulgwai, a lokacin
nan kuwa mutanen Mulgwai da Madube, da Cibok, su ne
masu fashin hanyar Barno zuwa ƙasar Adamawa. To, da muka
isa Mulgwai, sai mutanen Mulgwai suka gudu zuwa kurmi.
Muka bi su, muka iske su. Da muka taɓa ɗam faɗa kaɗan sai
suka watse. Ni kuma aka haɗa ni da soja bakwai muka tafi
Ngrabego don in kamo sarakunansu, da Mai Garisa da Mai
Nyanya. Na kamo Mai Garisa, amma Mai Nyanya ya tsere. Na
kawo Mai Garisa sansanimmu muka tashi daga Mude muka zo
Mafoni. Sai Mista Lorin da sojansa suka koma Gujiba, mu kuma
da Kyaftin Monde muka tafi Monguno. Daga Monguno sai
muka tafi Gaidam, sai kuma Gashuwa. A lokacin nan kuwa
sarkin Gashuwa shi ne Yarima Bolami, babban sarkin fashin
hanyar Kano zuwa Barno, a gabas da Gogaram. Gama ni da
kaina, ayarimmu, da muka tashi daga Garundole za mu Gogaram, sai Yarima Bolami ya zo kusa da gonakin Rinokuno yana
jiran ayarimmu. Mutanen Rinokuno ne suka ce ba su yarda ya
yi fashi a kusa da gonakinsu ba, gama su talakawan sarkin
Gogaram ne. Mai Sale sarkin Gogaram kuwa shi ya gaya
musu, kada su yarda wani ya taɓa ayarin da zai zo Gogaram.

Shi ke nan sai yaƙi ya tashi a tsakaninsu, Yarima Bolami ya soke mutuminsu guda. To, sabo da sanin halinsa, sa'ad da muka isa Gashuwa, sai muka kama shi muka tashi daga Gashuwa, muka wuce Albanjirori. Daga Albanjirori sai Daja. A Daja da dare sai Yarima Bolami ya gudu. Sai na ɗauki soja guda uku, muka bi shi, muka iske shi, muka kamo shi. Mun yi kusa da zangommu inda Kyaftin Monde ya ke, ba duka ba zagi, sai ya tsuguna yana waɗansu maganganu. Ko da ya faɗi sai ba rai, ya mutu.

Daga Daja sai muka bi hanyar Sheri, ta Maini, ta Kabi, muka je bakin Kogin Gashagar. Da muka isa wani gari wai shi Lamawana, sai muka iske rugar Tubawa, da Karekare waɗanda su ke fashi a arewacin ƙasar Barno. Da ganimmu ba su tsaya sun yi faɗa ba sai suka gudu. Sunayen manyansu Kedala Aserti da Kedala Guwod. Da muka tashi daga Lamawana, sai muka je Yau, muka bi bakin Cadi muka tafi Monguno. Muna Monguno muka sami labarin Sarkin Musulmi Attahiru ɗan Ahmadu ya zo Bima daga Sakkwato. Kyaftin Buram, da kamfanin sojansa na Gujiba, suka tare shi ya koma ya shiga Barmi, su kuma suka bi shi, suka shiga Ashaka suka tare shi. Sojan doki suna biye da shi, sai mu kuma muka tafi Ashaka. Muna Ashaka har Manjo Mash ya zo da rundunar sojansa, daga yamma, ya sauka a ƙofar Barmi. Mu kuma muka taso daga Ashaka, muka zo muka haɗu da Manjo Mash kamar ƙarfe tara da rabi na safe, aka fara yaƙi. A lokacin da yaƙi ya yi zafi, kamar ƙarfe biyar na maraice aka shigo cikin garin ana yaƙi, har ƙofar gidan sarkin Musulmi. Waɗansu mutane suka shiga cikin gidan sarkin Musulmi. Waɗansu suka shiga cikin masallaci. Ba a bar faɗa ba har ƙarfe takwas na dare tukuna, kana ya ƙare.

Kamar ƙarfe goma sha biyu na rana, aka harbi Manjo Mash da kibiya, bai daɗe ba ya mutu. Kuma a lokacin an harbi Kyaftin Buram, amma ya warke. Ga manyan sarakunan da ke tare da sarkin Musulmi a Barmi: Sarkin Bida Abubakar, da Sarkin Misau Ahmadu, da Sarki Tujjani Bashir, na ƙasar Futa (wanda Faransai suka koro ya zo Sakkwato) da Madawakin Kano Kwairanga, da Magaji 'Danyamusa na Kafi. Amma Sarkin Bida Abubakar, da Tujjani Bashir, an kamo su. Sarkin Misau Ahmadu da Magaji 'Danyamusa suka tsere, suka tafi Makka. Madawakin Kano Kwairanga kuwa aka kashe shi.

MUTUWAR SARKIN MUSULMI ATTAHIRU

SAI labarin mutuwar Sarkin Musulmi Attahiru. Da muka
taso daga Barmi, muka zo Ashaka, sai Mista Tompul, razdan
na Bauci, da Kyaftin Monde na Barno, da babban Baturen soja
wanda ya gaji Manjo Mash, suka nemo mutanen Barmi guda
uku, waɗanda suka san Sarkin Musulmi Attahiru. Sai muka
tafi Barmi. To, akwai wani kududdufi maras ruwa a gabas maso
kudu da kasuwar Barmi, a jikin ganuwar garin. A nan ne Sarkin
Musulmi Attahiru ya mutu. Mutanen dai da suka mutu sun yi
kusan ɗari. To, da muka zo wurin nan, sai aka bar mutanen
nan guda biyu a baya, aka zo da ɗaya wurin gawawwakin nan.
Sai mutumin ya nuna gawar sarkin Musulmi. Yana saye da
wando shuɗi, da riga fara, da rawani fari, da takalmi ƙwaf irin
na ɓallawa a ƙafa, da awaiki da laya ɗaya a damtsensa.

Sai kuma aka kawo ɗaya mutumin shi kuma ya nuna wannan gawar. Haka ma ɗayan ya nuna. Duka su uku mutum
ɗaya suka nuna. Akwai wani mutum a wurin kusa da ta sarkin

Musulmi an harbe shi da bindiga, an karya cinyoyinsa duka
biyu da bindiga, yana zaune abin tausayi. Da muka zo wurinsa
muka tsaya, muka ga bai mutu ba. Sai na gaishe shi, na tam-
baye shi labarin sarkin Musulmi. Akwai wata gawa a gabansa,
sai ya ce da ni, "Da ni da wannan ɗanuwana muna can gindin
garu. Sai muka ji sarkinMusulmi ya faɗi. Muka sheƙo da gudu.
Muna kawowa nan, sai aka harbe mu. Ni aka karya cinyoyina,
ɗanuwana kuwa ya faɗi ba rai." Kuma ya ce idan muka duba
cikin gawawwakin nan, muka ga mai shuɗin wando, da farar
riga, shi ne Sarkin Musulmi Attahiru.
Allahu Akbar, Allah ya ji ƙansa amin. To, a haka aka tab-
batad da mutuwar sarkin Musulmi a Barmi. Daga nan sai
muka komo Nafaɗa. Daga Nafaɗa muka wuce zuwa Fika da
waɗansu soja, domin a lokacin da mu ke sansanin Ashaka,
mun aiki Maina Barna wurin Sarkin Fika Sule, ya aiko mana
da abinci. Sai ya hana ya koro manzommu. Maina Barma
shi ne wanda ya zama sarkin Damagaram, wanda Faransai
suka naɗa. Daga baya ya ce tsakanimmu da shi sai yaƙi. To,
sabo da haka da aka ci Barmi, sai aka tafi wurinsa. To, da muka
ƙetare Kogin Nafaɗa, muka isa Ngalda, sai muka gamu da
'ya'yansa guda biyu, Maina Kura da Maina Gana, a nan.
Suka tare mu, sai na kai su wurin Kyaftin Monde. Shi Maina
Kura shi ne Mai Disa, wanda ya zama sarkin Fika, uban sarkin
Fika na yanzu. Ya ce ubansu ya yi rashin hankali, amma su da
manyan gari ba su son yaƙi, sabo da haka suka zo wurin Bature.
Sai Kyaftin Monde ya ce da su, to, sai mu tafi garinsu. Sai
muka zo ƙofar Fika, kyaftin ya ce wa 'ya'yan sarki, su je su
gaya wa ubansu ya zo. Sai suka tafi wurinsa. Da suka jima
suka komo wurimmu. Suka ce mu yi haƙuri su za su yi ƙoƙari
su kawo shi, domin su ba su son yaƙi. To, sai muka koma wani
ɗan tudu, gabas maso kudu da garin, muka sauka. Har kamar
ƙarfe huɗu na maraice, sarki bai zo ba. Sai Kyaftin Monde ya
ce in kirawo 'ya'yan sarkin. Da suka zo, sai ya ɗebi rabin
kamfanin soja, muka shiga gari tare da Maina Disa babban
ɗan sarkin, har ƙofar fada. Da muka zo, sai Kyaftin Monde
ya ce in shiga in yi kiran sarkin, sai na shiga. Da shigata sai
muka gamu da sarki yana fitowa. Na shaida masa, cewa ga
Bature a ƙofar gida yana jiransa. Da muka zo wurin Kyaftin
Monde, sai ya ce da shi mu tafi sansanimmu. Sarki yana
harama ya koma cikin gida sai Kyaftin Monde ya ce mu kama

shi. Muka kama shi. Da muka yi tafiya kaɗan sai ya faɗi, ya
ce wa mutanensa su harbe mu. To, a cikin garin kuwa ga 'ya-
'yansa Maina Gana, da Maina Kura, su kuma sun tare mu
babu dama harba kibiya. Sai muka bar shi, muka fito
muka komo sansanimmu.

Sai babban ɗansa Maina Kura ya ce mu yi haƙuri, zai yi
ƙoƙari ya kawo shi, amma zai tafi ya kawo Tunja Mama da
Malam Alhaji wurina tukuna domin in yi musu magana, su taimake shi su kawo sarkin. Gama su ne manyan gari, ba su ko son
yaƙi. Sai ya tafi ya kawo su. Na ce da su su yi ƙoƙari su kawo
sarki, ya zo su ƙulla amana da Bature. Na nuna musu misali
cewa, bai ga Sarkin Gwambe Umaru ba, da ya zo suka ƙulla
amana da Bature, ba ga shi nan lafiya ba ? Na ce idan ya ce
yaƙi zai yi, tun da sarkin Musulmi bai gagara ba, shi zai iya ?
Na ce su je su kawo shi. Sai suka tafi. Suka kuwa kawo shi
sansanimmu. Da ma an shirya soja ashirin da biyar, da zuwansa
sai aka kama shi aka aika da shi Gujiba. Sai muka naɗa ɗansa
Maina Kura, ya zama sarkin Fika, watau Disa uban sarkin
Fika na yanzu. Wannan duka a cikin shekara 1902 ne. Sai yaƙi
ya watse, mu kuma da Kyaftin Monde muka koma Monguno.

A cikin shekara 1903 Shehu Garbai ya ƙaura daga Monguno
ya koma Kukawa. A cikin shekaran nan Mista Yubi ya tafi
hutu. Mista Hawood ya ƙaurato da mazaunin razdan daga
Monguno zuwa Magumeri. A bayan wata shida Mista Yubi
ya komo daga hutu, sai Mista Hawood ya tafi Bauci, ya zama
razdan na Bauci, inda ya rasu daga baya.

A cikin shekara 1904 Gwamna Lugga ya biyo ta hanyar
Bauci ta Nafaɗa ya zo Magumeri, daga Magumeri sai ya tafi
Mafoni ya duba kamfanin soja. Daga Mafoni sai ya bi hanyar
Misau, sai Kukawa. To, a lokacin nan ne ya tabbatar wa
Shehu Garbai da sarautarsa, ya ba shi sanda da takobi, da lema,
da gado. A lokacin da gwamna ya zo Kukawa, Baturen soja
Manjo Kimbite da sojan doki suka biyo hanyar Kogin Yo
daga Kano, suka tari gwamna a Kukawa. Daga Kukawa sai
gwamna ya bi hanyar Yau zuwa Gaidam. To, a lokacin nan
ne aka ta da Gaidam Ballara, aka kawo shi Damageri. To,
daga Gaidam gwamna ya wuce zuwa Kano. A lokacin da
Gwamna Lugga ya zo Barno yana tare da ƙanensa Manjo
Lugga. A cikin shekaran nan ne, aka ta da mazaunin razdan

daga Magumeri aka kai Kukawa. Sai Mista Yubi ya kafa mazauninsa a Gonge, gabas da Kukawa kamar mil biyu.

A shekaran nan ne aka fara karɓar fiton kanwa a bakin Cadi, ana buga wa ko wane dutsen kanwa hatimi. Wuri 116 shi ne kuɗin fiton dutsen kanwa. A cikin shekaran nan ne, Mista Yubi ya yi kiran Sarkin Biu Mai Garga, watau kakan sarkin Biu na yanzu zuwa Magumeri. Lokacin da aka yi kiransa, ya ƙaurato daga Biu ya zo Pelamulta, da aka aika kiransa da fari ya ji tsoron zuwa. To, sai na haɗa masinja da wani mutum mai suna M. Mustafa, wanda ya taɓa zama a wurinsa, suka tafi Biu, ya waye masa kai. Sai suka zo Magumeri, aka ba shi sandan sarauta. Da mutanen Biu suna cewa idan sarkin Biu ya bar ƙasar Biu ya tafi wata ƙasa zai mutu. To, ya zo Magumeri ya koma Biu lafiya. Da va dawo daga Magumeri, bai tsaya a sabon garinsa Pelamulta ba, sai ya wuce zuwa kufan ubansa Mai Mari, shi ne Biu ta yanzu. Kuma a shekaran nan ne Tubawa suka tafi Kaigama Kakami da yaƙi a tsakanin Gashagar da Yo. Suka yi masa muguwar ɓarna, suka kashe masa dawakai kamar 53, da mutane da dama. A cikin shekaran nan ne aka fara rarraba ƙasashen hakimai, watau ajiya. Kuma ko wane ajiya yana da sanda gwargwadon darajarsa. Akwai mai daraja ta biyu, akwai mai daraja ta uku, da ta huɗu kamar dai sarakunammu na yanzu. Kuma akwai lawanai, watau dagatai. Su kuma suna da sanda mai daraja ta biyar. Kuma a lokacin nan ne, wani Bature da a ke kira Boyd Alexander, ya zo ƙasar Barno, tare da yaronsa Mista Lobis, da niyyar wucewa ƙasar Hartum daga Barno. Shi ya yi wa hakimin ƙasar Margi, Kacalla Mammadu Kaku, bulala sabo da bai kawo wa leburansa abinci da wuri ba. Kacalla Mammadu Kaku ya yi ƙararsa wurin razdan na Barno, Mista Yubi. Sai Mista Yubi ya sa shi shari'a ya yi masa hukunci. A lokacin nan ne mutanen Barno suka fara ganin adalcin Turawa, suna cewa shari'arsu babu zaɓe.

Shi wannan Bature, daga Barno sai ya ƙetare Cadi ya shiga ƙasar Faransi har ya kai gabas da Wadai cikin ƙasar Wadai. Akwai wata 'yar ƙungiya, wadda a ke kiran kabilarta Masalit, a nan suka kashe shi. Amma Lobis ya tsira ya gudu ya zo Maiduguri. Mista Yubi ya bai wa Lobis takarda ya tafi wurin Turawan Faransi a Farlomi suka tafi har inda aka kashe Boyd

Alexander, suka taho da ƙasusuwansa Maiduguri, aka binne. Yanzu haka kabarinsa yana nan a Maiduguri.

Haka kuma akwai wani Bature wanda ya zo ƙasar Barno, tare da Likita Barth, yau fiye da shekara ɗari. Shi kuma ya mutu a wani gari mai suna Maduwari a ƙasar Kanumbu, kusa da Cadi. Sunansa Mista Overweg. Mista Yubi ya sa ni in yi binciken inda aka binne shi. Na sami wata tsohuwa mai shekara kamar 80, a lokacin nan. Ita ta nuna mini wurin kabarinsa, na shaida wa Mista Yubi. Ya zo muka tone wurin, muka iske ƙasusuwansa. Muka ɗebo ƙasusuwan muka kawo Maiduguri muka binne. Yanzu haka kabarinsa yana nan a Maiduguri.

Haka kuma Mista Bedded, di'on da yafara zuwa Barno, tare da Mista Yubi a cikin 1902, wanda ya mutu a Monguno. Shi kuma muka tono ƙasusuwansa, muka kawo Maiduguri muka binne. Yanzu haka shi kuma ka barinsa yana Maiduguri.

A cikin shekaru 1902 zuwa 1906 Tubawa na arewa suka gallabi ƙasar Barno da hare-hare, a arewacin Kukawa, da yammacin Kukawa, suna ɗibar shanu da raƙuma. Sabo da haka aka bai wa Kacalla Kakami, wanda ya ke zaune a Yo, a kan iyaka, sojan doki 25, domin su taimake shi tsare ƙasa. A lokacin nan ne muka ga abin mamaki da ban dariya. Akwai wani Batube wai shi Hindimi. Daga kan iyakar Kacalla Kakami, aka fafaro shi. Da ya ga ba zai tsira ba, ya ga ramin dabgi, sai ya yi tsalle ya bar doki, ya shiga cikin ramin dabgin. Kacalla Kakami ya zo ya tsaya a bakin ramin, ya ce a tona. Aka yi ta tonon ramin nan, har aka gaji, ba a same shi ba. Sai daga baya aka sami labari bai mutu ba, ya fita. Amma mun ji bayansa duk ya ƙuje.

A cikin shekarar 1907 aka ga Kukawa ba ta cancanta ta zama babban birnin Barno ba, sabo da ƙarancin ruwa, da kuma zamantowarta gefe ainun.

Sai Mista Yubi ya yi shawara da Shehu, suka ga ya kamata a ta da Kukawa, a mai da ita Maiduguri, wurin da ya ke kusa da tsakiyar ƙasar Barno. Ga kuma wurin noma mai kyau, ga shi kuma tana da babbar kasuwa sananniya. Kuma hanya ta fito daga yamma ta ratsa Barno zuwa gabas, ga isasshen ruwa.

Sabo da haka aka ƙaurato daga Kukawa aka kawo ta Maiduguri, a cikin 1907. Mista Yubi ya kafa gidan razdana Mafoni, tsakaninsu kamar mil biyu.

Shehu kuwa ya kafa garinsa a Kalwa, a kusa da Maiduguri, sai Mista Yubi ya ce ya kamata a kira wannan wuri Maiduguri, domin shi ne sanannen suna a ƙasar. Shehu kuwa ya ce zai kira nasa garin Yerwa. Wannan shi ne dalilin kiran sunan Yerwa da Maiduguri, a yanzu.

A cikin 1908 Arnan Cibok suka shahara da fashe-fashe tsakanin Barno da Adamawa. Suna kashe fatake suna ɗibar kayansu. A lokacin nan ne suka kashe wani akawu mutumin Saliyo, sunansa Mista Cock, da ya tashi daga Maiduguri za shi Yola. Da aka ga sha'aninsu ya shahara, sai aka kawo musu yaƙi, da sojan doki da sojojin ƙasa, amma kafin a ci su sosai, an yi kamar wata uku. Domin suna da babban dutse, da ma yawancinsu, gidajensu duk a kan dutsen su ke. Dutsen kuwa yana da kogo. A cikin kogon kuma akwai ruwa da yawa a kwance. Sun rigaya kuwa sun tara abincinsu cikin kogon.

Da yaƙin ya yi tsanani, sai Yahi Ganama da jama'arsa suka shiga cikin kogon. Sai aka sa soja suka tsare bakin ramin. Su kuwa sai su laɓaɓo bakin ramin da dare su harbo kibiya ga sojojin. Ran nan sai muka tafi bakin ramin da Mista Yubi. A nan ne na gwada arziki. Mista Yubi ya ce da ni in gaya wa Yahi Ganama, ya kamata su fito daga cikin ramin nan, su zo a yi amana, yaƙi ya ƙare. Na sunkuya a bakin ramin, ina kiran Yahi Ganama. Ya amsa. Ina cikin gaya masa jawabin Mista Yubi, sai suka jefo mini kibiya, amma ba ta same ni ba.

Suna cikin ramin har abincinsu ya ƙare, sa'an nan suka fito, daga nan yaƙi ya ƙare.

Iyakar kashi na farko na labarin Mai Maina ke nan

References

Abraham, R. C.
  1962. *Dictionary of the Hausa Language.* 2d ed. London:
  University of London Press.
Ajayi, Jacob
  1965. *Christian Missions in Nigeria 1841–1891.* London:
  Longmans.
Alexander, Boyd
  1907. *From the Niger to the Nile.* 2 vols. London: Arnold.
Alexander, Herbert
  1912. *Boyd Alexander's Last Journey.* London: Arnold.
Bargery, G. P.
  1934. *A Hausa-English Dictionary.* London: Oxford University Press.
Barth, Heinrich
  1857–59. *Travels and Discoveries in North and Central
  Africa.* 3 vols. New York: Harper and Brothers. Reprint.
  London: Frank Cass, 1965.
  1862. *Collection of Vocabularies of Central-African Languages.* Gotha: Justus Perthes. Reprint. London: Frank
  Cass, 1971.
Benton, P. Askell
  1912. *Notes on Some Languages of the Western Sudan.*
  London: Oxford University Press. Reprint. *The Languages
  and Peoples of Bornu.* London: Frank Cass, 1968.
  1913. *The Sultanate of Bornu.* Translated from the German

of Dr. A. Schultze. London: Oxford University Press. Reprint. London: Frank Cass, 1968.

Bindloss, Harold
    1898. *In the Niger Country*. Edinburgh: Blackwood.

Boahen, A. Adu
    1962. "The Caravan Trade in the Nineteenth Century." *The Journal of African History* 3: 349–59.
    1964. *Britain, the Sahara, and the Western Sudan 1788–1861*. London: Oxford University Press.

Bovill, E. W.
    1958. *The Golden Trade of the Moors*. London: Oxford University Press.

Caillié, Réné
    1830. *Travels Through Central Africa to Timbuctoo*. 2 vols. London: Colburn & Bentley. Reprint. London: Frank Cass, 1968.

Crowther, Samuel A., and Taylor, John C.
    1859. *The Gospel on the Banks of the Niger*. London: Church Missionary House. Reprint. London: Dawsons, 1968.

Crozier, F. P.
    1932. *Five Years Hard*. London: Jonathan Cape.

Curtin, Philip D., ed.
    1967. *Africa Remembered: Narratives by West Africans from the Era of the Slave Trade*. Madison: University of Wisconsin Press.

Davies, John G.
    1956. *The Biu Book*. Zaria: NORLA.

Denham, D., Clapperton, H., and Oudney, W.
    1828. *Narrative of Travels and Discoveries in Northern and Central Africa, in the years 1822, 1823, and 1824*. 2 vols. London: John Murray.

[Dorugu]
    [1932a]. *The Story of Dorugu*. London: The Sheldon Press.
    [1932b]. *Hausa Tales Told by Dorugu and Others*. London: The Sheldon Press.

Dubois, Félix
1897. *Tombouctou la mystérieuse*. Paris: Ernest Flammarion.

East, Rupert, trans.
1939. *Akiga's Story*. London: Oxford University Press.

Flint, John
1960. *Sir George Goldie and the Making of Nigeria*. London: Oxford University Press.

Forde, Daryll, ed.
1956. *Efik Traders of Old Calabar*. London: Oxford University Press.

Gentil, Émile
1902. *La chute de l'empire de Rabeh*. Paris: Librairie Hachette.

Graham, Sonia F.
1966. *Government and Mission Education in Northern Nigeria 1900–1919 with special reference to the work of Hanns Vischer*. Ibadan: University Press.

Greenberg, J. H.
1946. *The Influence of Islam on a Sudanese Religion*. New York: American Ethnological Society. Monograph No. 10.

Hair, P. E. H.
1967. *The Early Study of Nigerian Languages: Essays and Bibliographies*. Cambridge: The University Press. West African Language Monographs, No. 7.

Hassan, Mallam, and Shu'aibu, Mallam
1952. *A Chronicle of Abuja*. Translated by F. Heath. Ibadan: University Press. Reprint. Lagos: African Universities Press, 1962.

Haywood, A., and Clarke, F. A. S.
1965. *The History of the Royal West African Frontier Force*. Aldershot: Gale and Polden.

Hiskett, M.
1966. "Materials Relating to the Cowry Currency of the Western Sudan, Part 2." *Bulletin of the School of Oriental and African Languages* 29: 339–66.

Hodgkin, Thomas, ed.
1960. *Nigerian Perspectives: An Historical Anthology*. London: Oxford University Press.

Hoffmann, Carl
1963. *A Grammar of the Margi Language*. London: Oxford University Press.

Hogben, Sidney J., and Kirk-Greene, A. H. M.
1966. *The Emirates of Northern Nigeria*. London: Oxford University Press.

Hourst, E. A. L.
1898. *French Enterprise in Africa*. Translated by Mrs. Arthur Bell. London: Chapman and Hall.

Italiaander, Rolf, ed.
1967. *Heinrich Barth: Im Sattel durch Nord- und Zentralafrika. Reisen und Entdeckungen in den Jahren 1849–1855*. Wiesbaden: F. A. Brockhaus.

Johnston, H. A. S.
1967. *The Fulani Empire of Sokoto*. London: Oxford University Press.

Kirk-Greene, A. H. M.
1956. "Abbega and Durogu [*sic*]." *West African Review* 27, no. 348: 865–69 (Sept.).

1957. "Link with Lugard." *West Africa,* p. 1179 (Dec. 14), p. 1203 (Dec. 21).

1958a. *Maiduguri and the Capitals of Bornu*. Zaria: NORLA.

1958b. *Adamawa Past and Present*. London: Oxford University Press. Reprint. London: Dawsons, 1969.

1959. "The Death and Burial of Adolf Overweg." *West African Review* 30, no. 378: 227–28 (March).

1962. *Barth's Travels in Nigeria*. London: Oxford University Press.

1965. "A Preliminary Note on New Sources for Nigerian Military History." *Journal of the Historical Society of Nigeria* 3: 129–47.

1968. "The Niger-Sudan Expeditionary Force, 1897." *Journal of the Society for Army Historical Research* 46: 49–56.

Kopytoff, Jean H.
1965. *Preface to Modern Nigeria*. Madison: University of Wisconsin Press.

Langa-Langa
1922. *Up Against It in Nigeria*. London: Allen & Unwin.

Macleod, Olive
1912. *Chiefs and Cities of Central Africa*. Edinburgh: Blackwood.

Maimaina
1958. *Labarin Maimaina Na Jega, Sarkin Askira*. Zaria: Gaskiya Corporation.

Mattei, Commandant
1890. *Bas-Niger, Bénoué, Dahomey*. Grenoble: Vallier.

Meek, Charles K.
1931. *Tribal Studies in Northern Nigeria*. 2 vols. London: Kegan Paul.

Miller, Walter
1936. *Reflections of a Pioneer*. London: Church Missionary Society.
1950. *An Autobiography*. Zaria: Gaskiya Corporation.

Mockler-Ferryman, A. F.
1902. *British Nigeria*. London: Cassell & Co.

Muffett, D. J. M.
1964. *Concerning Brave Captains: being a history of Kano and Sokoto and of the last stand of the Fulani forces*. London: André Deutsch.

Nadel, S. F.
1942. *A Black Byzantium*. London: Oxford University Press.

Orr, Charles J. W.
1911. *The Making of Northern Nigeria*. London: Macmillan. Reprint. London: Frank Cass, 1965.

Pedraza, Howard J.
1960. *Borrioboola-Gha: the story of Lokoja*. London: Oxford University Press.

Perham, Margery
1956. *Lugard: the Years of Adventure*. London: Collins.
1960. *Lugard: the Years of Authority*. London: Collins.

Perham, Margery, and Bull, M., eds.
   1963. *Diaries of Lord Lugard*, vol. 4. London: Faber.
Petermann, August
   1854. *An Account of the Progress of the Expedition to Central Africa, performed by order of Her Majesty's Foreign Office, under Messrs. Richardson, Barth, Overweg and Vogel, in the years 1850, 1851, 1852, and 1853*. Gotha: Justus Perthes.
Raphael, John R.
   (n.d.) *Through Unknown Nigeria*. London: Werner Laurie.
Robinson, Charles H.
   1899. *Dictionary of the Hausa Language*, vol. 1. Cambridge: The University Press.
   1900. *Nigeria, Our Latest Protectorate*. London: Horace Marshall & Son.
Rodd, Francis R.
   1926. *People of the Veil*. London: Macmillan.
Schön, J. F.
   1862. *Grammar of the Hausa Language*. London: Church Missionary House.
   1876. *Dictionary of the Hausa Language*. London: Church Missionary House.
   1885. *Magána Hausa*. London: Society for Promoting Christian Knowledge.
   1886. *African Proverbs, Tales, and Historical Fragments*. London: Society for Promoting Christian Knowledge.
Schubert, Gustav von
   1897. *Heinrich Barth, der Bahnbrecher der deutschen Afrikaforschung*. Berlin: Dietrich Reimer.
Smith, M. F.
   1954. *Baba of Karo*. London: Faber & Faber.
Smith, M. G.
   1960. *Government in Zazzau*. London: Oxford University Press.
   1967. "A Hausa Kingdom: Maradi Under Dan Baskore, 1854–75." In Daryll Forde and P. M. Kaberry (eds.),

West African Kingdoms in the Nineteenth Century, pp. 93–122. London: Oxford University Press.

Temple, Charles L.
1918. *Native Races and their Rulers.* Cape Town: Argus. Reprint. London: Frank Cass, 1968.

Tremearne, A. J. N.
1912. *The Tailed Head-Hunters of Nigeria.* London: Seeley, Service.

[1914]. *The Ban of the Bori.* London: Heath, Cranston & Ouseley. Reprint. London: Frank Cass, 1968.

Trimingham, J. Spencer
1959. *Islam in West Africa.* London: Oxford University Press.

1962. *A History of Islam in West Africa.* London: Oxford University Press.

Urvoy, Y.
1949. *Histoire de l'empire du Bornou.* Mémoires de L'Institut Français d'Afrique Noire, No. 7. Paris.

Vandeleur, Seymour
1898. *Campaigning on the Upper Nile and Niger.* London: Methuen.

Vaughan, James H.
1964a. "Culture, History, and Grass-roots Politics in a Northern Cameroons Kingdom." *American Anthropologist* 66: 1078–95.

1964b. "Religion and World View of the Marghi." *Ethnology* 3: 389–97.

1965. "Folklore and Values in Marghi Culture." *Journal of the Folklore Institute* 2: 5–24.

Vischer, Isabelle
1917. *Croquis et Souvenirs de la Nigérie du Nord.* Paris: Attinger Frères.

Willcocks, General Sir James
1904. *From Kabul to Kumassi.* London: John Murray.

Index